Appreciations

[of the seminar, "Women: Masters or Mothers?]

One lecture I came across on your website is "Masters or Mothers?" I listened twice in full and many times in pieces. I took notes, did research, and had a few discussions with *mātājīs* of different backgrounds and cultures. Most everything was covered in that series of lectures on the topic of women in society that I so desperately needed to hear. It connected so many dots for me. Immediately, I understood why I suffered so much in this lifetime on so many levels. Not only why I suffered but why most of the women and actually all of society are suffering now too.

Adrianna
[Maryland, USA]

I feel very grateful to the devotee who gave me this lecture series titled "Women: Masters or Mothers?" delivered by H. H. Bhakti Vikāsa Swami, which helped me to understand the reasons and logic behind all the prescribed Vedic injunctions defining the roles and duties of a soul in a woman's body. Ultimately, the goal of all the prescribed rules and regulations is to elevate the soul to a higher consciousness, or in other words, to help the soul to advance spiritually.

Mahārāja exposes the truth behind the duplicity of this material world created by Māyā, which women fail to understand due to their conditioned nature. He explains everything in such a clear, simple, and convincing manner that an ordinary and fallen soul like myself, and all others keen to find out the truth, can understand all the points.

He takes important teachings in certain sections of the *śāstras* prescribed for women and explains why they are to be followed, and why certain roles are not recommended for women to take up, as it is harmful for their spiritual advancement. He helped me to understand how the role of a woman as a wife is to submissively serve her husband attentively and consistently in favorable and unfavorable circumstances.

These classes are so powerful that they are capable of purifying us from various *anarthas* and misconceptions from so many lifetimes, which are rooted deep in our hearts and in our subconscious mind due to attachment to the material body and a reluctance to give up our false ego. I recommend all women to listen to these classes of such a pure soul like Mahārāja, who is capable of purifying them of their false ego.

Veena Kanchan
[Chartered Accountant, Mumbai]

Comments on the First Edition

Working on Bhakti Vikāsa Swami's book *Women: Masters or Mothers?* has been inspirational in helping to deepen my understanding of Śrīla Prabhupāda's example and instructions and has shown that we must carefully avoid the onslaught of the degraded mentality of Kali-yuga.

Madana-mohana-mohinī Devī Dāsī
[disciple of Śrīla Prabhupāda – Prabhupāda Village, North Carolina, USA]

Dear Ladies,

The choice is yours. The modern society is going in the wrong direction at a very high speed, and those women who want to escape from degradation can escape by following the guidelines in this book. Women in the modern age especially need such guidance, because this is now not available to us from any other source. By imitating the Western and materialistic lifestyles, the degradation among Indians is now even worse than that among Western people. The result is social calamities like divorce, gang rapes, child abuse, abortion, murders, etc. To stop these things, or at least escape from them, we women should use our intelligence to read this book and implement the teachings in our lives and thus benefit ourselves and the society. I was about to be spoiled by so-called women's education, career etc., but fortunately I escaped by following the instructions of my spiritual master,

His Holiness Bhakti Vikāsa Swami, and by the guidance of my devotee husband. I am now living very peacefully by being a housewife and a mother to my son.

Gīta Govinda Devī Dāsī
[resident of Māyāpur]

This book discusses all the important aspects of a woman's life, such as marriage, childbirth, education, and career, and provides the authorized Vedic perspective on them, being full of relevant quotes from Śrīla Prabhupāda's teachings and the *śāstras.* It encourages open-minded readers to question their own preconceived notions and the fact that today's society largely rejects traditional culture, which was superior, as primitive and exploitative. It describes in detail how accepting the real Vedic culture is not only beneficial for society in general but is particularly so for the members of ISKCON, as it provides an atmosphere which is most conducive for practicing spiritual life.

Women: masters or mothers? It is not actually a question of being one or the other. As Bhakti Vikāsa Mahārāja explains: "In Vedic culture, a woman may certainly be a 'master' in the sense of overseeing and being the queen of the home, or in the sense of being highly expert." This book suggests that women do not have to necessarily work with other men outside of their homes to be "empowered," but instead have a more powerful contribution to make by following their innate tendencies and being ideal wives and mothers at home by ensuring that the family is well taken care of. The need of the hour is indeed to return to traditional gender roles for, as Mahārāja points out, "ISKCON already has many devotees competent to deliver learned lectures, but we have yet to demonstrate to the world a better way of life based on stable, happy families." This book is a must-read for both men and women, because they must work together towards having stable Vaiṣṇava families across the entire ISKCON society.

Indirā-sakhī Devī Dāsī
[resident of Māyāpur]

Women: Masters or Mothers? is refreshingly different in that it makes us halt and review the direction our movement is taking and the path that we, its individual members, are treading.

His Holiness Bhakti Vikāsa Swami appears to have delved deep into the recesses of Śrīla Prabhupāda's mind and instructions before coming up with a searchlight to show us the way ahead.

This book draws attention to the danger for ISKCON in assimilating ideas wholesale from mainstream society, in the course of preaching.

It makes an urgent appeal to members to practise Kṛṣṇa consciousness without striking compromises with materialistic society. It shows how such compromises harm, hamper, and slow us down and how it could even eventually derail our movement.

While containing a wealth of advice on how female members of our movement might make their lives successful, the relevance of this book is by no means restricted to Vaiṣṇavīs alone.

This book has answered questions that troubled me and put to rest a growing sense of disquiet that I had been experiencing as a result of what I observed around me.

I urge those who are wary of picking up *Women: Masters or Mothers?* to disabuse their minds of prejudice and preconceived notions, and to take a good, hard look at what it proposes.

Su-gītā Vāṇī Devī Dāsī
[Māyāpur/Thiruvanantapuram]

This book makes no apologies for its stand on rules and roles. The controversial topic of the female-bodied soul is ongoing; one should understand it carefully, because it's not about putting down females but defining the use of the bodily machine for elevation. Even for the male-bodied there are defined rules according to one's duty. In Kṛṣṇa consciousness neither is put down, yet for both male or female a role is defined within certain parameters, the aim being elevation to Kṛṣṇa consciousness. There are two pathways from the fine to gross, and vice versa – the finest being spirit soul, where there is no distinction, all being feminine/servitors. Yet this platform is a very elevated position. One cannot, simply by bodily designation, claim to be on the supreme platform, where one of the features is extreme humility. This book attempts to address that issue. Another point that comes out in this topic is that although many of the confidential associates of Lord Caitanya were *sakhīs* or *mañjarīs,* they took male forms on this plane for preaching purposes – something to contemplate and meditate on.

Bhakta Piyush and Mādhavī Devī Dāsī
[residents of Māyāpur]

WOMEN

Masters or Mothers?

Books Authored by Bhakti Vikāsa Swami

A Beginner's Guide to Kṛṣṇa Consciousness
A Message to the Youth of India
Brahmacarya in Kṛṣṇa Consciousness
Glimpses of Traditional Indian Life
Jaya Śrīla Prabhupāda!
Lekha-mālā
My Memories of Śrīla Prabhupāda
On Pilgrimage in Holy India
On Speaking Strongly in Śrīla Prabhupāda's Service
Patropadeśa
Śrī Bhaktisiddhānta Vaibhava (three volumes)
Śrī Caitanya Mahāprabhu
Śrī Vaṁśīdāsa Bābājī
Vaiṣṇava Śikhā o Sādhana (Bengali)
Women: Masters or Mothers?

Books Edited or Compiled by Bhakti Vikāsa Swami

Rāmāyaṇa
The Story of Rasikānanda
Gauḍīya Vaiṣṇava Padyāvalī (Bengali)

WOMEN
Masters or Mothers?

A monograph for members of ISKCON
(the International Society for Krishna Consciousness)

Revised and Enlarged
(Second Edition)

Bhakti Vikāsa Swami

ISBN 978-93-82109-29-7

www.bvks.com

books@bvks.com

First Edition (February, 2015): 1,000 copies
Second Edition (April, 2015): 2,000 copies

The words *Conversation, Lecture, Letter,* and *purport* indicate quotations taken from published editions by or involving Śrīla Prabhupāda. *Conversation* subsumes all types of discussions with Śrīla Prabhupāda, variously classified by the Bhaktivedanta Archives as Morning Walks, Press Conferences, Room Conversations, etc. All such quotations are copyrighted by The Bhaktivedanta Book Trust International, Inc.

Published by Bhakti Vikas Trust, Surat, India.
Printed in India.

His Divine Grace

A. C. Bhaktivedanta Swami Prabhupāda

(Founder-*ācārya* of International Society for Krishna Consciousness)

Everything will be satisfied. Just like our women, Kṛṣṇa conscious – they are working. They don't want equal rights with the men. It is due to Kṛṣṇa consciousness. They are cleansing the temple, they are cooking very nicely; they are satisfied. They never said that "I have to go to Japan for preaching like Prabhupāda." They never say. This is artificial. Kṛṣṇa consciousness means work in his constitutional position. The women, men – when they remain in their constitutional position, there will be no artificial.

(Śrīla Prabhupāda, Conversation, 27 May 1974)

Contents

Preface to the Second Edition xvii
Introduction xxi

Part One 1

The Direction of the Kṛṣṇa Consciousness Movement: Merge with Modern Society, or Present the Varṇāśrama-dharma Alternative?

Devotees' Concern with and Approach to Social Issues 1
Kṛṣṇa Consciousness Is Largely Incompatible with Modern Culture 6
Scientism, Liberal Humanism, and Selfishness 8
Hedonistic Civilizations Are Doomed 10
Traditional Societies and the Dharmic Culture of India 12
Śrīla Prabhupāda's Outlook Was Not Mundane 14
Śrīla Prabhupāda Wanted to Introduce Divine Varṇāśrama-dharma 15
"Varṇāśrama-dharma Is External" 17
Devotees Need Varṇāśrama-dharma 19
Varṇāśrama-dharma (the Perfect Institution) Must Be Based On Kṛṣṇa Consciousness 20
Varṇāśrama-dharma Inculcates Selflessness 24
A Revolution of Consciousness 24
Varṇāśrama-dharma for Overcoming Sexual Desire 26
Śrīla Prabhupāda Slowly and Carefully Introduced Vedic Culture .. 28
Shared Cultures of Traditional Societies 30
"Preach Now, Varṇāśrama-dharma Now" 31
Śrīla Prabhupāda's Vision for Kṛṣṇa Conscious Farms 31
Rural Living Affords More Time for Kṛṣṇa Consciousness 33

Accepting Kṛṣṇa's Social System 35
An Experimental Revolution 36
ISKCON's Disconnect with Varṇāśrama 36
Traditional Culture Is Misunderstood 37
Slaughterhouse-education and Child Labor 38
Indian Culture and ISKCON 40
Preaching of Traditionalism in the West 42
An Overview of Religious and Political Reform 44
Ṛtvik Folly 45
The Basic Mistake of All Reformers 47
Understanding the Issues – Siddhānta 49
ISKCON Lite 51
ISKCON Has the Solution 52

Part Two 56

Women: Masters or Mothers?

Section One

Why Śrīla Prabhupāda Opposed Feminism 57
Demons Promote a Puffed-up Concept of Womanly Life 60
Respect for Women in Indian Culture 61
Feminism in ISKCON 63
Nasty Effects of Feminism Within ISKCON 67
Misunderstanding Śrīla Prabhupāda's Adjustments 69
Tweaking History by Blaming the Men 77
A Case Study: Yamunā Devī Dāsī 80
The Transformation of Women's Roles 82
Lust, Greed, and Exploitation 86
Sigmund Freud and His Followers 88
Sex, Dissatisfaction, and Family Decline 90
Men and Women Are Different 91
Feminist Folly 92
Demonic "Broad-mindedness" 101
Why Women Need Protection 102

Independent Women Are Unprotected, Exploited, and Unhappy.... 107
The Vital Role of Gṛhasthas 109
Women Should Be Married (Gṛhasthas, Not Sannyasis, Should Protect Them) 110
Women in Bengal 111
Illicit Sex in the Name of Religion 113
Fire and Butter 114
Even Paramahaṁsas Are Cautious About Female Association 115
Devotees Must Reject Feminism 116

Section Two

Fulfilling Women's Potential – As Mothers 121
Children Are the Victims 126
Frustration Due to Unrealistic Expectations 128
Early and Late Marriage 128
Arranged Marriage 133
"Love Marriage" 137
The Real Formula for Marital Success 138
Homemakers and Working Wives 139
The Scourge of Divorce 140
Discouraging Divorce Among Devotees 143
Divorce Can Be Averted 144
Family Planning and Big Families 144
Joint Families 147
Polygamy 147
Education for Girls: Chastity and Cooking 152
Victory for a Woman 156
Hopeless Women Become Feminists - Men Should Become First-class 157
Some Misconceptions of Men 159
Duties of Married Men 161

Section Three

Women As Leaders 167
Women As Gurus 170

Women Giving Classes and Leading Kīrtanas 173
Dancing 174
Menstruation 176
Calling Women "Prabhu" 180
Traditional Culture Is Still Appreciated 183
The Way Forward 185

Part Three 188

Gurudevis and Grandmothers 189
Feminist Rhetoric on Dandavats 195
"Sannyasinis".. 200
On the Subject of Female Diksha Gurus 202
Krsna Conscious Motherhood 213
Time for a Revolution 223
Playing the Hindu card 229

Suggested Further Reading 240
Acknowledgements 241
About the Author 242

Abbreviations

Bg: *Bhagavad-gītā*
Cc: *Śrī Caitanya-caritāmṛta*
SB: *Śrīmad-Bhāgavatam*
ppt: Bhaktivedanta purport

Preface to the Second Edition

The first edition of this book was released just a few weeks ago. However, several important points were not included therein, due to time constraints in the rush to make it available for the GBC* meetings in Māyāpur in early 2015.

Shortly after the first edition went on sale in Māyāpur, the Executive Committee (EC) of the GBC ordered the confiscation of the banners and posters used to promote it. (The banners and posters consisted of quotes from the text of the book along with photos of the front cover.)† Soon thereafter, I received an email from Anuttama Dāsa, on behalf of the EC, part of which went as follows:

> One of the primary purposes of the Māyāpur Festival is to create a sense of community, friendship, and camaraderie among ISKCON devotees.
>
> It is the opinion of the EC that the tone of the banners and posters used to promote your books run contrary to that goal and values. We respect that devotees have a right to a variety of opinions, but we believe those opinions need to be expressed in a way that doesn't offend or demean others.
>
> The EC received several complaints about the banners, and upon discussing, decided they should remain down. Their tone, in our estimation, was derogatory, disturbing, and divisive.

---

* GBC – Governing Body Commission.

† See: www.bvks.com/wmm_posters

> Śrīla Prabhupāda instructed the leaders of ISKCON to come to Māyāpur every year to discuss "Unity in Diversity." While we may differ in viewpoints and methods of serving His Divine Grace, there is a need to maintain civility in our chosen ways of communicating.
>
> We (the EC members) have not read the book yet, and we reserve our opinion on such. We have not restricted or prohibited the sale of the book.

It is not my intention to offend or demean anyone, nor to unnecessarily incite disturbance or division. However, before we stress unity, let us first be united in understanding Śrīla Prabhupāda's teachings and in acting accordingly. As I stated in *My Memories of Śrīla Prabhupāda:*

> Remembrance of Śrīla Prabhupāda, love for Śrīla Prabhupāda, praise of Śrīla Prabhupāda, and service to Śrīla Prabhupāda must all be based on obeying Śrīla Prabhupāda. Otherwise, such sentiments are superficial, hypocritical, and devoid of the potency to fulfil Śrīla Prabhupāda's mission of spreading Kṛṣṇa consciousness all over the world.*

In *On Speaking Strongly in Śrīla Prabhupāda's Service,* I wrote:

> According to the principle of unity and diversity that Śrīla Prabhupāda often stressed, the Kṛṣṇa consciousness movement can and should accommodate a variety of approaches toward the practice and propagation of devotional service. Yet in many cases the difference is not simply of approach, but a fundamental divergence in understanding what Kṛṣṇa consciousness entails and of the very purpose of the Kṛṣṇa consciousness movement.†

I respectfully submit that it is unrealistic to cite "unity in diversity" without conceding that a fundamental divergence

---

* Lecture: How to Glorify Śrīla Prabhupāda <www.bvks.com/2180>

† Lecture: Limitations of Unity in Diversity <www.bvks.com/20062>

exists within ISKCON over the issue of gender roles. The divergence is so deep that even a presentation (such as this book) that consists of reasoned arguments, backed by copious quotes from Śrīla Prabhupāda, is likely to be seen as derogatory, disturbing, and divisive by devotees who maintain a contrary perspective, whereas others are appalled by the male-female dynamic that for several years has been emanating from ISKCON's leadership. Clearly, my stating this will not please the feministic elements in ISKCON's leadership.

Notwithstanding the EC's claims of negative reports, the book sold well in Māyāpur, and seemed to be especially well received by many female devotees. Furthermore, a major turnaround in ISKCON's social polity took place just after the book's release; a proposal to bring *varṇāśrama-dharma* onto the ISKCON agenda was almost unanimously accepted by the GBC. Nevertheless, I have chosen to retain within this book much that might seem to be anachronized by that decision (for instance, the chapter "ISKCON's Disconnect with Varṇāśrama"), to at least underscore the enormous task of reorienting a society that has for an entire generation been adrift in this regard.

Although (in my perhaps not very humble opinion) the first edition stated a powerful case, this second edition is more comprehensive, having undergone considerable revision and expansion. May it be pleasing to Śrīla Prabhupāda and his faithful followers.

Introduction

Within the International Society for Krishna Consciousness (ISKCON), as in the great world around us, there are innumerable issues under discussion – political, social, economic, academic, scientific, etc. Many of the controversies in ISKCON center around the point "Should we pragmatically try to blend with modern society and adjust our teachings for the sake of preaching, or idealistically strive to create a Kṛṣṇa conscious revolution via *varṇāśrama-dharma?*"*

Obviously, these two vectors are not mutually exclusive. Every follower of Śrīla Prabhupāda accepts that ISKCON is meant for preaching Kṛṣṇa consciousness. And preaching in today's world necessitates various adaptations. But how far should we go? What is permissible and what is not? For example, should we have rock bands or just stick to traditional *kīrtana?* Do we incorporate the roles that contemporary Western society ascribes to women and homosexuals, or stick to Śrīla Prabhupāda's stated stance, which nowadays is widely viewed as antiquated, meanly discriminating, and unfair?

One reason for dispute is that Śrīla Prabhupāda made adjustments for Western preaching yet also repeatedly emphasized the superiority of Vedic culture and the need to introduce it. Should Śrīla Prabhupāda's cultural adjustments be permanently institutionalized, or taken further? Or should we rather adopt more of the "Indian-ness" that Śrīla Prabhupāda bequeathed us, by moving closer toward orthodox

---

* Lecture: Social Cooperation or Defiance <www.bvks.com/10457>

Vedic culture? Some devotees give greater importance to Śrīla Prabhupāda's willingness to adjust, while others emphasize the necessity to make real moves toward his stated objective for *varṇāśrama-dharma* as the social enactment of Kṛṣṇa consciousness, to offer an ideal alternative for today's unhappy world. The dichotomy is largely between the traditional and the modern, or Western.

Throughout this tract, I often use the word *traditional* to refer to the way of life that characterized India in the past and is widely followed still, as distinguished from modern or Western attitudes and norms (which are also extensively integrated into Indian life today). In some places, I also use the word *traditional* to refer to ancient cultures that in certain significant ways parallel the Vedic. My frequent use of the word *natural* indicates that which is according to the universal order, as ordained by the Supreme Lord.

Unless specifically indicated, my repeated references to feminism and feminists pertain particularly to those in the secular world, some manifestations of which are discussed herein. Although I argue that feminism within ISKCON is a reflection of that in the broader society, and is deeply influenced by it, I do not mean to insinuate that any devotees of ISKCON propound the more extreme and pernicious forms of feminism.

ISKCON's cultural divide is not unique. Similar controversies are playing out in many other religious institutions. For instance, both within ISKCON and in various Christian denominations, some mentors tend to privilege the perceived needs of individuals over the preservation of marriages, and thus are considerably more inclined to recommend divorce to couples undergoing serious marital discord; whereas other mentors, such as myself, will generally advise to tolerate many difficulties rather than undermine the sacred institution of marriage. Some people will protest that the latter approach messes up lives, especially those of women. But many will acquiesce: "Yes, this is what we need to hear. This kind of guidance is good for us."

My basic argument is that the attempt to incorporate within ISKCON any viewpoints or belief systems derived from mainstream society risks compromising the authenticity of the *saṅkīrtana* movement and disconnecting us from Śrīla Prabhupāda's mercy. I espouse that the traditional Indian way of life is the best for human stability and peacefulness – for making the best bargain out of a bad situation – and that only the Vedic system is really suitable for facilitating progress in Kṛṣṇa consciousness.* I particularly state this position: female followers of Śrīla Prabhupāda should adopt the role of mother rather than master.

Much of what is stated herein is especially applicable to the current situation in India, and will be more germane and intelligible for devotees who live there – although nearly all of these points would have been obvious to the general populace of past generations everywhere, and still will be obvious to the few remaining sane persons in these culturally challenged times.

Unfortunately, it cannot be expected that everyone will accept everything in this book – especially since one of its purposes is to counteract the erroneous propaganda that Śrīla Prabhupāda treated men and women equally in all respects. Even devotees who generally appreciate the recommendations herein might circumstantially be unable to follow them. For instance, many devotees are virtually locked into modern society, certain women are practically obliged to go to work, some couples

---

* Seminar: A Traditionalist Approach to Kṛṣṇa Consciousness <www.bvks.com/7224>

are unable to beget children, and some devotees who never wanted to divorce are presented with no other choice by their recalcitrant spouse.

Clearly, modern society is different from the Vedic civilization as Śrīla Prabhupāda has described it, and to follow Vedic culture is easier said than done. To perform devotional service according to the manner that Śrīla Prabhupāda has presented often necessitates defying conventional norms. As stated by Lord Kṛṣṇa in the *Bhagavad-gītā:*

> What is night for all beings is the time of awakening for the self-controlled; and the time of awakening for all beings is night for the introspective sage.[1]

Notwithstanding the inevitable difficulties that will arise in attempting to adopt the values described herein, my hope is that many devotees will, as far as possible, try to gravitate toward them, according to each individual's degree of conviction and specific circumstances.

Part one of this book is based on and developed from a lecture titled "The Basic Mistake of All Reformers" (given on 15 January 2013 in Vellore, India);* part two is from a three-session seminar titled "Women: Masters or Mothers?" (held on 13–14 June 2009 in Secunderabad, India).† Part three mostly consists of previously published articles – three by myself on topics related to ISKCON's gender issues, another by Phalinī Devī Dāsī on the same theme, plus two more of mine that are apposite to the direction of the Kṛṣṇa consciousness movement. These articles are reproduced here almost exactly as they first appeared, without editorial corrections or addition

* www.bvks.com/10309

† www.bvks.com/1244

1. Bg 2.69.

of diacritical marks. Part three also includes the previously unpublished "Playing the Hindu Card," and in this second edition a newly published essay by Revatī Devī Dāsī titled "Motherhood in Kṛṣṇa Consciousness."

This tract outlines general principles, but a huge body of research will be required to establish the details of *varṇāśrama-dharma.* Although many related topics, such as how men and women should dress and interact, also require considerable discussion, all such details will have to be covered in forthcoming books.* This volume is directional, and by no means exhaustive. It also features many generalizations and personal views of mine (albeit derived from a perspective grounded in *śāstra*). It is not presented in an academic manner, in the sense of including meticulously fashioned arguments accompanied by comprehensive information and references.

I crave the indulgence of the readers, should they find some points herein to be repetitive, for "repetition of something is necessary in order that we understand the matter thoroughly, without error."[1]

Bhakti Vikāsa Swami

---

* I have examined many of these topics (in further but not full detail) in various recorded talks, many of which are included in the DVD that accompanies the hard copy of this book (see inside back cover). These are also available online (see footnotes).

Cited hyperlinks to third-party web pages are archived at: www.bvks.com/wmm_citations

1. Bg 2.25, ppt.

PART ONE

The Direction of the Kṛṣṇa consciousness Movement:

Merge with Modern Society, or Present the Varṇāśrama-dharma Alternative?

Devotees' Concern with and Approach to Social Issues

Why should devotees be at all concerned with social issues? Shouldn't we just speak about Kṛṣṇa and topics directly related to Kṛṣṇa consciousness? Certainly, devotional service is ultimately a purely spiritual process, yet within this world psychological and social factors undeniably influence persons who are trying to cultivate spiritual consciousness. The outlook and attitudes of an aspiring transcendentalist will necessarily be affected by his previous impressions and by how he lives and acts within society.* In that regard, within the *Bhagavad-gītā* and *Śrīmad-Bhāgavatam,* Vedic social organization is discussed, along with the direct delineation of Kṛṣṇa consciousness. For instance, the Seventh Canto of *Śrīmad-Bhāgavatam* features an extended section wherein Nārada, who is famous as a *brahmacārī,* explains the various duties of the four social orders, and also the duties of women and related matters. And various *śāstras* (*Brahma-vaivarta Purāṇa, Mahābhārata, Śiva Purāṇa*) record graphic dialogs wherein Nārada inquires about and is instructed on the nature of women. Śrīla Prabhupāda also often discussed such subjects and gave many insights and directions pertaining to them.†

Śrīla Prabhupāda made it clear that a major objective of ISKCON's is to reform human society, so that the general populace may more easily take to Kṛṣṇa consciousness.[1] To achieve this stated goal of Śrīla Prabhupāda's, the members of the Kṛṣṇa consciousness movement must be clear about

* Lecture: Issues or Nāma-bhajana, Or Both? <www.bvks.com/20053>

† Lecture: Social Direction Needed in a Misled Age <www.bvks.com/2210>

1. As outlined in the "Seven Purposes of the International Society for Krishna Consciousness" and in many places elsewhere within the corpus of Śrīla Prabhupāda's teachings.

the social vision that he gave us, so that we can methodically work to effect it within the overall society. As with all other endeavors undertaken for the sake of Kṛṣṇa, our approach toward reforming society must begin with our *ācāryas'* vision, as they have explained it from the *śāstras* (authorized revealed scriptures). This means that our social vision is primarily realized from the verses of the *Bhagavad-gītā As It Is, Śrīmad-Bhāgavatam, Śrī Caitanya-caritāmṛta,* and especially the commentaries on them written by ISKCON's founder-*ācārya,* Śrīla Prabhupāda. Our social vision should be based on Śrīla Prabhupāda's books, because he ascribed the highest authority to them.*

In the following quotation, based on the text of *Śrīmad-Bhāgavatam,* Śrīla Prabhupāda explained the importance of *varṇāśrama-dharma:*

> The effect of adhering to the institution of *varṇāśrama* is gradual elevation to the spiritual platform and liberation from material bondage. By following the principles of *varṇāśrama-dharma,* one gets the opportunity to associate with devotees. Such association gradually awakens one's dormant propensity to serve the Supreme Personality of Godhead and frees one from all the basic principles of sinful life. One then gets the opportunity to offer unalloyed devotional service to the Supreme Lord, Vāsudeva.[1]

Or, as Śrīla Bhaktivinoda Ṭhākura put it:

> The main reason for the cultivation of *varṇāśrama-dharma* is to maintain the body, develop the mind, perform good works for society, and learn spiritual topics, all with the goal of developing pure devotional service. Who can deny the

---

* Lecture: Vaiṣṇava Ācāryas' Social Initiatives <www.bvks.com/165>

1. SB 5.19, summary.

> necessity of the *varṇāśrama* institution as long as the living being is bound up in the human body? If it is abandoned, and the above-mentioned four principles are lacking, the *jīva* will go astray and no good whatsoever will accrue to him. One should, therefore, strictly adhere to the rules governing *varṇāśrama* for the sake of the mind, society, and one's advancement in Kṛṣṇa consciousness. But the observance of *varṇāśrama-dharma* is not the sole business of the *jīva.* Therefore, with the assistance of *varṇāśrama-dharma,* one must cultivate pure devotional service. The purpose of the *varṇāśrama* institution is to facilitate the practice of devotional service.[1]

Śrīla Prabhupāda often emphasized the necessity and urgency of establishing *varṇāśrama-dharma:*

> There should be a thorough overhauling of the social system, and society should revert to the Vedic principles, that is, the four *varṇas* and the four *āśramas.*[2]

> The whole world has now become hell. So the Kṛṣṇa consciousness movement is a very important movement. It is overhauling the whole human – social, political, religious. So those who are engaged in the Kṛṣṇa consciousness movement should be very, very responsible, sober, try to understand the situation, and take shelter of Kṛṣṇa, and everything will become very successful.[3]

Thus Śrīla Prabhupāda's social vision of establishing *varṇāśrama-dharma,* derived from *śāstra* and the desire of the previous *ācāryas,* is clear and is stated profusely throughout his recorded teachings. Yet conversely, an alternative social vision that is not based on Śrīla Prabhupāda's books has become predominant within ISKCON. This vision was articulated in

---

1. *Jaiva Dharma* 3.4.
2. SB 4.29.54, ppt.
3. Lecture, 4 Dec 1973.

1998 by Jyotirmayī Devī Dāsī in her paper "Women in ISKCON in Prabhupāda's Times,"[1] which provided a manifesto for a brand of affirmative-action feminism within ISKCON. Therein she wrote:

> Authenticity of the Proposed Arguments
>
> Our subject here deals with the social application of Kṛṣṇa conscious principles, not with philosophical knowledge. Therefore many of the arguments given here do not come from Prabhupāda's books but from conversations between Śrīla Prabhupāda and his disciples in daily encounters, most of which of course did not get recorded. Many devotees do not trust these "Prabhupāda said," but Prabhupāda himself gave his opinion about these "Prabhupāda said." In a reunion in Māyāpur in 1975, the GBC told Prabhupāda: "There are so many 'Prabhupāda said'; better only accept what is in the books and tapes."
>
> Śrīla Prabhupāda answered: "No, what I say in talks also, many things I say are not in my books." (From Himāvatī.)* My information is coming from a notebook in which, all along the years, I noted the anecdotes related to me by devotees who lived closely with Prabhupāda or by devotees who received these stories from these first disciples. My other stories, which are irrefutable, are from Śrīla Prabhupāda's letters.

There are many difficulties with the above-stated argument, but I will briefly discuss two of the most problematic. First, the social vision articulated by Jyotirmayī Mātā is not based on statements from Śrīla Prabhupāda's books. Although she sometimes does cite Śrīla Prabhupāda, she emphasizes that her main argument depends primarily on anecdotes about Śrīla Prabhupāda recounted by other devotees; and she states that

* Another "Prabhupāda said"!

1. www.dandavats.com/?p=14535 (retrieved 25 Dec 2014).

her citations from Śrīla Prabhupāda's published letters (albeit "irrefutable") are only secondary evidence. For her, anecdotal testimony is prime.

But Śrīla Prabhupāda told us: "Everything I have wanted to say I have said in my books."[1] And in a letter, he wrote: "They misunderstand me. Unless it is there from me in writing, there are so many things that 'Prabhupāda said.'"[2] This is "irrefutable" counterevidence to Jyotirmayī Devī Dāsī's main argument, yet she attributes more weight to the anecdote by Himāvatī Devī Dāsī, whose testimony cannot be considered irrefutable.

The second, and maybe even more troubling, problem with Jyotirmayī's social vision is that she disconnects the "philosophical knowledge" presented in Śrīla Prabhupāda's books from "the social application of Kṛṣṇa conscious principles," which she infers from unrecorded anecdotes. Even if the anecdotes are one hundred percent accurate, they nonetheless must be understood in light of what Śrīla Prabhupāda has presented in his books. Her distinction between "philosophical knowledge" and "application" is improper, on the principle that a definite unity of thought pervades all of Śrīla Prabhupāda's statements, whether recorded or not. Hence, for followers of Śrīla Prabhupāda, any authentic social vision for ISKCON or beyond must derive its authority primarily from Śrīla Prabhupāda's books.

This principle of unity can be understood from an exchange with Professor Staal, wherein Śrīla Prabhupāda stated: "As the goal of spiritual realization is only one, love of God, so the Vedas stand as a single comprehensive whole in the matter of transcendental understanding. Only the incomplete views of various parties apart from the bona fide Vedic lines of

1. Letter from Tamāla Kṛṣṇa Goswami, 20 Jul 1977.

2. Letter, 2 Sep 1975.

teaching give a rupturous appearance to the *Bhagavad-gītā*."[1] Similarly, since Śrīla Prabhupāda perfectly represents a bona fide Vedic line, his statements should also be assumed to be "a single, comprehensive whole in the matter of transcendental understanding." And therefore any bona fide vision of a Kṛṣṇa conscious society must mainly derive from Śrīla Prabhupāda's books. As a general principle, statements made by Śrīla Prabhupāda in his books are more authoritative than other of his statements – which certainly are valuable, but only if accepted as secondary evidence.

Feminism within ISKCON is further discussed in Part Two of this book.

Kṛṣṇa Consciousness Is Largely Incompatible with Modern Culture

Śrīla Prabhupāda forthrightly and untiringly pointed out the defects of modern society, because he wanted to awaken people to their plight and give them the truth of Kṛṣṇa consciousness, which is the only panacea for the myriad troubles of mankind.* He referred to the "soul-killing civilization"[2] and "the civilization of polished cats and dogs,"[3] and analyzed the whole situation thus:

> The completely bewildered material civilization is wrongly directed toward the fulfillment of desires in sense gratification. In such civilization, in all spheres of life, the ultimate end is sense gratification. In politics, social service, altruism, philanthropy, and ultimately in religion or even in salvation, the very same tint of sense gratification is ever-increasingly

* Lecture: Modern Civilization is a Failure, Kṛṣṇa Consciousness is the Only Solution <www.bvks.com/1176>

1. *Science of Self-Realization*, ch. 3m.
2. *Īśopaniṣad*, mantra 3, ppt.
3. SB 1.8.5, ppt.

predominant. In the political field the leaders of men fight with one another to fulfill their personal sense gratification. The voters adore the so-called leaders only when they promise sense gratification. As soon as the voters are dissatisfied in their own sense satisfaction, they dethrone the leaders. The leaders must always disappoint the voters by not satisfying their senses. The same is applicable in all other fields; no one is serious about the problems of life.[1]

Indubitably, modern society fits Kṛṣṇa's description of the demons as given in chapter sixteen of the *Bhagavad-gītā*.* It is a distinctly unpleasant civilization, characterized by monstrous efforts to amass wealth and to develop industry, science, the military, and educational institutions dedicated to spewing out ever more useless knowledge – all for the sake of outdoing and dominating others. Being based on *dehātma-buddhi* (the bodily concept of life) and the quest for sense gratification, it has a completely different outlook from the Vedic.† A prime example is the modern attitude regarding women's role in society.

Devotees should understand that the endeavor to be Kṛṣṇa conscious while operating on a template that is basically demonic will simply not work. Kṛṣṇa has prescribed a particular way of life (*varṇāśrama-dharma*), with rules and regulations to be followed and attitudes to be imbibed, and therefore it is foolish and arrogant to think that we have a better idea than Kṛṣṇa, or to consider it acceptable to neglect Kṛṣṇa's prescription.

On Śrīla Prabhupāda's order, and by his mercy, the preaching of Kṛṣṇa consciousness is continuing throughout the world.

---

* Lecture: Modern Society - Full of Hypocrite Demons <www.bvks.com/2173>

† Lecture: Values of Western World are Opposite to Values of Kṛṣṇa Consciousness <www.bvks.com/2048>

---

1. SB 1.2.10, ppt.

Persons who become inspired by that preaching and desire to become Kṛṣṇa conscious will want to know how to best practice devotional service. But the praxes of Kṛṣṇa consciousness do not go well with modern culture, because today's lifestyle is based on sense gratification, whereas Kṛṣṇa consciousness ultimately requires that we forswear even the thought of sense gratification.

However, most devotees today have little choice but to try to make the best use of a bad bargain, because ISKCON has not yet developed the *varṇāśrama* alternative that Śrīla Prabhupāda mandated.

Scientism, Liberal Humanism, and Selfishness

The predominant worldview of modern society is a pastiche called liberal humanism, which is derived from the so-called "scientific outlook" and misleads people into thinking that there is no supreme controller, no absolute reality, that everything came into being without an ultimate cause, and that the universe is going on automatically according to some impersonal scientific laws.* The Big Bang theory postulates that once upon a time there was nothing, whence (inexplicably) came everything – for no reason and with nothing or no one having caused it. This baloney posing as science is a product of scientism, the dogmatic belief that science can explain everything in materialistic terms.† It admits no existence of the spiritual, and affords no goal of life other than to satisfy personal desire. All of this parallels Lord Kṛṣṇa's statement in the *Bhagavad-gītā* (16.8) regarding the godless outlook, and certifies this toxic society to be demonic.

* Lecture: Liberal Humanitarianism <www.bvks.com/10788>

† Seminar: The Challenge of Scientism <www.bvks.com/10947>

Liberal humanism is a largely atheistic development that promotes the primacy of human beings, both individually and collectively, and claims to be guided by rationalism and evidence rather than religious faith or established doctrines. It is a distinctly Western enterprise, with roots tracing back 2,500 years to the Greek philosopher Protagoras, a self-proclaimed agnostic who declared that "man is the measure of all things" and emphasized human subjectivity as the determinant of all understanding. More recent seminal Western thinkers who have furthered the evolution of liberal humanism include Voltaire, Rousseau, Darwin, Marx, Freud, Sartre, and other speculators who were "materially engrossed, being blind to the knowledge of ultimate truth."[1]

Liberal humanism translates into moral relativism: the theory that there is no fixed standard of right and wrong, that morality is "user definable." Notwithstanding any higher ideals that some humanist philosophers have aspired for, the overall social outcome of liberal humanism is the piggish attitude of "Eat, drink, and be merry, for tomorrow we shall all be dead" – that all beings live but once and therefore everyone should peacefully coexist and be free to pursue personal happiness to the extent that it causes no harm to others.

Liberal humanism promotes personal rights (especially in recent times, women's rights and gay rights) in the pursuit of "the kingdom of God without God."[2] Although meant to be altruistic, the actual result of emphasizing individual rights is the culture of selfishness – "Get what you can" – acting for one's own interests with little consideration for others or willingness to sacrifice for them. Such selfishness typifies modern society and underlies its prominent noxious

---

1. SB 2.1.2, verse translation.

2. SB 9.10.50, ppt.

tendencies – exploitation, envy, lust, greed, anger – all of which underlie the terrible problems that face mankind today, including ecological disaster, marital disruption, psychological disturbances, meaningless violence, and cheating by the bankers, politicians, and big corporations. All such anomalies are rooted in the mean spirit of selfishness, which itself is rooted in envy of Kṛṣṇa.

Hedonistic Civilizations Are Doomed

In his purport to verse 16.7 of the *Bhagavad-gītā*, Śrīla Prabhupāda stated that in every civilized society there are religious rules for governing behavior, which are established by God, but that demons do not want to accept such rules. It thus follows that by Vedic standards, Western society is uncivilized and demonic. Although Western thought is deeply contaminated by the lower modes of nature, the West considers itself the paragon for the rest of the world – that its lifestyle and values are the apex of human evolution, that Western civilization has at last got it right, whereas everyone in the past, and those today who are not as advanced, are simply wrong and need to be reformed, and, if necessary, by force.

However, pervading serious social problems and a deeply discontent population should be sufficient evidence that liberal humanism has failed to create peace and harmony. For instance, "Today nearly twenty percent of Americans have seen a [psycho-] therapist, and twenty percent are on some kind of medication for anxiety and depression."[1] Actually, almost everyone in the world suffers mentally due to pursuing a wrong goal of life. People become frustrated and desperate because they center their existence around sensual pleasure (especially sex) and clutter their lives with gizmos and gadgets

1. www.well.wvu.edu/articles/dispelling_the_top_eight_therapy_myths (retrieved 12 Sep 2014).

– cell phones, air conditioners, and whatnot. Their minds also are cluttered, with innumerable desires, anxieties, and misconceptions, a big pile of mental garbage that all amounts to spiritual emptiness.

And decadence leads to disaster. Civilizations that degrade into hedonism lose all moral strength and are overrun, as was the fate of the once-mighty Babylonian and Roman empires.

Western sociologists have noted that their civilization is decaying and cannot endure. As far back as the 1920s, Oswald Spengler, a German, published a series of works titled *The Decline of the West,* describing Western civilization as one wherein the populace constantly strives for the unattainable, thus making Occidental man a proud but tragic figure, for while he struggles and creates, he secretly knows that his actual goal will never be reached.

Of course it is easy to cast "the West" as one horrendous villain, but we should bear in mind that we are discussing complex social situations in a general way. Actually, in their everyday dealings many people in the West are civil, helpful, and polite. By no means are all Westerners enamored of the misplaced values of their society, which prioritizes the obscene accumulation of wealth by a few over the wellbeing of the masses, who are themselves but programmed consumers set up for exploitation. The crass, inhuman commercialism symbolized by Coca-Cola, MacDonald's, and Monsanto, and by Hollywood, Madison Avenue, and Wall Street (to name but a few), proclaim a spiritual bankruptcy that typifies the entire Western world.

Even if it does not soon collapse physically, politically, or economically or be smashed militarily, Western civilization is already condemned by its godless, inhuman pursuit of money and sense enjoyment. It beggars incredulity that devotees, who are blessed with access to the Divine Reality, would wish to cozy up to such a condemned society.

Traditional Societies and the Dharmic Culture of India

Traditional societies are based on religious ethics, on the understanding that what we do today affects our future, even beyond the grave, that there is both sin and piety, which derive from an ultimate, transcendent standard of good and evil.*

The moral relativist sees no wrong in, for instance, homosexual behavior: "What's the harm in consensual sex between two people of the same gender? They don't harm anyone." But persons with "the vision of eternity"[1] know that sex is meant for procreation, and therefore "recreational" sex is sinful, and that because homosexual union cannot produce a child, it is illicit sexual indulgence. It is harmful because illicit sex impedes each participant's progress on the path of self-realization. Furthermore, it is harmful to promote that it is not harmful.

Conversely, traditional societies emphasize the duty of each person toward the whole.† The concept of duty is particularly enshrined in the multilayered concept of dharma, which is the cornerstone of India's spiritual civilization. Life being complex, dharma can be very subtle and difficult to ascertain. Hence, for the guidance of humankind, many *śāstras* describe conflicting dharmas and their resolution – for instance, "Is it acceptable to

* Lecture: Traditional Morality and Contemporary Degradation <www.bvks.com/20138>

† Lecture: Everyone Speaks of Rights; No One Considers Duty <www.bvks.com/2094>

1. From Śrīla Prabhupāda's rendering of Bg 13.32.

kill one person in order to save two lives"? Indeed, the whole story of the *Mahābhārata* is a record of the differing responses of dharmic and adharmic persons to an intricate web of dilemmas.* And the *Bhagavad-gītā,* the philosophical crest jewel within the *Mahābhārata,* develops from Arjuna's being confused about his duty. He was obliged to join his brothers in battle, yet he felt that no intrinsic good could come from it – so should he fight or not?[1]

Still today, albeit in often-corrupted forms, dharma largely defines India and especially Hinduism. Undeniably, contemporary Indian society is beset by myriad social problems, which may well be a reason why some Western devotees are wary of what they see as an "Indianization" of the Kṛṣṇa consciousness movement. But the genuine Indian culture (*varṇāśrama-dharma*) is pervaded by a sense of dharma, which provides a natural basis for and is practically inseparable from Kṛṣṇa consciousness.†

Even though India, or Bhārata, has to a large extent lost its original values, it still nurtures vital cultural factors (derived from the ancient understanding and practice of *varṇāśrama-dharma*) that are conducive to Kṛṣṇa consciousness and are noticeably absent in contemporary Western culture. A prominent example is the annual gathering of millions for bathing in the sacred river Gaṅgā at Prayāga-rāja (Allahabad); and it is estimated that every twelve years, forty million people converge there on Makara-saṅkrānti, one of the main bathing days. It is easy to see that Vedic culture still stands strong in India (although with the march of Kali-yuga, traditions are on the wane there as well).

---

* Lecture: Dilemmas of Dharma <www.bvks.com/2239>

† Lecture: India - Ancient and Modern <www.bvks.com/5034>

1. See Bg 2.7.

Śrīla Prabhupāda's Outlook Was Not Mundane

Many people who were dissatisfied with straight American life became attracted to Śrīla Prabhupāda's starkly different alternatives, but time showed that not all were ready to fully follow him. Knowingly or unknowingly, numerous devotees carry with them the baggage of worldviews developed from the speculations of various demons (Darwin, Marx, Freud, et al).* For them, some of Śrīla Prabhupāda's teachings, particularly those regarding gender roles and non-egalitarianism, are very difficult to accept. Most newcomers to Kṛṣṇa consciousness (especially in the West) are steeped in these kinds of wrong understandings and have zero knowledge of dharmic principles, roles, and duties. Even after they have begun the steady practice of Kṛṣṇa consciousness, they do not imbibe such ideals – one reason being that such topics are hardly encouraged or discussed within ISKCON.

But a major objective of Śrīla Prabhupāda's mission was to, as far as possible, reestablish pristine Vedic culture, including early marriage, polygamy, and a non-egalitarian social system. To most people raised in the modern ethos, such concepts will seem unrealistic, bizarre, primitive, and repressive.

Hence the dichotomy of a movement that theoretically follows Śrīla Prabhupāda but is actually much influenced by persons whose outlook is largely antithetical to the culture that he represented. Because Śrīla Prabhupāda's social outlook is disliked by many of his so-called followers, it is now not uncommon to hear statements such as "I agree with Śrīla Prabhupāda's spiritual teachings but not his material teachings," nor unusual to encounter the notion that Śrīla Prabhupāda's social outlook was influenced by his education

* Lecture: How Culture Influences Devotees <www.bvks.com/1613>

in a British-run school, whence (it is supposed) he imbibed Victorian attitudes.* However, a better understanding is that any similarities between Victorian morality and Śrīla Prabhupāda's position are because Victorian ethics match the directions of *śāstra.*

It is not that Śrīla Prabhupāda was just old-fashioned and out of sync with contemporary "progressive" thought. Yet persons who are perhaps unwittingly "attracted by demonic and atheistic views"[1] derived from the liberal humanistic culture in which they were raised, try to portray Śrīla Prabhupāda as having been influenced by mundane ideas.

Śrīla Prabhupāda always emphasized that he was presenting perfect knowledge, he himself having strictly adhered to guru, sadhu, and *śāstra.* It was through *śāstra-cakṣur* (the eye of *śāstra*) that he discerned various problems in human society and offered solutions to them. He always claimed to abide by *śāstra,* and would extensively quote *śāstra* to substantiate his statements. He did not attempt to introduce anything contrary to the principles of *śāstra.* He therefore was an ideal *ācārya* – one who knows the principles of *śāstra* and how to apply them in different times, places, and circumstances.

Śrīla Prabhupāda Wanted to Introduce Divine Varṇāśrama-dharma

In discussing *varṇāśrama-dharma,* it is most important to clearly distinguish between the original, divine method (*daiva-*

* See http://www.dandavats.com/?p=12095 (retrieved on 22 Apr 2015).

The Victorian era is broadly the latter part of the 19th century, when Victoria was the British monarch and middle-class morality was notably conservative, especially in regard to sexuality and gender roles. This era was also the Empire period, during which Britain achieved unprecedented influence throughout the world.

1. From Śrīla Prabhupāda's rendering of Bg 9.12.

varṇāśrama) and its present perverse manifestation as *āsura-varṇāśrama,* the caste system based solely on birth.* Devotees must clearly understand this difference, both to disabuse others and to not themselves re-create a new kind of caste system in the name of *varṇāśrama-dharma.*† It was *daiva-varṇāśrama-dharma* that Śrīla Prabhupāda advocated even in his earliest writings. He increasingly emphasized it after establishing Kṛṣṇa consciousness in the West.‡

> Hearing his conversations and lectures in chronological order gives us the chance to examine the evolution of Śrīla Prabhupāda's *varṇāśrama* presentation over time. During the earliest days he presents *varṇāśrama* as an ideal social structure, but one which is probably not possible for the present age. Nevertheless, even in that early period, he is intent on creating *brāhmaṇas* – devotees who would provide a "head" for society, giving it sound spiritual guidance. During the middle period, he proposes that ISKCON's *brāhmaṇas* provide the leadership to create a model of *varṇāśrama* in which the rest of the world can also be included. In the final phase, he presents *varṇāśrama* as an important preaching tool and a structure to be implemented initially "within our ISKCON society," with devotees in the Kṛṣṇa consciousness movement participating at every level.[1]

As Śrīla Prabhupāda famously stated: "Fifty percent of my work is not complete, because I have not established *varṇāśrama-dharma.*"[2] And: "I have only done fifty percent of what I want to do. The farms have to be done. If they are established,

* Lecture: Systematic and Chaotic Varṇāśrama <www.bvks.com/1041>

† Lecture: About Caste System <www.bvks.com/1112>

‡ Lecture: Śrīla Prabhupāda's Varṇāśrama Mission <www.bvks.com/145>

1. From the introduction to *Varṇāśrama-dharma* (comp. Hare Kṛṣṇa Devī Dāsī).
2. Cited by several devotees, e.g. Abhirāma Dāsa, as quoted in the book entitled *Varṇāśrama-dharma.*

varṇāśrama will be established."[1] While recognizing that it is unfeasible to fully revive *varṇāśrama-dharma* in Kali-yuga,[2] Śrīla Prabhupāda desired to do so as far as possible.[3]

"Varṇāśrama-dharma Is External"

Śrī Caitanya Mahāprabhu's famous statement that *varṇāśrama-dharma* is external (*eho bāhya*)[4] should be understood contextually, especially considering that *śāstra* recommends, and Vaiṣṇava *ācāryas* uphold, that aspiring devotees should act according to *varṇāśrama* norms at least until they have attained the perfected stage.[5]

Śrīla Prabhupāda explained:

> *Eho bāhya.* Caitanya Mahāprabhu was interested only on the spiritual platform. He rejected the material side. Our position is different. We are trying to implement Kṛṣṇa consciousness in everything. And Caitanya Mahāprabhu personally took *sannyāsa.* He rejected completely material. *Niṣkiñcana.* But we are not going to be *niṣkiñcana.* We are trying to cement the troubled position of the ... That is also in the prescription of *Bhagavad-gītā.* We are not rejecting the whole society. Caitanya Mahāprabhu rejected everything: *eho bāhya.* Rejected meaning "I do not take much interest in this." *Bāhya:* "It is external." He was simply interested in the internal, the spiritual. But our duty is that we shall arrange the external affairs all so nicely that one day they will come to the spiritual platform very easily, paving the way. And Caitanya Mahāprabhu, personality like that, they have nothing to do with this material world. But we

---

1. *TKG's Diary,* 10 Aug.
2. SB 1.1.11, ppt.
3. Conversation, 14 Feb 1977.
4. Cc 2.8.59.
5. See SB 3.29.15, 11.20.9.

> are preaching. Therefore we must pave the situation in such a way that gradually they will be promoted to the spiritual plane.[1]

"External" does not mean unnecessary. It means "extrinsic to the essence," or that which is not required for those who are in full Kṛṣṇa consciousness. External activities are unavoidable for persons who are outside the spiritual realm, and *varṇāśrama-dharma* offers guidance regarding how to act in this external world to persons who wish to leave it and return to the spiritual abode. Analogously, a hospital patient must undergo therapy; by accepting a course of blood transfusions, enemas, surgeries, x-rays, and so forth, he should become sufficiently fit to be discharged and return to healthy society, after which he no longer has any need for medical treatment. Similarly, persons who are outside the spiritual world but want to get inside must perform activities within this material world, and they should do so according to *varṇāśrama-dharma.**

It must be iterated that devotees who stress Śrīla Prabhupāda's order to establish *varṇāśrama-dharma* are fully aware that it is neither the goal of life nor the best means to attain that goal (especially in this Kali-yuga, when chanting of the holy names is the *yuga-dharma* and *varṇāśrama-dharma* cannot be followed very punctiliously). Still, "even if there is some temporary disturbance in the execution of the *varṇāśrama-dharma* principles, they can be revived at any moment.[2] To the degree that it can be instituted, *varṇāśrama-dharma* is needed for devotees, and actually for the entire world, if at all sanity is to be restored within it.†

* Article: Varṇāśrama and Bhakti <www.bvks.com/reader/articles/varnasrama_and_bhakti>

† Lecture: Varṇāśrama is External to Bhakti, but Still Required <www.bvks.com/10717>

1. Conversation, 14 Feb 1977.

2. SB 5.19, summary.

Devotees Need Varṇāśrama-dharma

Although devotional service is transcendental, most devotees are not fully on the transcendental stage and therefore require to practice *varṇāśrama-dharma.* Even great *ācāryas,* who for their own sake do not need to follow the worldly rules of *varṇāśrama-dharma,* nevertheless act on the platform of *varṇāśrama-dharma* to educate others. For example, that is why Śrīla Bhaktisiddhānta Sarasvatī superficially stepped down to the level of *sannyāsa* (a stage of *varṇāśrama-dharma*). Previously he had been leading a visibly renounced life akin to that of Gaurakiśora Dāsa Bābājī, yet after he adopted *sannyāsa* he availed of big buildings, automobiles, and stylish clothing, just to teach others how to become Kṛṣṇa conscious while living in this world.

However, very few devotees are anywhere near the plane of the great *ācāryas.* Most of us, if we are honest, will have to admit that we struggle with base material desires. And even if a devotee considers himself to be fully realized, others might discern that he is delusional. It is easy to proclaim and advertise, but it is not so common to actually be a pure, spotless devotee, free from all material attraction. Philosophically, we all accept that we are not man or woman, black or white, Indian or Chinese – that as spiritual beings we are all intrinsically equal – yet we should realistically admit that almost all devotees are actually not on the topmost spiritual platform, and that we therefore need to conduct our lives accordingly.

Although in one sense all devotees are on the transcendental platform, most seem to not be very firmly situated thereon, as suggested by the not infrequent sexual falldowns within ISKCON. Such falldowns are likely to remain common unless the movement adopts significantly stricter adherence to the *varṇāśrama-dharma* principle of restricting interaction between the sexes.

Śrīla Prabhupāda was once asked, "We have the perfect philosophy, the perfect way of life, and the perfect guru [Śrīla Prabhupāda], so why do we have so many problems in our society?" And Śrīla Prabhupāda replied, "Because the *brahmacārīs* and sannyasis mix too much with the women."[1]

Śrīmad-Bhāgavatam (7.12.9) states:

> Woman is compared to fire, and man is compared to a butter pot. Therefore a man should avoid associating even with his own daughter in a secluded place. Similarly, he should also avoid association with other women. One should associate with women only for important business and not otherwise.

In his purport to this verse, Śrīla Prabhupāda explains:

> If a butter pot and fire are kept together, the butter within the pot will certainly melt. Woman is compared to fire, and man is compared to a butter pot. However advanced one may be in restraining the senses, it is almost impossible for a man to keep himself controlled in the presence of a woman, even if she is his own daughter, mother, or sister. Indeed, his mind is agitated even if one is in the renounced order of life. Therefore, Vedic civilization carefully restricts mingling between men and women. If one cannot understand the basic principle of restraining association between man and woman, he is to be considered an animal. That is the purport of this verse.

Varṇāśrama-dharma (the Perfect Institution) Must Be Based On Kṛṣṇa Consciousness

As a complete social system, *varṇāśrama-dharma* not only assists in sensual control but also offers a comprehensive solution for modern crises. Whereas today's civilization induces people to pursue unreal and abnormal aspirations

1. Told by Girirāja Swami.

that inevitably end in frustration (if not disaster), *varṇāśrama-dharma* enables both men and women to find fulfillment in their natural roles. *Varṇāśrama-dharma* regulates the lower propensities and channels them toward higher propensities.

Although egalitarianism is supposed to provide equal opportunities, almost inevitably "might makes right" and the weak are exploited. Vedic culture is more realistic, for it recognizes that people are different and have different needs and capabilities, and accordingly assigns commensurate functions to individuals, thus maximizing their opportunities for personal development.

Varṇāśrama-dharma is "the perfect institution for humanity."[1] Of course, the enactment of *varṇāśrama-dharma* can never be fully perfect, inasmuch as it is meant for regulating imperfection, for normalizing people who are affected by *māyā.* And without Kṛṣṇa consciousness, *varṇāśrama-dharma* must inevitably degrade.

Lord Kṛṣṇa created the system of four *varṇas* (*brāhmaṇa, kṣatriya, vaiśya,* and *śūdra*) according to quality and work,[2] concomitant with which is the system of four *āśramas* (*brahmacārī, gṛhastha, vānaprastha,* and *sannyāsa*). Śrīla Prabhupāda gave an overview of *varṇāśrama-dharma* as follows:

> Human life is meant for understanding one's relationship with the Supreme Lord and acting in that relationship. Any human being can do this by dovetailing himself in the service of the Lord while discharging his prescribed duties. For this purpose human society is divided into four classes: the intellectuals (*brāhmaṇas*), the administrators (*kṣatriyas*), the merchants (*vaiśyas*), and the laborers (*śūdras*). For each class there are prescribed rules and regulations, as well as

1. SB 4.24.53, ppt.
2. Bg 4.13, verse translation.

occupational functions. The prescribed duties and qualities of the four classes are described in the *Bhagavad-gītā* (18.41–44). A civilized society should be organized so that people follow the prescribed rules and regulations for their particular class. At the same time, for spiritual advancement they should follow the four stages of *āśrama,* namely student life (*brahmacarya*), householder life (*gṛhastha*), retired life (*vānaprastha*) and renounced life (*sannyāsa*)....

Those who strictly follow the rules and regulations of these eight social divisions can actually satisfy the Supreme Lord, and one who does not follow them certainly spoils his human form of life and glides down toward hell. One can peacefully achieve the goal of human life simply by following the rules and regulations which apply to oneself. The character of a particular person develops when he follows the regulative principles in accordance with his birth, association, and education. The divisions of society are so designed that many people with different characteristics can be regulated under those divisions for the peaceful administration of society and for spiritual advancement as well. The social classes can be further characterized as follows: (1) One whose aim is to understand the Supreme Lord, the Personality of Godhead, and who has thus devoted himself to learning the Vedas and similar literatures is called a *brāhmaṇa.* (2) A person whose occupation involves displaying force and administering the government is called a *kṣatriya.* (3) One who is engaged in agriculture, herding cows and doing business is called a *vaiśya.* (4) One who has no special knowledge but is satisfied by serving the other three classes is called a *śūdra.* If one faithfully discharges his prescribed duties, he is sure to advance toward perfection. Thus regulated life is the source of perfection for everyone. One who leads a regulated life centered around devotional service to the Lord attains perfection.[1]

---

1. From *Teachings of Lord Caitanya,* ch. 27.

Succinctly, *varṇāśrama-dharma* is the natural, practical, and efficient organization of human society as ordained by the Supreme Lord, whereby people are engaged in work according to their individual propensities and dispositions, while also regulating their senses and offering the results of their labor for Kṛṣṇa's satisfaction. Everyone is obligated to worship the Supreme Lord according to the facility he has been given, in a spirit of devotional service. The spirit of service, of dharma, of duty – doing what is right as opposed to what feels good – is inculcated in *varṇāśrama-dharma,* and matures into perfection as pure devotional service. As expressed by Tamāla Kṛṣṇa Goswami:

> The Vedic culture provides equal opportunities for all devotees to advance in Kṛṣṇa consciousness. With intelligence, it recognizes psychophysical differences between the sexes as well as between individuals within each sex, while at the same time maintaining a spiritual equality. This allows for an individual to utilize his or her abilities maximally. And it also ensures the peaceful continuation of normal relationships within the family and in the greater society at large. Although modern critics may doubt the value of such an ordered social structure, they should bear in mind that the Vedic social system has been successful for millions of years, having been created by Lord Kṛṣṇa Himself. We do not believe that the present so-called civilization, despite its constant innovations, will be able to stand the similar test of time.[1]

In a dharmic society, none of the law-abiding citizens feel oppressed or despised. Rather, *varṇāśrama-dharma* promotes mutual sharing, appreciation, and service between all classes of people, and when practiced in Kṛṣṇa consciousness, it helps aspiring devotees to rise to the highest platform. However, if not practiced in Kṛṣṇa consciousness, *varṇāśrama-dharma*

---

1. *Servant of the Servant,* ch. 9.

is mundane and thus gives rise to the material disease of exploitation. The caste system arose in India because people lost the true spiritual focus of *varṇāśrama-dharma* and instead used it to exploit others. Śrīla Prabhupāda very much desired to introduce the genuine, ancient, and sound method of *varṇāśrama-dharma,* both to regulate his own disciples and to rectify the social ills that afflict the world today.[1]

Varṇāśrama-dharma Inculcates Selflessness

Everyone in this world has, at least to some extent, the inherent tendency toward selfishness and exploitation,[2] but *varṇāśrama-dharma* is designed to purify such proclivities and lead persons to a consciousness of selflessness. The whole system of dharma is meant to instill selflessness, following the ideals of exemplars like Lord Rāma, the Supreme Personality of Godhead in the form of an ideal king who is genuinely concerned about the welfare of his citizens.

Śāstra describes many other ideal characters, such as Mahārāja Śibi, who demonstrated selflessness and compassion by giving his body for the sake of a pigeon.[3] Such anecdotes are recounted to wean people from the attitude of exploitation and ultimately draw them toward the highest consciousness of full selflessness in pure love of Kṛṣṇa.*

A Revolution of Consciousness

There have been several major revolutions that have profoundly affected the course of modern history, prominent among which were the American, the French, and the Russian revolutions,

* Lecture: The Dharma of Being Happy <www.bvks.com/11112>

1. Conversation, 14 Feb 1977.

2. See Bg 7.27.

3. See SB 1.12.20, ppt.

and even more so the Industrial Revolution. The French Revolution and the Russian Revolution were fought to supplant the incumbent hierarchy with a more egalitarian society. The American Revolution was for kicking out the British. As Śrīla Prabhupāda noted, "The point is that when people become unhappy, they revolt. That was done in America, that was done in France, and that was done in Russia."[1] The Industrial Revolution was a different kind of upheaval, which engendered several kinds of unforeseen disastrous effects, among them the unprecedented ability to conduct warfare and wreak destruction in ever more sophisticated and devastating ways.

"Revolution" means "a return to the original point," yet for all their bravado and radical changes, all these revolutions simply continued to perpetuate material existence, characterized by eating, sleeping, mating, and defending, all in forgetfulness of Kṛṣṇa. But Śrīla Prabhupāda's "revolution in the impious life of a misdirected civilization"[2] is a revolution in the fullest sense of the term. It is a revolution of consciousness, of going back to our original, pure consciousness of love of God. This revolution affects all aspects of human life and proposes to revamp social organization on a basis that is completely different from that of any revolution conceived in terms of alternative formats for eating, sleeping, mating, and defending.* As such, Śrīla Prabhupāda's revolution is the antidote for all imperfect and misleading revolutions, and is particularly a rejection of the civilization that evolved in the wake of the Industrial Revolution.

Śrīla Prabhupāda's revolution does not require guns and bombs, tanks and drones, or even an inordinate emphasis on politics. The social aspect of his revolution, of going back to the land for living simply and cooperatively in service to God,

* Lecture: A Revolution Against Materialism <www.bvks.com/20004>

1. *The Science of Self-realization,* ch. 6d.

2. SB 1.5.11, verse translation.

is the greatest possible societal revolution. It is not about who amasses money and power, for it rejects these as criteria on which to base a civilization. It is a nonviolent revolution for undermining the entire foundation of materialistic society – whether manifest as democracy, socialism, or whatever – by cutting out of the money-culture and establishing peaceable living in pursuance of love of God.

Śrīla Prabhupāda's revolution is a revolutionary concept of revolution.* It is a revolution of consciousness. People should evolve from the consciousness of trying to enjoy this world to the consciousness of living in it for the sake of serving Kṛṣṇa. A revolution of consciousness might sound vague or impractical, but Śrīla Prabhupāda – himself eminently pragmatic in everything that he did – envisaged a workable reorganization of society, with a shift to agrarian-centered economy and rural life, and with specialized, distinct duties for *brāhmaṇas, kṣatriyas, vaiśyas,* and *śūdras,* according to inherent qualities and disposition. People should marry young and never divorce – quite a revolutionary concept in the modern world. The distinctly feminine role of women as mothers and wives, and subordinate to men, is definitely a contentious point for many people today (but by no means all). And women should become wives before becoming mothers – not the other way around.

Varṇāśrama-dharma for Overcoming Sex Desire

A few years after Śrīla Prabhupāda's establishing of ISKCON, it became apparent that many of his disciples, despite having practiced devotional service for some time, would again fall away. Such is common in the West, where the fever of sense gratification is so high that certain sinful practices, such as

* Lecture: Śrīla Prabhupāda's Strategies for Revolution <www.bvks.com/20189>

illicit sex and gross intoxication, are considered normal and even desirable; so it is very easy even for practicing devotees to succumb to temptations for indulging in such abominable activities.

It is stated in the *Bhagavad-gītā* (3.36): *anicchann api vārṣṇeya balād iva niyojitaḥ,* "being impelled to sinful acts, even unwillingly, as if engaged by force." Some devotees who actually wanted to be Kṛṣṇa conscious were just pulled away as if driven by their senses. To safeguard against such cases, Śrīla Prabhupāda wanted to introduce *varṇāśrama-dharma,* the social system given by Kṛṣṇa (*cātur-varṇyaṁ mayā sṛṣṭaṁ guṇa-karma-vibhāgaśaḥ*),[1] to help his disciples remain on the standard of Kṛṣṇa consciousness, by adhering to the four regulative principles and by daily chanting sixteen rounds of the *mahā-mantra.* Even more ambitiously, Śrīla Prabhupāda proposed to regulate all of humankind so that people worldwide may avail of Vedic culture (also termed *varṇāśrama-dharma,* or *sanātana-dharma,* or the ancient culture of pious Indians), which is more conducive for adopting Kṛṣṇa consciousness.

Aspiring devotees need to follow *varṇāśrama-dharma* to help them rise to the perfect platform. *Māyā* is very, very powerful, and to suppose that she is easy to overcome is foolishness. The basic principle of this *māyā,* of material existence, is the attraction between male and female:

> *puṁsaḥ striyā mithunī-bhāvam etaṁ*
> *tayor mitho hṛdaya-granthim āhuḥ*
> *ato gṛha-kṣetra-sutāpta-vittair*
> *janasya moho 'yam ahaṁ mameti*

> The attraction between male and female is the basic principle of material existence. On the basis of this misconception, which ties together the hearts of the male and female, one becomes attracted to his body, home, property, children, relatives and

1. Bg 4.13.

> wealth. In this way one increases life's illusions and thinks in terms of "I and mine."[1]

Varṇāśrama-dharma is required to help in overcoming the sexual impulse. As Śrīla Prabhupāda explained:

> What is the big plan behind these regulative principles? The big plan is: here is the attraction – *puṁsaḥ striyā mithunī-bhāvam* – to cut down this attraction between male and female. This is the big plan. Otherwise there is no need of *varṇāśrama-dharma. Varnāśrama* means to train the candidates gradually to become free from this entanglement of man and woman. This is the basic principle.[2]

> The entire Vedic system teaches one to avoid sex life so that one may gradually progress from *brahmacarya* to *gṛhastha,* from *gṛhastha* to *vānaprastha,* and from *vānaprastha* to *sannyāsa* and thus give up material enjoyment, which is the original cause of bondage to this material world.[3]

According to the rules of *varṇāśrama-dharma,* men and women are to be separated to a large extent because unless there are systems to regulate the association between men and women, sexual attraction increases, leaving little hope for spiritual advancement. Therefore *varṇāśrama-dharma* society has strict rules to protect both men and women from their lower natures, and especially to preserve women's respectability and chastity.

Śrīla Prabhupāda Slowly and Carefully Introduced Vedic Culture

Although Śrīla Prabhupāda came to the West with spiritually revolutionary intents, he adapted and adjusted as necessary,

1. SB 5.5.8.
2. Lecture, 30 Oct 1976.
3. SB 7.12.7, ppt.

to some extent integrating local norms and practices, as was required for introducing Kṛṣṇa consciousness in such an alien ethos. At the outset, while clearly expressing his spiritual aim, he spoke little about his social plans. As an expert teacher, he did not attempt to do the impossible among the wild and uncouth hippies who mostly comprised his early followers. Perceiving that "Vedic culture is a very difficult civilization for the Westerners,"[1] he first induced them to take *prasāda,* chant Hare Kṛṣṇa, and hear Vaiṣṇava philosophy, without introducing many of the finer points of Vedic culture. Indeed, initially Śrīla Prabhupāda largely overlooked the free mixing of young men and women (although he did ask those of his disciples who were living together as couples to marry). In fact, it was not until several years after incorporating ISKCON that he began to press his disciples to institute *varṇāśrama-dharma* and its many attendant usages, all of which he had already extensively discussed in his books.

Śrīla Prabhupāda carefully introduced Lord Kṛṣṇa's ancient Vedic culture, according to the gradual awakening and growing receptivity of his audience. Step-by-step, he introduced more rules, thus steering his followers closer toward Kṛṣṇa consciousness as it had been practiced for generations in India. Having brought Kṛṣṇa consciousness to the West, he started to bring his Western disciples to India, with the express purpose of introducing them to the culture in which Kṛṣṇa consciousness can grow naturally, and he wanted his Western disciples to adopt it as far as possible. By observing the conduct of Indians in the 1970s, these early disciples were exposed to many cultural truths – for instance, that as a principle for spiritual advancement, men and women do not intermingle freely, let alone dance in close proximity. And having observed various long-established Vaiṣṇava practices in India, certain of his leading disciples began to implement them within ISKCON.

1. Conversation, 15 May 1976.

Shared Cultures of Traditional Societies

Many of the principles in Vedic *śāstra* and culture parallel those in religious traditions worldwide. Examples are sex allowed only within marriage, contraception and abortion considered sinful, and taboos on homosexuality. I remember as a child attending Catholic church in England; the men were on one side and the women on the other, and the women wore headscarves. But all that changed after the Second Vatican Council in the 1960s, which instituted many compromises. Nonetheless, up to the present in Russia and much of Eastern Europe (areas which are in many important ways more traditional and less hedonistic than Western Europe and the USA), elderly women are generally seen wearing headscarves. Muslim women still cover their head (if not their whole body) in public – which some people think is inhumanly restrictive but is appreciated by a chaste woman as being cultured and dignified.

Śrīla Prabhupāda similarly described:

> Even fifty or sixty years ago in Calcutta, all respectable ladies would go to a neighboring place riding on a palanquin carried by four men. The palanquin was covered with soft cotton, and in that way there was no chance of seeing a respectable lady traveling in public. Ladies, especially those coming from respectable families, could not be seen by ordinary men. This system is still current in remote places. The Sanskrit word *asūrya-paśyā* indicates that a respectable lady could not be seen even by the sun. In the oriental culture this system was very prevalent and was strictly observed by respectable ladies, both Hindu and Muslim. We have actual experience in our childhood that our mother would not walk even next door to observe an invitation; rather, she would go in either a carriage or a palanquin carried by four men.[1]

---

1. Cc 1.13.114, purport.

"Preach Now, Varṇāśrama-dharma Now"

Some devotees have posited that we should just preach instead of getting sidetracked by contentious social issues: "The world is going to hell and the urgent need is to propagate Kṛṣṇa consciousness. We can deal with other issues later. Right now we should do whatever is necessary to get people to chant Hare Kṛṣṇa, in comparison to which whatever else they do or think is inconsequential."

We are not advocating to stop preaching. But as long as we are not serious about instituting *varṇāśrama-dharma,* we will continue to experience the same problems that prompted Śrīla Prabhupāda to emphasize it. In other words, the syndrome will continue – that from our preaching, people will take up Kṛṣṇa consciousness but will then either leave or regress to a very low level. Especially as this organization grows, we must consider how to teach newcomers to conduct their life in Kṛṣṇa consciousness. We must establish norms of behavior suitable for Vaiṣṇavas and should be clear as to what our various roles are.

The need to demonstrate traditional Vedic culture as a better way of life is an intrinsic aspect of Śrīla Prabhupāda's vision. He famously said "Work now, *samādhi* later"[1] and indirectly repeatedly said "Preach now, *varṇāśrama-dharma* now." He did not tell us to put it off until later. He wanted it now. That is his order, and we should try to implement it.

Śrīla Prabhupāda's Vision for Kṛṣṇa Conscious Farms

Three months before departing this world, Śrīla Prabhupāda stated:

---

1. Quoted in *Servant of the Servant* (Tamāla Kṛṣṇa Goswami), ch. 13.

> This is the next aspect of Kṛṣṇa consciousness which I wish to push forward. On these farms we can demonstrate the full *varṇāśrama* system. If these farms become successful, then the whole world will be enveloped by Kṛṣṇa consciousness. I am very happy to see fresh vegetables, fresh fruits, grains, the devotees taking sumptuous *prasāda* and chanting Hare Kṛṣṇa. This is the actual meaning of human life.[1]

From a 1980 edition of *Back to Godhead:*

> ISKCON is dedicated to showing people how to live a simple, happy, God conscious life. Before Śrīla Prabhupāda passed away, he said he had established half of his work – millions of Kṛṣṇa conscious books were being printed and distributed – now the Kṛṣṇa conscious farming communities should be developed. Our city temples introduce people to Kṛṣṇa philosophy, and now people can come to our farms and see how one should live in a simple, self-sufficient, God conscious manner.[2]

One devotee couple, disciples of mine, recently left their middle-class city life to move to a Kṛṣṇa consciousness farm with no running water or electricity. Their main reason in doing so was for the sake of their two young children, to save them from having to grow up in the city culture. About three months after their move, I visited that farm (in Gujarat), and upon seeing them I exclaimed that their faces had become dark and bright – dark from exposure to the sun and bright with happiness. They expressed their great satisfaction at now being able to daily rise early and spend all day working alongside devotees and living peacefully, away from the noise and stress of the metropolis, absorbed in Kṛṣṇa conscious activities without having to mix with materialistic people or divert their attention to money making.

---

1. Letter, Tamāla Kṛṣṇa Goswami to Hari Śauri Dāsa, 10 Aug 1977.
2. BTG 15–03/04.

This was what Śrīla Prabhupāda wanted, and undoubtedly he is very pleased with those of his followers who have gone back to the land. But it is not meant to be just a few brave individuals here and there. Śrīla Prabhupāda's open and clear order to the leaders of ISKCON is to form ideal, self-sufficient eco-villages, with devotees producing their own food and conducting a simple yet cultured life. If and when we, as a movement, take this mandate seriously, then surely many members of the public will be attracted to the spiritual joy, peace, prosperity, purity, and harmony of Kṛṣṇa conscious rural life. Indeed, Śrīla Prabhupāda predicted that "millions of people would join our farms."[1]

Rural Living Affords More Time for Kṛṣṇa Consciousness

We generally encourage people who are interested in the process of Kṛṣṇa consciousness to remain in the flow of modern society and just add Kṛṣṇa to their life. But most people in the modern world – especially in India, where work hours are very long – do not have time to properly practice Kṛṣṇa consciousness. For his disciples living in temple communities, Śrīla Prabhupāda set a minimum standard of four hours of *sādhana* in the morning and one-and-a-half hours in the evening. However, the majority of initiated devotees today are in the work force and don't have time for proper *japa* or *kīrtana*, or to associate with devotees, or to read Śrīla Prabhupāda's books. Unfortunately, many devotees find it difficult to maintain their initiation vow of chanting sixteen rounds per day. Or their chanting may often be squeezed in among activities, such as dressing the kids before leaving for work. Maybe at the workplace they are able to fit in one or two rounds while others are on coffee break. In this and

1. Śrīla Prabhupāda Remembrances (video transcript), ch. 50.

many other ways, modern rat-race life is not at all suitable for advancement in Kṛṣṇa consciousness.

Mercifully, Śrīla Prabhupāda gave us not only a philosophy but also practical directions for making progress toward the actual goal of life. Although in many ways it is easier to "go with the flow," that choice is inadvisable when the flow is toward hell. Modern civilization is not only flowing toward hell – practically it already is hell. People who deny belief in hell don't recognize that they are living in hell right here. So Śrīla Prabhupāda went against the flow, although he did not totally reject everything in the world today, because preaching means to make a connection with people and then attempt to elevate them from their present position toward the ultimate goal of Kṛṣṇa consciousness.

Particularly for devotees who are very serious to practice pure devotional service, Śrīla Prabhupāda wanted to establish farm communities so that they would have sufficient time to practice Kṛṣṇa consciousness.* Generally it is thought that farm life means much arduous work – which is true of commercial farming – but that is not the case if we just take what we can manage, living simply and producing what we need.

So long as we fail to implement Śrīla Prabhupāda's revolutionary *varṇāśrama* farms, it will be difficult for anyone other than renunciants and a few exceptional *gṛhasthas* to practice Kṛṣṇa consciousness at even the minimum level that Śrīla Prabhupāda recommended for making positive advancement. Moreover, by living according to the terms dictated by modern society, we are likely to be increasingly compromised by it.†

* Lecture: Śrīla Prabhupāda's Master Plan for Gṛhasthas <www.bvks.com/2180>

† Lecture: Vedic Culture Helps to Remember Kṛṣṇa <www.bvks.com/2261>

Accepting Kṛṣṇa's Social System

Devotees may feel justified in wanting to largely adapt to the modern lifestyle. They typically argue along these lines: "We tried *varṇāśrama-dharma* but it didn't work, so better not to continue – maybe some time in the future"; "In the name of demarcation of the sexes and protection of women there was exploitation, so it is best to forget all of that. Such is unsuitable for today's world. Or at least we aren't yet ready for it." But such reasoning aligns us with the worldview of Western civilization, which developed out of protest against misapplied traditionalism, and which Śrīla Prabhupāda repeatedly and unreservedly declared to be demonic.[1]

Man is a social animal, and therefore mankind cannot but follow some sort of social system. If devotees do not adopt *varṇāśrama-dharma* – Kṛṣṇa's social system – then we will have to take shelter of whatever system is around us, which presently is a society that encourages people to act against their real self-interest, by encouraging intoxication, prostitution, gambling, slaughterhouses, and cheating and exploitation at every possible level. While living in such an environment, it is very difficult for people who are practicing Kṛṣṇa consciousness to withstand the negative force of social pressure. Of course, not all devotees fall into gross gratification, but many clearly become adversely affected by the values, the way of thinking, and the activities of nondevotees. Therefore, a major project that Śrīla Prabhupāda promoted was to establish *varṇāśrama-dharma* farming communities for demonstrating to the world how, by depending on the land, cows, and Kṛṣṇa, everyone can live simply, happily, peacefully, and healthily, free from the pernicious effects of the "soul-killing civilization."[2]

---

1. For instance, in Bg 16.8, ppt.

2. *Īśopaniṣad,* mantra 3, ppt.

Again, it may not be easy to quickly change one's way of thinking. Even if one agrees with these principles, it could for various reasons be very difficult to implement them. Nonetheless, reform is needed, and reform begins with understanding of principles.*

An Experimental Revolution

It is a fact that there were serious shortcomings in most of our initial attempts to introduce within ISKCON the protection of women and cows and to also establish *gurukulas* (Vedic schools). Consequently, many devotees became apprehensive about continuing with the *varṇāśrama* experiment, because especially in the Western world, implementation of such changed values and lifestyle could only be an experiment. And experiments are conducted by trial and error; things will go wrong. From another perspective, the *varṇāśrama* initiative is also not experimental, in the sense that it is Kṛṣṇa's timeless system. Again, it is a revolution: going back to original principles. Even if this revolution is taken to be experimental, we must have faith that, if strived for with intelligence, patience, and sincerity, it can and will work, because Śrīla Prabhupāda and Kṛṣṇa want it.†

ISKCON's Disconnect with Varṇāśrama

Within ISKCON, the contention that we should preach now and think about *varṇāśrama-dharma* later (if at all), has overshadowed the "preach now, *varṇāśrama-dharma* now" prescription given by Śrīla Prabhupāda.

* Seminar: Principles for Establishing Varṇāśrama Communities <www.bvks.com/11134>

† For a comprehensive discussion of the experimental nature of *varṇāśrama-dharma,* listen to "Varnāśrama: Into Uncharted Waters." <www.bvks.com/10279>

Most devotees fail to appreciate the relevance of *varṇāśrama-dharma* to the *saṅkīrtana* movement. Indeed, the importance of implementing *varṇāśrama-dharma* is largely ignored and discredited. For instance, there is not a single mention of it on the official website of ISKCON's Governing Body Commission, which presents the strategic planning, policies, and goals that the GBC envisions for the society.*

ISKCON is perceived as a preaching mission, and any undertaking (including the establishment of *varṇāśrama-dharma*) that is not seen as direct preaching tends to be considered less important. However, the *saṅkīrtana* movement aims at propagating pure devotional service, which demands a pure way of life, which in turn is dependent on certain regulative principles, which are fundamental to *varṇāśrama-dharma*. Importantly, a major aspect of *varṇāśrama-dharma* is the regulation of male-female interactions, based on the timeless Vedic knowledge of how men and women perceive themselves and each other, and the specific roles that they are expected to assume.†

Traditional Culture Is Misunderstood

Especially in the West, most people consider that modern society, based on democracy, liberty, equality, and human rights, axiomatically constitutes the highest form of civilization, and that no other form of societal organization could conceivably be better, and that even to question these values renders a person a dangerous deviant.‡ The possibility or desirability of creating a *varṇāśrama-dharma* society is beyond their imagination. Yet persons who have been raised in India have at least some idea that there could be a wholly

* http://gbc.iskcon.org/ (as of 6 Jan 2015)

† Lecture: ISKCON's Forgotten Mission <www.bvks.com/20209>

‡ Lecture: Liberté, Égalité, Fraternité - All Nonsense <www.bvks.com/2192>

different way of living, for (ironically) it was only after India's political independence (in 1947) that her established cultural usages began to rapidly deteriorate, and many vestiges of her original civilization are still extant.

Common among advocates of supposed human rights is to harp on the "evils" of Indian culture, especially targeting the caste system and arranged marriage. Such righteous moralists cannot at all comprehend the spiritual basis of these practices and therefore conclude that it is all very wrong. Sometimes persons, including even devotees, who are overly influenced by such attitudes fear that a restoration of *varṇāśrama-dharma* and traditional Indian customs would necessarily mean a return to the caste system.* Yet actually, despite its perversions, the caste system as it was widely practiced until only recently still retained some of the advantages of pristine *varṇāśrama-dharma.* The potter was simply a potter; he didn't aspire to become a movie star. The barber was a barber; his duty was clear. There was no need for him to speculate or think "Well, now I should start a business." Business is not the dharma of a barber. He cuts hair and nails and performs some functions at weddings. That is what barbers do, and that's all. His son automatically has a fixed profession, with no anxiety about his future means of sustenance. The procedure was easy to understand and to follow. People understood that their place in society was determined by their previous karma, and they were more or less satisfied with that.

Slaughterhouse-Education and Child Labor

This modern society inflicts violence on its members, beginning with the children. Child abuse begins at birth, by inculcating a misguided aim of life, but it worsens when kids are sent to school to be indoctrinated in the mindset for them

* Lecture: Misconceptions about Varṇāśrama <www.bvks.com/20226>

to become another dispensable cog in someone else's machine. Hence universal education, touted as a hallmark of genuine civilization, is actually a hoax.* Śrīla Prabhupāda defined the true goal of education to be character formation,[1] yet at the schools and colleges students learn to have illicit sex with each other or sometimes also with their teachers. Śrīla Prabhupāda noted: "The whole system of education is geared to sense gratification, and if a learned man thinks it over, he sees that the children of this age are being intentionally sent to the slaughterhouses of so-called education."[2] †

The goal of education today is to secure a financially lucrative job. Most middle-class parents in India direct their children to study to become doctors, engineers, accountants, or similar well-paying and respectable professions, irrespective of whether the children themselves actually want it. Consequently, most people today, highly educated or otherwise, spend their entire life doing something that they don't like, just for the money it brings. Some youths graduate after twenty years of education but with no vocation. No posts are available, and they must accept some petty job that not only doesn't pay much but won't even pay off the debt for their education.

In the Vedic system, however, children are trained from the beginning to work concordant to their inborn psychophysical propensities.‡ I have seen boys, maybe only eight or ten years old, of Marwari mercantile families, working in the family shop and dealing with customers while their father tends to other customers. I have also seen a sculptor of religious icons

* Lecture: School Means Contamination, Manipulation not Education <www.bvks.com/236>

† Lecture: Fairly Tales and Reality Education <www.bvks.com/10424>

‡ Lecture: Vedic and Modern Education <www.bvks.com/7170>

1. Bg 8.28, ppt.
2. SB 1.1.22, ppt.

training his young sons on the job. The boys not only learn a profession early on, but also develop a close bond with their father and their family culture. Technically this is child labor, which is not only illegal but is particularly abhorrent to liberal humanists, who pontificate that children should learn academics in school so as to be competent to work more efficiently later on.

Indian Culture and ISKCON

Some devotees who promote the molding of Kṛṣṇa consciousness into a Western format seem to adamantly dislike Śrīla Prabhupāda's instructions concerning the adoption of "Indian" culture. They prefer to emphasize the morally decrepit position of India today – "dirt everywhere, the caste system, polluted cities and rivers, rape, corruption..."

It is undeniable that India has become debased. Mass acceptance of Western culture began in the cities. A recent example is that first some sophisticated city girls started to wear tight jeans and T-shirts, and gradually such fashions are now finding their way to smaller towns. It hasn't yet come to most villages, but it won't be long before it does. Yet it is illogical to opine that Indian culture is all bad, and that because India is now off course we should not try to reintroduce her unparalleled spiritual culture (even though Śrīla Prabhupāda insisted that we do so). Moreover, to criticize the India of today is irrelevant, for our mandate is not to follow either modern Indian culture or modern Western culture, but actual culture – Kṛṣṇa's culture – as given in *śāstra* and presented by Śrīla Prabhupāda.

Undoubtedly, India currently faces tremendous social challenges, as indeed every country does, including the Western nations. One major challenge that non-Western nations must confront is the deliberately propagated myth of Western cultural superiority, which is widely considered axiomatic, especially in India. But Śrīla Prabhupāda would have nothing of it, and neither should his followers. He noted: "Bhārata-varṣa, India, is the most sacred place within this universe";[1] and "Whoever has taken birth in the land of India – this happens due to a huge amount of past pious activities – this is not an ordinary thing. I saw as I traveled all over the world, though at present Indians have fallen down from their original position, that India's culture is the highest in the universe."[2] Anyone from overseas who visits India, if not a totally dull materialist, cannot but be struck by the deeply spiritual underpinnings that pervade life in India even today, notwithstanding the increasingly mundane veneer.*

Clearly, India is neglecting the spiritual substance of her own culture and pursuing the wrong direction of the rest of the world, with ever-increasing industrialization, urbanization, and commercialism. Most of the supposedly spiritual organizations of India are simply bogus and have no clue how to actually rectify matters. Many of them contribute to the confusion by offering courses in topics such as stress-relief and personality development, aimed at training people to integrate and cope with the current demonic lifestyle.

At least Śrīla Prabhupāda's followers should know that everything he did and said was meant for the benefit of all living beings, in accord with the famous Vedic injunction *sarve sukhino bhavantu* – "May all be happy" – notwithstanding that traditional Vedic prescriptions concerning social stratification and gender are often anathema for persons who are steeped in illusory conceptions of happiness.†

---

* Lecture: The Value of Indian Culture <www.bvks.com/7140k>

† Seminar: Vedic Culture and ISKCON Today <www.bvks.com/516>

---

1. Lecture, 8 Apr 1975.

2. Lecture, 13 Oct 1976; quoted in *A Transcendental Diary* (Hari Śauri Dāsa), vol. 2.

Preaching of Traditionalism in the West

Within ISKCON there is a cultural divide, between devotees who think that we need to repackage ourselves to be relevant to modern society and those who maintain that we should stick closer to time-honored Indian usages, as were described by Śrīla Prabhupāda. The controversy has centered especially on two issues, both of which concern women in Kṛṣṇa consciousness: 1) should women be allowed to act as official initiating gurus? and 2) should women be addressed as *prabhu?**

"Modernists" point out that while establishing Kṛṣṇa consciousness in the West, Śrīla Prabhupāda himself introduced many adjustments. While that is true, Śrīla Prabhupāda also gave many instructions and anecdotes concerning the traditional Vedic way of life, explicating that he wanted his disciples to reestablish that culture, principally by establishing *varṇāśrama* communities and social roles.

Yet some devotees are reluctant to accept Śrīla Prabhupāda's *varṇāśrama* initiative, opining that to uphold such controversial points – particularly the non-equality of the sexes – is a major obstacle to the spreading of Kṛṣṇa consciousness. Their argument is that life for devotees in the West will be in many ways less challenging if we largely blend into the mainstream, by adopting the social norms and attitudes, and the clothes, music, food, etc., that are distinctly Western rather than Indian, and that to do so would also make it easier for newcomers to embrace Kṛṣṇa consciousness.

A major problem with this proposition is that in doing so we run counter to the cultural revolution that Śrīla Prabhupāda introduced along with the philosophy and practices of Kṛṣṇa consciousness. Food, dress, names, daily habits, etc. – Śrīla

* These topics are discussed on p. 170 and p. 180 respectively.

Prabhupāda had his disciples change them all. By relinquishing the culture (and thus to a large extent the outlook) that Śrīla Prabhupāda bestowed, we lose much of our uniqueness and identity and thus fail to offer a comprehensive alternative to a way of life that many intelligent people perceive to be palpably failing.

Establishment of *varṇāśrama-dharma,* along with the best of traditional Indian culture, is central to Śrīla Prabhupāda's desire that the Kṛṣṇa consciousness movement be a dynamic, inspiring, educational, and exemplary alternative to the misguided modern civilization. And as his followers, we are duty-bound to accept the challenge to demonstrate *varṇāśrama-dharma* as a way of living on our own terms, or rather Kṛṣṇa's terms, rejecting those dictated by predatory corporations and politicians.*

Nor is it impossible to present to people who are at least somewhat open-minded about traditional social roles that, for instance, men and women have different mentalities and different needs, or that women should care for their children full-time and consequently must in many ways be dependent upon their husband.†

It is not that these ideas come from a completely different dimension of existence. Some years ago, in a widely broadcast Australian TV show about devotees, an interviewer asked some of the women how they felt about being subordinate, and they answered that they felt happy to be protected. And the show was well received. So while these points about social duties (like much else of the teachings and practices of Kṛṣṇa consciousness) may be difficult for people to grasp,

* Lecture: Our Varṇāśrama Responsibility <www.bvks.com/10903>

† This issue is further discussed in the next section – "Women: Masters or Mothers?"

gradually they can become accepted, especially if devotees practically demonstrate happy Kṛṣṇa conscious communities that actually work.

An Overview of Religious and Political Reform

Some 600 years previously, the Reformation in Western Europe inaugurated the Protestant religion in protest against the worldliness of the Roman Catholic Church and its popes. "We believe in Jesus and the Bible, but forget the Pope. We do not accept any ecclesiastic authority." (It was way ahead of the *ṛtvik* movement!) But with the increasing prominence of enlightenment, humanist, and secular values, eventually Protestantism itself, and indeed all religion, came to be protested against. Karl Marx's pronouncement "Religion is the opiate of the people" insinuated that just as those who are addicted to opium live in a hallucinatory world and are docile and hence easily manipulated, religion is merely a device to keep people in ignorance and subjugation.* Although Marx struck a chord with many, he presumed the misappropriation of religion to be its very essence, overlooking the fact that not all religionists are scheming charlatans and that, however much it might be misused, the true heart of religion is genuine spiritualism. Rejecting the shallowness of religion as he adjudged it (at face value), Marx substituted it with his own shallow doctrines. And many similarly shallow people followed him (and several other supposed philosophers) in rejecting religion.

Another casualty of the ongoing secularization of the West, and eventually of the entire world, was monarchy, which previously had been the standard polity all over the world. Kings (or the equivalent) were everywhere understood to be embodiments

* Lecture: The Opiate of the People <www.bvks.com/10952>

of the divine. In India, each maharaja was known as *naradeva* (a god among men), as per Kṛṣṇa's statement in the *Bhagavad-gītā* (10.27) *narāṇāṁ ca narādhipam:* "I am represented among men by the king." However, beginning in the West, one by one the kings were removed, because they were exploiting instead of protecting the population. Wherever monarchy has been retained (most famously in the United Kingdom, but also in Belgium, Denmark, Holland, Monaco, Sweden, Thailand, etc.), the royalty are mere figureheads with negligible political power. As Śrīla Prabhupāda noted: "Formerly the kings were very responsible for the welfare of the citizens. When the kings were not responsible, then gradually government by the people was introduced."[1]

Kings were rejected for being tyrannical, but the end of monarchy did not bring an end to tyranny. For instance, both in France and in Russia, the dethroning and execution of monarchs was followed by extended periods of mass violence. In Russia ensued the brutal history of communism, which during the twentieth century accounted for the slaughter by communist regimes of an estimated 85 to 100 million of their own peoples (not including many more killed in external wars). So by no means did tyranny end along with monarchy – just that the system changed.

Ṛtvik Folly

Similarly, in and around ISKCON there has been an attempt to remove gurus. Devised several years after Śrīla Prabhupāda's departure from this world (in 1977), *ṛtvikism* was meant to counter abuses of the guru system that arose post-1977 by providing the simplistic solution that Śrīla Prabhupāda alone continues to initiate all aspiring disciples within ISKCON for

1. Lecture, 3 Jan 1969.

all time into the future. But the short history of *ṛtvikism* has shown it to be incapable of curbing the kind of vice that tends to arise in religious organizations. *Ṛtvikism* has simply added one more deviation: the abandoning of the guru system, which is enshrined in *śāstra* and tradition. Although *ṛtvikists* claim that Śrīla Prabhupāda is their initiating guru, there is no precedent in genuine Vaiṣṇavism for accepting initiation from a guru who is not physically present in the world.

Of course, Śrīla Prabhupāda is the guru of all generations of ISKCON members (and, as the founder-*ācārya,* has special significance for them), but then so also Rūpa Gosvāmī, Sanātana Gosvāmī, and all other previous *ācāryas* are gurus for all subsequent generations of Gauḍīya Vaiṣṇavas. Still, the established practice is to take *dīkṣā* from a physically present devotee. The notion that due to so many problems with gurus in ISKCON we can simply bypass the gurus and make Prabhupāda our guru derives from the classic error of all would-be reformers: misapplication of a principle does not mean that the principle should be altogether rejected.*

Never in a thousand years of reading Śrīla Prabhupāda's books could anyone come to the conclusion of *ṛtvikism.* The same is true of the proposition to establish gender parity for devotee women; it is an idea imported from secular society. And because both *ṛtvikism* and "Vaiṣṇava feminism" (an oxymoron) do not derive from guru, sadhu, or *śāstra,* the protagonists of these two doctrines seek to justify their position by the heterodox and dangerous hermeneutic that Śrīla Prabhupāda is so special that he could override guru, sadhu, and *śāstra,* and that he actually did so to establish *ṛtvikism* and feminism. Moreover, in their zeal to establish their fanciful speculations, they cite Śrīla Prabhupāda yet give far less importance to the authority and importance of *śāstra* and tradition than

* Lecture: Ṛtvikism is Self-defeating <www.bvks.com/1104>

did Śrīla Prabhupāda and all the previous *ācāryas.** Śrīla Prabhupāda often warned against such an attitude by quoting:

śruti-smṛti-purāṇādi- pañcarātra-vidhiṁ vinā
aikāntikī harer bhaktir utpātāyaiva kalpate

Devotional service of the Lord that ignores the authorized Vedic literatures like the *Upaniṣads, Purāṇas,* and *Nārada Pañcarātra* is simply an unnecessary disturbance in society.[1]

The Basic Mistake of All Reformers

Across various civilizations throughout history, a repeated mistake has been to reject a principle due to its having been misused. For instance, a common rationale is: The king is bad, so kill the king and institute democracy, fascism, socialism, communism, or whatever. But the principle that someone should be in charge, a representative of God who has been trained to take care of the people, is actually a much better system, and instituted by God (Kṛṣṇa) Himself.

During the 1980s, I experienced military rule in Bangladesh, overseen by one Ziaur Rahman, a former army officer who had taken over the government. From what I observed, his rule was not very oppressive. Most of the people were scattered in villages throughout the country, growing food and passing simple, tranquil lives with few luxuries, in much the same way that generations of their ancestors had previously lived, their main anxiety being how to sufficiently feed their family. It made little difference to them what system was extant, for their rulers were far distant and hardly seen or even heard of. And actually, the country was relatively peaceful, and political

* This important point is analyzed in *What about Śrīla Prabhupāda's Books?: A paramparā critique of "Women in ISKCON in Prabhupāda's Times"* by Kṛṣṇa-kīrti Dāsa <www.siddhanta.com/2015/04/18/what-about-srila-prabhupadas-books>.

1. E.g., quoted in Bg 7.3.

matters were quite clear (if not to everyone's taste). But then Ziaur Rahman was assassinated, and a subsequent attempt at democracy resulted in chaos in the cities, with continual political unrest, regular rioting, and trade and communication disrupted throughout the country. Of course, Ziaur Rahman was certainly not an ideal leader by Vedic standards; but to me, the comparative calm and order of his somewhat benign dictatorship seemed more workable than the unruly "rule of the people" that followed.

The real solution to poor monarchy is not democracy, but to strive to reinstitute genuinely godly monarchy.* Admittedly, in the modern age it seems very difficult to attempt this. So we set up another system, thinking we can do something better. But it doesn't work.

Manmade solutions never work, because men are imperfect. (Feminists will surely agree with this. But women also are not perfect, nor is feminism, which is just another backlash against exploitation; it has no positive basis.) Even the seemingly best of manmade (or women-made) schemes inevitably end in grief.† We may think that we have discovered something better, but it is wise to follow the old rules; they have been given for all time and for a very good purpose. Hence, notwithstanding the inevitable major hurdles in doing so, the only real solution to humankind's woes is to restore the principles that God, in His perfect wisdom, has given for our benefit. We have to do what Kṛṣṇa says, as recorded in *śāstra*.

The Kṛṣṇa consciousness movement must choose either to try to implement Śrīla Prabhupāda's orders regarding *varṇāśrama-*

* Lecture: Vedic Governance <www.bvks.com/10987>

† "That happiness which is derived from contact of the senses with their objects and which appears like nectar at first but poison at the end is said to be of the nature of passion." (Bg 18.38)

dharma, or to accommodate itself with the modern world. Of course, this is not a completely black-and-white issue, because we cannot avoid some level of adjustment with contemporary society, nor can we just flick a switch and turn on *varṇāśrama-dharma.* But we should at least know where we are supposed to be going, and make serious steps in that direction. To avoid Śrīla Prabhupāda's *varṇāśrama* mandate is *guror avajñā,* disobedience to the order of the spiritual master. If we instead try to increasingly adapt ourselves with nondevotees, we risk minimizing our connection with Śrīla Prabhupāda.

Understanding the Issues – Siddhānta

Some devotees emphasize Śrīla Prabhupāda's call for unity in diversity,[1] which he identified with the philosophy of *acintya-bhedābheda,*[2] and they cite that Śrīla Prabhupāda did not like his disciples to fight. Of course, it is true that Śrīla Prabhupāda did not like his disciples to fight among themselves. But this doesn't mean that, on the plea of keeping the peace and fostering unity in diversity, all kinds of fabrications, concoctions, distortions, and speculations should be allowed to circulate within ISKCON.* Śrīla Prabhupāda's own response to various misconceptions that were sometimes propagated within ISKCON was not to simply say "Well, it is alright – just chant Hare Kṛṣṇa." Rather, he took swift and firm action and clearly pointed out the correct path to follow.

Śrīla Prabhupāda often quoted *Śrī Caitanya-caritāmṛta* 1.2.117:

> *siddhānta baliyā citte nā kara alasa*
> *ihā haite kṛṣṇe lāge sudṛḍha mānasa*

* Lecture: Navigating ISKCON's Multiculturalism <www.bvks.com/10670>

1. Letter, 18 Oct 1973.

2. See SB 4.7.54, ppt.

> "Do not be lazy in the matter of understanding *siddhānta*. *Siddhānta* means proper philosophical conclusion, and one's mind becomes firmly attached to Kṛṣṇa if it is applied to grasping *siddhānta*."[1]

Devotees should not simply take sectarian positions on various issues but should try to understand – according to guru, sadhu, and *śāstra* – the actual *siddhāntas* involved.

Ideas have consequences.[2] For instance, Marx and Engels had an idea, the major consequence of which was that a large part of the world came under Communist regimes. Or there is the idea that life has arisen by chance from matter and that different species have evolved by natural selection, and one consequence is that people have become atheistic; another is that abortion is euphemized as the removal of unwanted tissue. People think nothing of the daily slaughter of millions of animals because they believe that animals are just dull creatures who are meant to be eaten by humans. But the fact is that mankind must suffer the consequences of such grossly sinful activities. Ideas have consequences, and most ideas in the world today are very wrong.

Some devotees propose to seek a happy medium between "excessive Indianization" and "excessive Westernization." But rather, we should try to deeply comprehend and appreciate Śrīla Prabhupāda's mission, according to his stated teachings, rather than attempting to harmonize according to our own understanding.

Acting on the basis of a wrong understanding can never yield a good result. A poisoned tree gives poisoned fruit. Devotees are duty-bound to understand proper *siddhānta* and to

---

1. Translation by Bhakti Vikāsa Swami, as quoted from transcript.
2. This is the title of a book by Richard M. Weaver, published in 1948.

combat all wrong ideas, whenever and wherever they appear, including, most importantly, within ISKCON itself, the society that is meant to give to the world all the right ideas and their practical application.

ISKCON Lite

Guru means "heavy." Kṛṣṇa consciousness is heavy, serious, substantial. But nowadays there is a tendency to present it as light, with supposed preachers within ISKCON preaching such things as "Don't make it difficult. Don't observe so many rules." One of our devotees was told "Don't come to *maṅgala-ārati.* Why put yourself to so much trouble?"

Step-by-step, things are going down. Contemporary ISKCON culture is a concoction of something somewhat Western, somewhat Indian, and overall not very compelling or substantial. Recently at the opening of a beautiful new ISKCON temple in South India, the only cultural program for the public was a mantra-rock dance. Maybe that would have been acceptable if many other, more traditionally Vaiṣṇava, presentations had also been organized. But as the only function, it was definitely an imbalance. When preaching becomes substituted by entertainment, we become light, not guru.

Although Śrīla Prabhupāda clearly instructed his disciples to institute *varṇāśrama-dharma,* the movement that is now being conducted in his name has abandoned this project and is instead heading the opposite way. It is lamentable that despite Śrīla Prabhupāda's followers being well aware of his order to go back to the land, they are instead returning to their old materialistic ways.

ISKCON Has the Solution

When the whole society is misdirected – and what is right, people think is wrong, and what is wrong, people think is right – undoubtedly it is a daunting assignment to introduce what is actually right, what is actually beneficial and auspicious in the highest and best possible way. But by the grace of Śrīla Prabhupāda, his followers have the solutions to all of the modern world's afflictions, plus his order to propagate and establish those solutions at both the fully spiritual and the social level. Therefore, despite the inherent difficulties in doing so, Śrīla Prabhupāda's followers are duty-bound to attempt the implementation of *varṇāśrama-dharma* – not that we should sheepishly acquiesce with the demonic society.

ISKCON alone has the genuine spiritual solution, but we cannot help the world if we ourselves also veer in the wrong direction. If ISKCON's present direction continues, soon there will be no meaningful difference between us and so many so-called spiritual leaders of today, except that they will have more members than we, because they are long-practiced and expert at cheating people.

Many pious people in India, who are concerned with the demise of their ancient culture and the ongoing mass conversion to anti-Vedic religions, have amazingly strong faith that ISKCON has the potential to restore Vedic culture to its pristine glory. Maybe when they read our books they assume that we are actually following the teachings within them. And we should be!

Here is a small compilation of quotes from the many instances wherein Śrīla Prabhupāda discussed *varṇāśrama-dharma:*

> The distinction between human life and animal life therefore begins with the scientific system of *varṇa* and *āśrama,* guided by the experience of the sages in relation with the demigods,

gradually rising to the summit of reestablishing our eternal relation with the Supreme Absolute Truth, the Personality of Godhead, Lord Śrī Kṛṣṇa.[1]

Occupational duties are known as *varṇāśrama-dharma* and apply to the four divisions of material and spiritual life – namely *brāhmaṇa, kṣatriya, vaiśya,* and *śūdra,* and *brahmacarya, gṛhastha, vānaprastha,* and *sannyāsa.* If one works according to the *varṇāśrama-dharma* system and does not desire fruitive results, he gets satisfaction gradually. Discharging one's occupational duty as a means of rendering devotional service unto the Supreme Personality of Godhead is the ultimate goal of life.[2]

If we do not take to the principles of *varṇāśrama-dharma* by accepting the four social orders (*brāhmaṇa, kṣatriya, vaiśya,* and *śūdra*) and the four orders of spiritual life (*brahmacārī, gṛhastha, vānaprastha,* and *sannyāsa*), there can be no question of success in life.[3]

It is essential that society be divided into four groups of men – *brāhmaṇas, kṣatriyas, vaiśyas,* and *śūdras.*[4]

Unless in the human society the *varṇāśrama* system is introduced, no scheme or social order, health order or any order, political order, will be successful.[5]

In order to rectify this world situation, all people should be trained in Kṛṣṇa consciousness and act in accordance with the *varṇāśrama* system. The state should also see that the people are engaged in satisfying the Supreme Personality of Godhead. This is the primary duty of the state. The Kṛṣṇa consciousness

---

1. SB 1.16.31, ppt.
2. SB 4.20.9, ppt.
3. SB 5.19.10, ppt.
4. SB 7.10.24, ppt.
5. Conversation, 18 Oct 1977.

movement was started to convince the general populace to adopt the best process by which to satisfy the Supreme Personality of Godhead and thus solve all problems.[1]

Unless human society is regulated by *varṇāśrama-dharma,* it is no better than a bestial society of cats and dogs.[2]

Because there is no institution to teach people how to become *brāhmaṇas, kṣatriyas, vaiśyas* and *śūdras* or *brahmacārīs, gṛhasthas, vānaprasthas,* and *sannyāsīs,* these demons want a classless society. This is resulting in chaotic conditions. In the name of secular government, unqualified people are taking the supreme governmental posts. No one is being trained to act according to the principles of *varṇāśrama-dharma,* and thus people are becoming increasingly degraded and are heading in the direction of animal life. The real aim of life is liberation, but unfortunately the opportunity for liberation is being denied to people in general, and therefore their human lives are being spoiled. The Kṛṣṇa consciousness movement, however, is being propagated all over the world to reestablish the *varṇāśrama-dharma* system and thus save human society from gliding down to hellish life.[3]

For peace and happiness in the material world, the *varṇāśrama* institution must be introduced. The symptoms of one's activities must be defined, and one must be educated accordingly. Then spiritual advancement will automatically be possible.[4]

If the process of *varṇāśrama-dharma* is introduced, even in this age of Kali, the situation of Satya-yuga can be invoked. The Hare Kṛṣṇa movement, or Kṛṣṇa consciousness movement, is meant for this purpose.[5]

---

1. SB 4.14.20, ppt.
2. SB 5.1.29, ppt.
3. SB 5.19.19, ppt.
4. SB 7.11.25, ppt.
5. SB 9.10.51, ppt.

Our next program will be to organize farming land to set an example to the whole world how people can be peaceful, happy, and free from all anxieties simply by chanting Hare Kṛṣṇa *mahā-mantra* and living an honorable life in Kṛṣṇa consciousness. In India especially people are religiously inclined. They like to live in village and also like to love Lord Rāma, Lord Kṛṣṇa. This idealism is running through their blood and veins. We have to organize their natural tendency and elevate them again back to home, back to Godhead.[1]

1. Letter, 19 Oct 1975.

PART TWO

Women: Masters or Mothers?

Section One

Why Śrīla Prabhupāda Opposed Feminism

Feminism is the claim that throughout history women have been victims of an oppressive patriarchal society. The typical feminist outlook may be summarized thus: "All men are guilty, both individually and collectively. Men have always exploited women, but now it is time to reverse the trend and prove that women are equal (or superior) to men. Women should not be bound by past social, religious, or legal restrictions, nor should their identity be tied to any man. They should exercise their rights, set their own destiny, and take over the societal roles, powers, and privileges that men have unjustly been holding since time immemorial. Women must be free to do whatever they like, how they like, whenever and wherever. They may have sex with as many partners as they wish, and choose to abort any pregnancies that occur."

Notwithstanding some valid claims of mistreatment of women, feminism is clearly not in line with the ultimate goal of *śāstra*. Śrīla Prabhupāda consistently repudiated the idea that women could be equal to men:

> *Prakṛti* means energy, just like *prakṛti* means woman. Naturally, a woman is under the control of the man. That is our Vedic system, and natural system also. However the women may claim equal rights, they are under the control of the man. That is natural.[1]

Not caring for political correctness, Śrīla Prabhupāda unreservedly opposed feminist notions – as evidenced, for instance, in the following exchange in New York:

---

1. Lecture, 17 Dec 1975.

Reporter: Are men regarded as superior to women?

Śrīla Prabhupāda: Yes, naturally. Naturally, woman requires protection by the man. In the childhood she is protected by the father, in youth she is protected by the husband, and in old age she is protected by elderly sons. That is natural.

Female Reporter: That goes against the thinking of a lot of people in America now. Do you know that?

Śrīla Prabhupāda: America, maybe, but this is the natural position. Women require protection.[1]

Śrīla Prabhupāda often spoke about the role of women because (according to Arjuna's words in the *Bhagavad-gītā*) the preservation of women's character is essential for the upkeep of civilization.[2] He identified the "puffed-up concept of womanly life" as a major factor in the distressed, chaotic state of modern society.[3] When a female journalist asked, "Would you say that women are inferior to men?" Śrīla Prabhupāda replied "Yes," and then explained why women should be subordinate to men. Eventually the incredulous journalist asked, "If women were subordinate to men, would it solve all of our problems?" And again Śrīla Prabhupāda said "Yes."[4]

Śrīla Prabhupāda maintained the Vedic position that a woman should have just one husband and stick to him. When an American woman challenged that Indian women are treated as slaves, Śrīla Prabhupāda responded that it is better to become the slave of one man than of hundreds.[5] On another occasion, he explained:

---

1. 5 Mar 1975.
2. Bg 1.40.
3. Bg 16.7, ppt.
4. Television Interview, 9 Jul 1975.
5. Conversation, 19 Mar 1976.

> Every woman should try to become maidservant of her husband, and every man should try to become the hundred-times servant of Kṛṣṇa. This is Indian civilization. Not that "Husband and wife – we are equal rights." In Europe and America, the movement is going on: "equal rights." That is not Vedic civilization. Vedic civilization is that the husband should be a sincere servant of Kṛṣṇa, and the wife should be a sincere maidservant of the husband.[1]

Dr. Stillson Judah, an informed and impartial religious scholar who sometimes dialogued with Śrīla Prabhupāda and highly regarded him, carefully studied ISKCON and in 1974 presented his findings as the book Hare Krishna and the Counterculture (which Śrīla Prabhupāda endorsed).[2] Therein, his depiction of Śrīla Prabhupāda's attitude toward women does not tally with that of ISKCON's feminists (who present Śrīla Prabhupāda as having treated his female disciples similarly to men, giving them all opportunities for varied services, including leadership):

> The position of women in the [ISKCON] society may not appeal to Americans interested in women's liberation. Swami Bhaktivedanta says that all women other than one's wife are to be considered as one's mother, and yet he regards them as prone to degradation, of little intelligence, and untrustworthy. They should not be given as much freedom as men, but should be treated like children; they should be protected all during their lives, by their fathers when young, later by their husbands, and in their old age, by their sons.... This view is largely consonant with the traditional one found in the ancient Indian law books. Females may not become presidents of any temple, nor occupy positions of authority. They may do the cooking, help with the devotional services and maintenance of the temple, and prepare the flower offerings for Kṛṣṇa.[3]

---

1. Lecture, 2 Mar 1976.
2. Conversation, 20 Jun 1975.
3. Judah, 1974:86.

Demons Promote a Puffed-up Concept of Womanly Life

Śrīla Prabhupāda's most widely distributed book, and the most essential for communicating the basics of Kṛṣṇa consciousness to the public, is *Bhagavad-gītā As It Is.* Therein Śrīla Prabhupāda wrote:

> [Translation of verse 16.7] Those who are demonic do not know what is to be done and what is not to be done. Neither cleanliness nor proper behavior nor truth is found in them.
>
> [Purport] In every civilized human society there is some set of scriptural rules and regulations which is followed from the beginning. Especially among the Āryans, those who adopt the Vedic civilization and who are known as the most advanced, civilized peoples, those who do not follow the scriptural injunctions are supposed to be demons. Therefore it is stated here that the demons do not know the scriptural rules, nor do they have any inclination to follow them. Most of them do not know them, and even if some of them know, they have not the tendency to follow them. They have no faith, nor are they willing to act in terms of the Vedic injunctions. The demons are not clean, either externally or internally. One should always be careful to keep his body clean by bathing, brushing teeth, shaving, changing clothes, etc. As far as internal cleanliness is concerned, one should always remember the holy names of God and chant Hare Kṛṣṇa Hare Kṛṣṇa Kṛṣṇa Kṛṣṇa Hare Hare/ Hare Rāma Hare Rāma Rāma Rāma Hare Hare. The demons neither like nor follow all these rules for external and internal cleanliness.
>
> As for behavior, there are many rules and regulations guiding human behavior, such as the *Manu-saṁhitā,* which is the law of the human race. Even up to today, those who are Hindu follow the *Manu-saṁhitā.* Laws of inheritance and other legalities

> are derived from this book. Now, in the *Manu-saṁhitā,* it is clearly stated that a woman should not be given freedom. That does not mean that women are to be kept as slaves, but they are like children. Children are not given freedom, but that does not mean that they are kept as slaves. The demons have now neglected such injunctions, and they think that women should be given as much freedom as men. However, this has not improved the social condition of the world. Actually, a woman should be given protection at every stage of life. She should be given protection by the father in her younger days, by the husband in her youth, and by the grownup sons in her old age. This is proper social behavior according to the *Manu-saṁhitā.* But modern education has artificially devised a puffed-up concept of womanly life, and therefore marriage is practically now an imagination in human society. Nor is the moral condition of woman very good now, although those who are married are in a better condition than those who are proclaiming their so-called freedom. The demons, therefore, do not accept any instruction which is good for society, and because they do not follow the experience of great sages and the rules and regulations laid down by the sages, the social condition of the demonic people is very miserable.

Notably, in this verse Kṛṣṇa did not directly mention women or female roles. Nevertheless, Śrīla Prabhupāda chose to comment on it by saying that women are to be protected at every stage of their life. And this essential point may be understood in relation to other descriptions within this same chapter, which concerns the demonic nature: failure to act according to the injunctions of *śāstra* necessarily leads to inauspiciousness, downfall, and misery.

Respect for Women in Indian Culture

Feminists are likely to view as psychopathic the *Manu-smṛti's* injunction against the independence of women. And it might be presumed that, accordingly, the lot of women in India is or was simply hellish – but this is incorrect.* Undeniably, women in India, as in other traditional cultures, were restricted and controlled (both being required for protection) and were expected to be reserved and submissive. Nevertheless, in Indian culture, dignified womanhood has always been revered as a manifestation of the divine feminine nature:

> According to the *varṇāśrama* system, generally the *śūdras* (laboring class) and ladies are not allowed direct participation in the higher religious functions. Only indirect participation is allowed for them, and they also do not get the sacred thread. Yet a *brāhmaṇa* boy can be found touching the feet of his mother! The mother will not touch the Deity of Nārāyaṇa, but her son who is worshiping Nārāyaṇa is touching her feet and taking her feet-dust.[1]

This paradox escapes those who suffer from typical Western linear thought and adjudge that the respect accorded to women is merely superficial, to trick them into subordination. Nonetheless, pristine Vedic society recognized that genuine civilization can exist only where chaste, dutiful women are protected, respected, and well cared for. Women are to be especially honored for their irreplaceable contribution as mothers.

In Indian culture the most oft-quoted saying about women is *mātṛ-devo bhava*: "Be one for whom the mother is a god."[2] And another famous maxim is:

yatra nāryas tu pūjyante ramante tatra devatāḥ
yatraitās tu na pūjyante sarvās tatrāphalāḥ kriyāḥ

* Lecture: Were Women Exploited in the Vedic Culture? <www.bvks.com/2188>

1. B. R. Śrīdhara. *The Golden Staircase*, ch. 4.
2. *Taittirīya Upaniṣad* 1.1.20.

> Where women are honored, the gods rejoice, and where women are not revered, all undertakings become fruitless. (*Manu-smṛti* 3.56)

Feminism in ISKCON

In the last half-century, the women's liberation movement has radically changed the secular world; and more recently, it has also radically changed ISKCON. As stated in *The Hare Krishna Movement: The Postcharismatic Fate of a Religious Transplant* (Bryant and Ekstrand, 2004):

> The society [ISKCON] is experiencing the stirrings of a suffragette movement reacting against the historical disempowerment and denigration of women, who have long been denied access to prominent roles as a result of the sannyasi (male, lifelong renunciant) culture and ethos developed in ISKCON in the 1970s."[1]

And indeed, this suffragette movement has had much effect within ISKCON.*

One chief complaint of the "suffragettes" was the lack of female representation in institutional positions. But during Śrīla Prabhupāda's manifest presence there were no female GBC members or temple presidents. Certainly, Śrīla Prabhupāda could have promoted either of these – but he did not. Furthermore, members of the *sannyāsa* order, who have always been male, have traditionally been at the head of Vedic society:

* The term "suffragette" was first applied to females in early twentieth-century Britain who militantly demanded the right to vote. Bryant and Ekstrand's use of it, as quoted herein, appears to be somewhat tongue in cheek.

1. "Introduction" (Columbia University Press: New York, 2004) page 5.

> In the *varṇāśrama* institution the sannayasi or the person in the renounced order of life, is considered to be the head or the spiritual master of all the social statuses and orders.[1]

And according to scripture, women are not allowed to act independently of male guardians. There is close correlation between these precepts and the lack of women in public positions of social or institutional authority in the ISKCON of the 1970s. During that period, fidelity to those precepts was inherent in ISKCON's social structure.

However, following the line of their secular counterparts, the suffragettes argued that it is these very precepts that caused the neglect and abuse of women throughout ISKCON's short history. As stated by Rādhā Dāsī, and quoted in an essay by Rukmiṇī Dāsī (who was a member of a delegation of women who presented this and other essays to the GBC body at their general meeting on 1 March 2000): "Our Vaiṣṇava society suffers when women are excluded from its public life, from decision-making, management, and formation of policy."[2] Note that they do not lay the blame on improper execution. Instead, they attack the precepts themselves, which have their origin in scripture and were preached extensively by Śrīla Prabhupāda. The GBC responded by stating that this presentation "brought a clearer understanding of the mistakes of the past and the need to provide equal and full opportunity for devotional service for all devotees in ISKCON, regardless of gender."[3] Since then, this feminist, non-*śāstric* notion of equality has been relentlessly pressed by ISKCON's leadership, and has resulted in the ever-

1. Bg 16.3, ppt.

2. "Presentation by Rukmini Dasi" (March 2000, Mayapur, India) ISKCON Communications Journal, #8.1 - January/June 2000.

3. GBC, "Section 500. HOLY PLACES AND SPIRITUAL COMMUNITIES: Women in ISKCON" 2 Mar 2000, ISKCON Governing Body Commission Society, 7 Jan. 2015 <gbc.iskcon.org/2012/01/31/2000/>

increasing presence of women in ISKCON's public life – its decision-making, adult education, management, and formation of policy. Affirmative action has included the appointing of women to positions of authority (without consulting the devotees who would become their subordinates) that Śrīla Prabhupāda never attributed to them, and of stipulating that women devotees should give public classes, even in the presence of sannyasis and other senior male devotees. In some ISKCON centers in the West, young women regularly teach courses to men and even supervise *brahmacārī* training(!), as if this were an accepted, proper standard.

Although the proponents of feminism within ISKCON refuse to call it feminism, several of ISKCON's suffragettes clearly embody the masculine traits that typify secular feminists – being socially outgoing, ambitious, and sometimes highly political and aggressive.

Given that Śrīla Prabhupāda was unequivocally opposed to feminism, no ISKCON member or contingent will overtly identify as a feminist, even though they promote and enact policies within ISKCON that parallel many of those of secular feminists. And at least Bryant and Ekstrand, as outside observers, had no qualms using the term "suffragette" (as quoted above).

Considering that most of Śrīla Prabhupāda's disciples were born and raised in societies that place much value on equality of the sexes, the influence of feminism within ISKCON is actually not surprising. Such notions of egalitarianism are non-Vedic, utopian, and bewildering to the intellect, inasmuch as they appear to be very reasonable but actually are not. Yet it appears that in the psyches of many devotees, such notions are so deeply rooted that even after years of hearing from Śrīla Prabhupāda, those devotees still fail to comprehend that while men and women are spiritually equal, they are materially and socially different. Granted, designations such as "man" and "woman" are illusory coatings over the pure soul, but to pretend that within mundane existence there are not significant bodily, psychological, and social distinctions is not only disingenuous, but – in its to attempt to make everything "all one" – is a manifestation of impersonalism.

Indeed, the unabashed promotion of feminism continues as vigorously within ISKCON as in the secular world. In "Women in ISKCON in Prabhupāda's Times," an example is cited that in the early days of ISKCON, men and women would together circumambulate Tulasī Devī, but that later on the practice was stopped by certain hard-core men. As a result of this published revelation, many ISKCON centers in the West reintroduced that men and women circumambulate Tulasī Devī together.

My personal experience of this change has not been good. A few years ago in an ISKCON center in Europe, while circumambulating Tulasī Devī I noticed that a female devotee was just to my left. So I moved to my right, only to almost bump into another woman who was next to me on that side. I then stopped circumambulating and stood at a distance. (The system of men and women circumambulating Tulasī Devī together has now been stopped in that temple, presumably because the devotees there can understand that it is improper.)

At a festival in another European temple, while standing in the crowded temple room, I was physically shoved out of the way by a woman devotee(?) who seemed in a hurry to go somewhere. And when I was invited to go onto the altar to bathe the Deities, I saw that there were only women in the altar area – five women and the Deities all in a cramped space, which hardly one more person could squeeze into. "I cannot go in there," I protested to the (male) devotee who had invited me. "But this is modern ISKCON," he laughingly replied. "Well, forget it. I'm not going." I don't want to sound whiny, but these are examples of attitudes and behavior that are unconducive to creating an ethos suitable for the spiritual progress of anyone, whether designated as male or female.

Another claim by ISKCON feminists is that gender parity is required in preaching, because otherwise devotees will be socially irrelevant. Even if this were true for the West (which is questionable), it should be considered that various other principles propagated by devotees – belief in karma, reincarnation, vegetarianism – were also at one time widely considered stupid or even anti-social, and that in course of time all of these have gained wide acceptance in the West. It is also true that in many parts of the world, promotion of gender parity is likely to be unwelcome. And yet another problem with the endorsement of gender parity is that people will notice the discrepancy between the instructions given by Śrīla Prabhupāda in his books and the actual practice by us who are supposed to represent him. So let us stick to our principles as enunciated in *śāstra,* instead of inordinately adjusting to local circumstances. Let us preach what Śrīla Prabhupāda preached, and with the faith that if we are sincere, Kṛṣṇa will reciprocate.*

Nasty Effects of Feminism Within ISKCON

A lady devotee from India informed me:

> Some years ago, my godbrother S. Dāsa took a break from his secular job here in India to serve in a temple in America at the behest of the local GBC there. In the following three years, he got to travel to various centers in the U.S. What he found most disturbing in most of the congregations he visited was the mood of misandry, or hatred towards men (among the women).

* For a scholarly analysis of the parallels between secular feminism and that in ISKCON, and of the denial of this by ISKCON's feminists, see: www.siddhanta.com/2015/01/06/language-ideology-and-the-womens-movement-in-iskcon/

> He wondered what sort of sentiments such women harbored toward their own gurus and toward Śrīla Prabhupāda. He eventually cut short his assignment and retreated to India.
>
> So it seems that man-hating women presume that they are hated by men, and respond accordingly – it's a vicious cycle.

Feminist proselytizers are determined to work their mischief also within India. A Bengali devotee told me that along the route of the Navadvīpa-dhāma *parikramā*, many villagers, both Hindu and Muslim, were visibly aghast to behold ISKCON Bengali women dancing vigorously in public. Those enthusiastically dancing women could not have dreamed of doing so had they never associated with their Western godsisters. Worse still, certain Western devotees come to the *dhāmas* in India and there preach denigration of *strī-dharma* to local women: "Why are you submissive to your husband?"* Some Indian Vaiṣṇavas have told me that after fifteen years of peaceful married life, they one day returned home and suddenly encountered their wife arguing and fighting with him. Her attitude had completely changed upon being told that her husband has been exploiting her, so she should stop serving him obediently and should instead "stand up for her rights."

Many Indian women who join ISKCON, especially those from village backgrounds, become influenced toward Western thinking. When they lived in their village, they were trained in traditional ways, but after coming to ISKCON they lose their culture by observing the behavior of the Western women, whom they naively presume to be superior (an impression that many Westerners also seem to hold – even though Western devotees should learn how to behave from cultured Indian devotees, not degrade the Indians by introducing their *mleccha* ways).

---

* *Strī-dharma* – the duties of women as prescribed in *śāstra* (e.g., SB 7.11.25–29).

Misunderstanding Śrīla Prabhupāda's Adjustments

It appears that many devotees have misunderstood some of Śrīla Prabhupāda's early adjustments to have been the standard to be followed for all future time – for instance, his allowing women to live in temple ashrams (for which some of his godbrothers disparaged him). On this point, Śrīla Prabhupāda commented:

> Sometimes jealous persons criticize the Kṛṣṇa consciousness movement because it engages equally both boys and girls in distributing love of Godhead. Not knowing that boys and girls in countries like Europe and America mix very freely, these fools and rascals criticize the boys and girls in Kṛṣṇa consciousness for intermingling. But these rascals should consider that one cannot suddenly change a community's social customs. However, since both the boys and the girls are being trained to become preachers, those girls are not ordinary girls but are as good as their brothers who are preaching Kṛṣṇa consciousness. Therefore, to engage both boys and girls in fully transcendental activities is a policy intended to spread the Kṛṣṇa consciousness movement. These jealous fools who criticize the intermingling of boys and girls will simply have to be satisfied with their own foolishness because they cannot think of how to spread Kṛṣṇa consciousness by adopting ways and means that are favorable for this purpose.[1]

This passage is often quoted by ISKCON feminists to substantiate their claim that the adjustments made by Śrīla Prabhupāda for his Western preaching should be perpetuated forever, thereby overriding the norms of countless generations of Vaiṣṇava culture. However, there is overwhelming evidence that Śrīla Prabhupāda wanted to replace what he called

1. Cc 1.7.32, ppt.

"the nasty Western culture."[1] Hence, the words "one cannot suddenly change a community's social customs" indicate that even though Śrīla Prabhupāda certainly wanted to change social customs in the West, he realized the impracticality of trying to suddenly and completely change everyone:

> In our society the girls and boys mix, intermingle together, and this is practically impossible to stop because you Western people are accustomed to the habit. Sometimes my godbrothers criticize me for intermingling of girls and boys. But there is no way out of it – you girls and boys will mix; even if I say [not to] they cannot avoid it. They sit separately in the temple and then outside mix again. So this was not possible from the beginning.[2]

> Sometimes in India, I am criticized that I keep women and men in the same temple. In India, that is not allowed; no women can live at night. They can come and go. But I defend myself that this is the system of the country – the women and men, they intermingle – how can I check it? Then the women – shall I not give them any chance for chanting Hare Kṛṣṇa? No, I shall give this chance to women even at the risk [of illicit sex].[3]

Within traditional Indian culture, many measures for separating the sexes were more stringent than can hardly be imagined today. An example is that commonly in public events, arrangements would be made so that men and women would not even see one another. Elderly people in India might remember the use of a bamboo screen for situations in which unrelated men and women would need to communicate. For instance, an Ayurvedic doctor (in those days only males were doctors) would examine a lady's pulse from behind a screen via a cotton thread tied around her wrist; he would not see the

1. Letter, 20 Jan 1976.
2. Letter, 30 Apr 1974.
3. Lecture, 28 Jul 1973.

woman. Similarly, through such a screen Śrīla Bhaktisiddhānta Sarasvatī Ṭhākura gave *harināma-dīkṣā* to one of his young female disciples.* Such apparently extreme measures were the external manifestation of a culture wherein much precaution was taken to prevent even impure thoughts, what to speak of improper interactions.

Still, although such norms had been in practice for thousands of years, it is probably impractical to try to quickly return to them, because most people today are clueless as to what constitutes proper behavior and, in fact, take right to be wrong and wrong to be right.[1]

Recognizing that it was difficult for his Western, and especially his female, disciples to accept much of the Vedic culture, Śrīla Prabhupāda did not force them to adopt traditional practices of gender separation. Yet he let them know that "the separation of man and woman is desirable,"[2] the very same principle he had outlined even before coming to America:

> The ladies [of Dvārakā] did not mix with the crowd on the street, and thus their respectability was perfectly observed. There was no artificial equality with the man. Female respectability is preserved more elegantly by keeping the woman separate from the man. The sexes should not mix unrestrictedly.[3]

Śrīla Prabhupāda was quite aware of the mindset of his Western female disciples, and often encouraged them to serve Kṛṣṇa in ways that were commensurate with their abilities and outlook. Doing so helped to kickstart the Kṛṣṇa consciousness movement in the West. Yamunā Devī Dāsī recalled:

---

* This is described in *Śrī Bhaktisiddhānta Vaibhava,* part 2, ch. 24, "Regarding Women." This chapter has many salient points about traditional gender roles.

1. See Bg 16.23–24 and 18.31–32.
2. Letter, 13 Nov 1975.
3. SB 1.11.24, ppt.

> As a strong and independent young woman I met Śrīla Prabhupāda in 1966 and took initiation in 1967. Had Śrīla Prabhupāda demanded conformity to orthodox roles for women as a condition of surrender, I, along with many of my godsisters, would probably not have joined ISKCON. That he did not is testament to his spiritual vision. He lovingly encouraged and engaged us in the service of the *saṅkīrtana* movement, and he consistently revealed himself to be *paṇḍitāḥ sama-darśinaḥ* – equal to all.[1]

Apart from Yamunā Devī Dāsī, many other female devotees have made outstanding contributions to Śrīla Prabhupāda's mission. For instance, Viśākhā Devī Dāsī is probably the most prolific photographer in the history of ISKCON. She and her husband, Yaduvara Dāsa, were photographers even before meeting Śrīla Prabhupāda – who fully encouraged them in their art – and together they have spent a lifetime in his divine service.

Śrīla Prabhupāda wanted to impart Vedic tradition, but he was also practical and therefore made concessions for his Western sons and daughters. In engaging female devotees in ways unprecedented in Vedic culture, he demonstrated extraordinary broad-mindedness. For example, he permitted women to perform Deity worship in public temples (which is disallowed in India), and to live, albeit separately, in the same ashrams as men. He made these cultural adjustments to facilitate the establishment of Kṛṣṇa consciousness in the West. This was Śrīla Prabhupāda's expertise and special mercy: to engage all fallen souls in Kṛṣṇa's service, even those from a background of very little real culture of any kind. He was unswerving in upholding absolute truths and principles, yet flexible when it came to inspiring and motivating individuals.

1. Yamunā Devī Dāsī, ISKCON Communications Journal #8.1 (January/June 2000).

His endeavor was to encourage people to chant the holy names and to engage in devotional service at whatever standard and in whatever way they could, with the aim of steadily elevating them. As he himself explained:

> It is the concern of the *ācārya* to show mercy to the fallen souls. In this connection, *deśa-kāla-pātra* (the place, the time, and the object) should be taken into consideration. Since the European and American boys and girls in our Kṛṣṇa consciousness movement preach together, less intelligent men criticize that they are mingling without restriction. In Europe and America boys and girls mingle unrestrictedly and have equal rights; therefore it is not possible to completely separate the men from the women. However, we are thoroughly instructing both men and women how to preach, and actually they are preaching wonderfully. Of course, we very strictly prohibit illicit sex. Boys and girls who are not married are not allowed to sleep together or live together, and there are separate arrangements for boys and girls in every temple. *Gṛhasthas* live outside the temple, for in the temple we do not allow even husband and wife to live together. The results of this are wonderful. Both men and women are preaching the gospel of Lord Caitanya Mahāprabhu and Lord Kṛṣṇa with redoubled strength.... Śrī Caitanya Mahāprabhu wanted to deliver one and all. Therefore it is a principle that a preacher must strictly follow the rules and regulations laid down in the *śāstras* yet at the same time devise a means by which the preaching work to reclaim the fallen may go on with full force.[1]

Hence, in the beginning days of ISKCON Śrīla Prabhupāda was very tolerant, but he then gradually revealed to his followers how they could improve in their service and behavior. He did what every teacher must do: first start with the basics, and only gradually introduce more developed concepts. Although

---

1. Cc 1.7.38, ppt.

he had a definite outlook on *strī-dharma,* he did not attempt to forcibly impose it, due to his observation that Westerners were simply not ready for it.

Still, along with introducing pragmatic adjustments, Śrīla Prabhupāda often spoke about Vedic culture and the necessity for establishing it, which includes traditional gender roles within the *varṇāśrama* system. While being lenient and seeing the spirit soul in everyone, he never (as some would have us believe) overrode the Vedic social teachings.

Within ISKCON it has been propagated, and is now widely accepted as fact, that some overly zealous men undermined the initial idyllic equality of, and loose mixing of, the sexes.[1] But this narrative obscures the fact that, on principle, Śrīla Prabhupāda approved the introduction of restrictions that reshape the gender equation – as evidenced not only by his numerous philosophical instructions, but also by his ordering, without inducement from others, at least one very significant change: "Now there should be one rule: that unless they are husband-wife, man and woman should not worship [Deities] together."[2] Had this command been fully instituted, several devotees would have been saved from disastrous falldowns, and ISKCON itself would have been spared much shame.

Quite early in the history of ISKCON, along with providing adjustments to accommodate his female disciples, Śrīla Prabhupāda specified that he wanted them to perform distinctively feminine duties. This pertained especially to the farm communities, which were meant to demonstrate the ideal of Kṛṣṇa conscious life:

---

1. For instance see www.dandavats.com/?p=14535 (retrieved 25 Dec 2014). Also: Dīnatāriṇī Devī Dāsī, *Yamuna Devi – A Life of Unalloyed Devotion.* Vol. 2, p. 58.

2. Conversation, 20 Jul 1976; see also *A Transcendental Diary,* vol. 5.

> The first thing is that whether the girls and women who live there are agreeable to work as I have suggested – namely 1) to take care of the children, both from health and educational point of view, 2) to keep the whole temple, kitchen, etc., very clean, 3) cooking, 4) churning butter.[1]

> A woman's real business is to look after household affairs, keep everything neat and clean, and if there is sufficient milk supply available, she should always be engaged in churning butter, making yogurt, curd, so many nice varieties, simply from milk. The woman should be cleaning, sewing, like that.[2]

Yet also for his female disciples who served in city temples, Śrīla Prabhupāda assigned duties specific to their constitution and nature:

> All the wives of our students should be especially trained up for Deity worship and cooking, and when possible they should go outside on the *saṅkīrtana* party with their husbands and others.[3] [N.B. "with their husbands"]

Even after having experienced public strictures for his anti-feminist stance, up until the last days of his manifest presence Śrīla Prabhupāda continued to iterate feminine duties for females: "Girls should be taught how to sweep; how to stitch, clean, cook; to be faithful to the husband, obedient to the husband."[4]

Clearly, Śrīla Prabhupāda wanted his Western lady disciples to overcome their cultural conditioning and accept the role of a Vedic wife. In 1976, he instructed a Western lady devotee, who previously had been a movie actress:

---

1. Letter, 24 Jun 1969.
2. Letter, 16 Feb 1972.
3. Letter, 18 Apr 1970.
4. Conversation, 29 Apr 1977.

> As a faithful wife, your duty is to follow your husband. That is your duty. ... Otherwise you will be hampered in your advancement in Kṛṣṇa consciousness. You are husband and wife and you have to follow the instructions of your spiritual master wherever you live. Simply one has to be in full Kṛṣṇa consciousness. Study the philosophy and try to distribute this philosophy. Where is the problem? I don't see the problem. Your duty is to keep peacefully with your husband, and his duty is to follow strictly the principles given to him by his spiritual master. You have got to live, so live cooperatively. ... A wife's duty is to remain faithful to her husband and if the husband is a pure devotee then both of them will be happy. What is the problem? [Referring to an Indian couple.] You see they are living happily, husband and wife. The culture is so nice amongst Indians that in any condition the husband and wife live very peacefully.

The lady devotee protested, "I've not been brought up in that culture," to which Śrīla Prabhupāda responded:

> If something is good you should accept. I know in your Western countries the ideas are different, but we have to pick up the best. In Vedic culture, the wife should remain faithful to husband. If the husband is bad then that is another thing. Your husband is not bad; he's a devotee. So what is wrong there? Don't disturb your mind. Follow what I have laid down and chant Hare Kṛṣṇa. Follow the regulative principles and read the books.[1]

Thus Śrīla Prabhupāda made various concessions that were necessary for establishing Kṛṣṇa consciousness in the West. Only gradually did he introduce gender-specific roles and separation of the sexes, basic *varṇāśrama* practices that have always been required within Vaiṣṇava society for protecting devotees from spiritual downfall. A relevant analogy: Whereas

1. From *My Glorious Master,* by Bhūrijana Dāsa.

normal circumstances call for careful driving at moderate speeds, in cases of emergency an ambulance might be driven extremely fast so as to reach the hospital as quickly as possible, even though such speeding drastically increases the risk of injury and death. Similarly, it would be dangerous to consider Śrīla Prabhupāda's early innovations to be the standard for Vaiṣṇavism for all time. By taking various risks, such as allowing the mixing of males and females, Śrīla Prabhupāda was able to introduce Kṛṣṇa consciousness within a culture that was devoid of the safeguards afforded by *varṇāśrama-dharma*. It was indeed a risk, for there certainly was danger, and factually many of his disciples did succumb to *māyā* – for which reason Śrīla Prabhupāda wanted to establish *varṇāśrama-dharma,* for the benefit of not only his followers but also the world.

Another analogy: Suppose Śrīla Prabhupāda were leading a *kīrtana* and steadily increased the tempo, yet the accompanying devotees failed to notice and continued to play instruments at a slower speed; and when informed that they should have increased the pace to keep in sync with Śrīla Prabhupāda, they protest: "We are playing in a way that Śrīla Prabhupāda has already approved." Similarly, although Śrīla Prabhupāda retained his basic aim of bringing Kṛṣṇa consciousness to the world, he gradually made changes in his approach – changes that many of his disciples seem to have either missed or been unable to adjust to. As Yamunā Devī Dāsī wrote:

> I tried to become more conscious of the behavior and etiquette some leaders in ISKCON were expecting of women, even though this was the antithesis of my prior experience and training.[1]

It is arguable that the same kind of concessions that Śrīla Prabhupāda made are still applicable, for the influence of feminism in the West is even more pervasive than previously.

---

1. *Yamuna Devi,* vol. 2, p. 25.

A counterargument is that Śrīla Prabhupāda's female disciples should have by now understood his mission and been able to groom themselves into more traditional roles, and should also be competent to refute objections by the public in regard to ISKCON women's non-feministic behavior.

Tweaking History by Blaming the Men

Followers of Śrīla Prabhupāda should know that whatever adjustments he made due to *deśa-kāla-pātra* – place (Western world), time (1960s), and persons (hippies)* – should eventually be replaced by the genuinely human cultural standards that he tirelessly advocated. Those of his female followers who feel that they were mistreated might consider that much of their suffering arose from their not having kept up with the tempo – i.e., by refusing to acknowledge that the ongoing changes in gender roles originated with and were desired by Śrīla Prabhupāda himself, who derived them from the very *śāstra* and tradition that he had come to establish. They are as if stuck in a conception of how Kṛṣṇa consciousness should be practiced, based on their cherished personal interactions with Śrīla Prabhupāda during an early phase of his preaching mission, and apparently do not want to see the broader picture of Śrīla Prabhupāda's later instructions, such as:

> You leaders see that the Kṛṣṇa conscious standards in regard to initiation, cleanliness, dress and activities of the devotees, the **restriction of association between men and women,** all be strictly followed. Devotional service cannot be done whimsically.[1]

---

* See quote above (p. 73). Although Śrīla Prabhupāda usually translates *pātra* as "circumstance," a more common meaning is "individual, person." (Śrīla Prabhupāda uses it in this way in SB 7.14.34, ppt.)

1. Letter, 1 Jan 1974.

In order to avoid blaming Śrīla Prabhupāda, they have instead wholly indicted those men who often rather crassly imposed gender demarcation – yet did so under the order of Śrīla Prabhupāda. For instance, Yamunā Devī Dāsī commented:

> Our society was dramatically growing and changing. Śrīla Prabhupāda was creating so many sannyasis, and the GBC was in place. **It was these men** who attempted to create a society-wide template on the position and treatment of women.[1]

Like their secular counterparts, the suffragettes have vigorously opposed those who have protested their feministic rewrite of history (in this case, that of ISKCON). Similarly, to "exonerate" Śrīla Prabhupāda from his centrality in ISKCON's changed gender equation, the suffragettes have had to recast him as being largely divorced from tradition and as having little empathy for the suffering of women. The following further example of history-tweaking claims that Śrīla Prabhupāda was aware of "the devaluation of women" yet allowed it due to his indulging of sannyasis:

> ... the situation began to change in the mid-1970s. By this time several male devotees had been initiated as sannyasis. They worked closely with Prabhupāda, particularly on various projects in India where they were exposed to very different cultural circumstances to those operating in the West. Looking back to this time, older devotees now see this situation as causal in the devaluation of women within the movement. With a desire to protect their own *āśrama* and their individual spiritual advancement, they saw the involvement of women as a problem.... Prabhupāda was certainly aware of some of the things which took place in this period. However, most devotees, in evaluating the changes in relation to Prabhupāda's original openness and equal treatment of women, believe that he allowed such things to happen to allay the fears of his newly

1. *Yamuna Devi*, vol. 2, p. 22 (emphasis mine).

> celibate male population and perhaps to help them with the difficulties that the renunciant lifestyle inevitably engendered.[1]

But if we analyze according to *śāstra* rather than by mundane social and psychological theories, then much of the suffering that female devotees have accused men of perpetrating can better be attributed to those females' misconception of equal rights, opportunities, and positions. As stated in *Bhagavad-gītā* (2.62–63), such desire leads to frustration, anger, and bewilderment. So, better to be happy by remembering Śrīla Prabhupāda's advice:

> Everything will be satisfied. Just like our women, Kṛṣṇa conscious – they are working. They don't want equal rights with the men. It is due to Kṛṣṇa consciousness. They are cleansing the temple, they are cooking very nicely; they are satisfied. They never said that "I have to go to Japan for preaching like Prabhupāda." They never say. This is artificial. Kṛṣṇa consciousness means work in his constitutional position. The women, men – when they remain in their constitutional position, there will be no artificial.[2]

By solely blaming men within ISKCON, the suffragettes have created an artificial gender divide that parallels that made by feminists in secular society. If they were more honest they would admit that their real problem is with certain of Śrīla Prabhupāda's teachings which at heart they do not agree with and do not want to accept.

A Case Study: Yamunā Devī Dāsī

Yamunā Devī Dāsī was maybe the best-known, highest regarded, and most loved among Śrīla Prabhupāda's female

---

1. "The Debate About Women In The Hare Kṛṣṇa Movement," by Kim Knott. ISKCON Communications Journal, #3.2, July/December 1995.

2. Conversation, 27 May 1974.

disciples. She became famous for her singing, cooking, Deity worship, missionary work, deep sense of dedication to Śrīla Prabhupāda, and her many saintly qualities. According to her own account, Śrīla Prabhupāda so much appreciated her abilities that he once considered inducting her as a "half member" of the GBC. He told her: "I was planning that you and Govinda Dāsī would be as one Governing Board member – half." She replied, "I don't think this would be very successful, because I have a female body, and it simply wouldn't work." And Śrīla Prabhupāda agreed.[1]

Her extensive biography* reveals the struggles that she, like many of her godsisters, underwent during the first clumsy (if not harsh) attempts to institute within ISKCON some semblance of traditional gender roles.

Being a self-professedly "strong and independent young woman" (as quoted above), Yamunā derived many bittersweet lessons amid the conservative culture of India. One occurred in January 1971 during the Ardha Kumbha-melā in Allahabad. As had always been her habit, she sat close to Śrīla Prabhupāda during his morning lectures:

> Throughout my early years of Kṛṣṇa consciousness, Śrīla Prabhupāda was so open and merciful to the ladies that we never felt the stricture of separation or division between us. So one morning this sannyasi brusquely approached me and said, "Yamunā, have you noticed where the other women are sitting?" I replied, "Yes, I have." They were seated in the back. He then said, "You should be sitting back there with them, not in the front by Śrīla Prabhupāda."[2]

* *Yamuna Devi – A Life of Unalloyed Devotion.* Dīnatāriṇī Devī Dāsī. (2 vols.) Unalloyed Inc., 2014.

1. *Yamuna Devi*, vol. 1, p. 343.
2. *Yamuna Devi*, vol. 1, p. 358.

For the next two days, Yamunā sat in the back. Then Śrīla Prabhupāda called her and asked why she did not like to hear from him anymore.

> I immediately burst into tears because I had no words to express how much I was appreciating his discourses on the life of Ajāmila. So I said, "I love to hear from you more than ever, Śrīla Prabhupāda. More than anything in the world, all I want is to hear from you." Prabhupāda inquired, "So why aren't you sitting where you usually sit?" I said, "A sannyasi told me that it was the etiquette that I sit far in the back with the ladies." Prabhupāda was quiet. Then he said, "Yes, that is the etiquette."[1]

Significantly, although Śrīla Prabhupāda initially engaged Yamunā Devī Dāsī in active, outgoing services, after she left her husband and started a rural ashram he wrote to her:

> Yes, you are right, women are generally after sense gratification. That is the disease. Chant twenty-four hours a day and don't dress nicely to attract men. It is better that you don't make a large program. Remain a humble program. In *bhakti* there is no grotesque program.* A humble program is better. We are doing all these grotesque programs to allure the masses. My Guru Mahārāja used to say that no one hears from a person coming from a humble, simple life. You remain always very humble.
>
> Sītā Devī, Mother Lakṣmī, wife of Lord Rāmacandra, went to live with Vālmīki Muni in a cottage. Although she was a king's daughter and a king's wife, she preferred to live very humbly in the cottage of Vālmīki Muni with two sons in the absence of Rāmacandra. That should be the ideal example. Women when not with husband must live very very humbly and simple life.[2]

* In this context, "grotesque" may be understood to mean "large, meant to attract attention."

1. Ibid.

2. Letter, 13 Jan 1976.

Although in some ways Śrīla Prabhupāda encouraged Yamunā in establishing her ashram, he had reservations about it – which, however, he did not directly express to her, but instead did so via a letter sent (on the same day as the letter quoted above) to the GBC man of the area wherein her ashram was situated:

> Regarding Yamunā and Dīna-tāriṇī, they want to live independently, that is the defect. A woman cannot live independent. According to the Vedic culture a woman is always to be protected by a man.

Privately, Śrīla Prabhupāda commented, "What can I do? They want to be independent."[1] As in several other cases, Śrīla Prabhupāda dealt with Yamunā Devī Dāsī according to her individual needs, and he recognized that some exceptional women can actually live as renunciants. Nevertheless, Śrīla Prabhupāda's having made certain concessions does not undermine the fact that his overall social manifesto, meant to be implemented by his followers, is *varṇāśrama-dharma* with all that it entails, including the non-independence of women.

The Transformation of Women's Roles

In Vedic culture, a woman may certainly be a "master" in the sense of overseeing and being the queen of the home, or in being highly expert. Nonetheless, her general social role is subtle and subdued, in accord with the feminine nature. She is to be subordinate to her master, her husband. Such a role is directly ordained and approved by the Supreme Personality of Godhead, who states: "As chaste women bring a gentle husband under control by their service, the pure devotees, who are equal to everyone and completely attached to Me in the core of the heart, bring Me under their full control."[2] *

---

* Lecture: A Woman Should Follow Her Husband <www.bvks.com/891>

---

1. *Yamuna Devi*, vol. 2, p, 75.
2. SB 9.4.66.

George Eliot, a celebrated English writer (who was actually a female but published her works under a male pseudonym), authored novels depicting the early period of the industrial revolution in England. Because capitalists needed workers for their factories, peasants' land was seized, thus compelling the peasants to move to the cities, where they lived and worked in extremely unhealthy conditions. In one novel, Eliot portrays a man who is dying due to such adverse conditions, and whose wife refers to him as "my master." In traditional English culture, a woman would consider her husband as master.

Actually, this same general understanding originally prevailed throughout the entire world, but all of that changed with the onset and spread of the industrial revolution. As was understood everywhere (and particularly in Vedic tradition), and as was encouraged by Śrīla Prabhupāda, the foremost duty (dharma) of a woman is to be a housewife, and her natural propensity is household work. She is a wife, mother, grandmother, cook, cleaner, and guide to the children. In Sanskrit she is called *gṛha-lakṣmī,* "the goddess of fortune within the home," or *gṛhiṇī* (commonly rendered in Hindi as *gharwālī*), "the female in the home." Such was the understanding the world over. In English is the (now almost defunct) saying: "A woman's place is in the home."

The modern idea is that women should be out competing in the world, showing that they are as capable as men. However, women become attractive and powerful by their feminine qualities of shyness, service, and submissiveness, and not by imitating men. If the wife serves her husband well, and if he is responsible and not simply a loafer, he becomes inspired to work hard for her and provide everything she needs.* That is actually a much better arrangement for her, because without having to go out to work she still gets what she wants.

* As suggested by SB 6.19.17.

The astrological treatise *Bṛhat-jātaka* (chapter 24) states that if a woman is destined to achieve worldly opulences, such as wealth and fame, they will come to her through her husband. She does not have to do anything other than her own dharma.

Admittedly, all of this is anathema to many modern women, because they seek fulfillment through a career. And their very desire to do so is complexly linked with the historical transformation from an agrarian to an industrial economy, and the almost complete shift in the values, norms, and usages that accompanied the age of technology. One effect was that women's work, which had been performed in the home, lost its economic value, because much of the housework that they used to do could now be done by machines. Additionally, by utilizing artificial contraception they were now bearing fewer children.

As per Betty Friedan, author of the highly influential *The Feminine Mystique* (1963), the storybook-perfect housewives of her time were "bored and listless" and "nervous and jittery." Of the women whom she interviewed, a surprising number were regularly treated by psychotherapists or often took tranquillizers; and several had attempted suicide. Many also were engaged ("in fact or in fantasy") in extramarital affairs. To Friedan, their plight was obvious: "They had uncommon gifts of intelligence and ability nourished by at least the beginnings of higher education – and the life they were leading as suburban housewives denied them the full use of their gifts."[1] Friedan reasoned that if women do not use their natural gifts in livelihoods commensurate with their abilities, the idleness of their domestic home life will be the cause of their perpetual misery.

---

1. Betty Friedan, *The Feminine Mystique* (New York: Norton, 1963) 2001 edition.

But there are serious problems with being a career woman. Later and more rigorous studies have shown that the extramarital affairs that Friedan presumed were caused by household boredom did not cease when women found their way into the workforce. Instead, the workplace offered further opportunity for illicit affairs. As reported by a recent study: "Some researchers have found that around one-half of participants who had cheated on their partner and who sought therapy (due to problems in their primary relationship) had met their extradyadic partner [paramour] through their work."[1] The same researchers also report that several studies had also found an association between adultery and higher education: "Highly educated persons are more likely to report engaging in infidelity than less educated individuals." And as part of their own findings, they report: "There are no significant gender differences in the report of infidelity." In other words, the entrance of women en masse into the Western workforce secured "equality" at the cost of sexual restraint.*

Verily, Arjuna's concern (Bg 1.37–43) for the degradation of women and consequent failure of society is not some prudish anachronism. Rather, he speaks to our modern circumstances, for today's society is a full-blown population of *varṇa-saṅkara.*† Hence Śrīla Prabhupāda's advice, meant for today's world: "There should be a thorough overhauling of the social system, and society should revert to the Vedic principles, that is, the four *varṇas* and the four *āśramas.*"[2]

* "Career women" are further discussed on pp. 122–23.

† Lecture: Adharma is a Problem <www.bvks.com/179>

1. Kristen P. Mark, Erick Janssen, Robin R. Milhausen, "Infidelity in Heterosexual Couples: Demographic, Interpersonal, and Personality-Related Predictors of Extradyadic Sex." Retrieved: 12 February 2011, Springer Science+Business Media, 9 Jan. 2015 <http://www.kinseyinstitute.org/publications/PDF/Infidelity%20in%20hetero%20couples.pdf>.

2. SB 4.29.54, ppt.

Notwithstanding the illusory excitement of being a "woman of the world," the highest boon awaits those devotee women who execute *strī-dharma* in accord with the directions of *śāstra:*

> The woman who engages in the service of her husband, following strictly in the footsteps of the goddess of fortune, surely returns home, back to Godhead, with her devotee husband, and lives very happily in the Vaikuṇṭha planets.[1]

Lust, Greed, and Exploitation

As Lord Kṛṣṇa states in the *Bhagavad-gītā,* there are three gates leading to hell – lust, anger, and greed – which intelligent persons should give up.[2] But today's permissive society promotes all three of these vices, especially lust. Television, cinema, and the internet unabashedly and unrelentingly tout lust, anger, violence, and greed. The dangers of lust are described by Lord Kṛṣṇa in the *Gītā;* it covers one's intelligence.[3] Yet, the peddling of lust is the main feature of today's liberal and "progressive" world.

How can we propose that humankind will be very nice and peaceful and that everyone will be happy, when lust, anger, and greed – lust being the root of them all – are promoted? Lust and greed cannot make anyone happy. On the contrary, they cause tremendous discontent, because they can never be fulfilled. They are emblematic of "happiness" in the mode of passion, which is like nectar in the beginning but poison at the end.[4] In today's ridiculously oversexed society, women are the main sufferers, because they are more often and more seriously exploited. Lust is so strong that commonly even children – both boys and girls – are sexually exploited, even

1. SB 7.11.29.

2. Bg 16.21.

3. Bg 3.39.

4. Bg 18.38.

by their closest relatives. Lust causes people to lose all sense of discrimination, all sense of right and wrong (as described in Bg 16.7, cited above). They then see others as mere bodies meant to satisfy their lust. They do not stop to reason or consider that that body is actually their sister or daughter. But this is the mentality of pigs.

The inordinate promotion of sexuality is the root cause of myriad problems within today's highly disturbed world. People are programmed to relentlessly indulge their sexual appetites: "In modern civilization, sex life is the focal point for all activities. Wherever one turns his face, he sees sex life predominant."[1] Women in particular are encouraged to be unchaste. What would formerly have been considered sluttish behavior is now heralded as virtue, as an assertion of women's independence and empowerment. Yet these same women, who freely mix with and entice men, will later complain that they have been sexually exploited.

Free mixing of the sexes must incite lust, which results in premarital sexual contact. Sex before marriage is devoid of commitment and responsibility. Marriage means a commitment to be responsible to one's family and to the whole community. But in animalistic society, a girl is picked up by a boy and together they enjoy sex. But what is she left with? She loses her virginity and her respectability, all for some fleeting titillation.

And due to the habit of intermingling with assorted sexual partners before marriage, people continue to do so even after being married "religiously." So what is the point of marrying at all? Indeed, many people (especially in the West) simply do not bother to marry; they just live together until they feel like switching to someone else. All of this is very sinful and uncivilized – like cats and dogs, as Śrīla Prabhupāda would say.

---

1. SB 1.1.1.

In India (until only recently), free mixing between boys and girls, even in schools, was unthinkable; and up to about a century ago, the idea of sending girls to school could hardly be imagined, and was considered an abomination. Even now in India, men and women do not mix very freely. Innocent teenagers who are sent to Westernized educational institutions are actually induced there to mix freely. Similarly, young people from small towns in South India who land IT jobs in Bangalore, or in the call centers, are induced to drink, smoke, have illicit sex, and thus become well degraded so as to fit into the lifestyle there. Of course, in the Western world, people do not need such special training. They are raised with sense gratification, without even a hint that anything could be wrong with it. But an increasingly bewildered and clueless populace within India is fast becoming the norm there as well.

Sigmund Freud and His Followers

A few years ago in Foyle's (a famous bookshop in London), I came across a large room dedicated to a special exhibition of books by and about Sigmund Freud, the founder of psychoanalysis, whose speculations have deeply influenced the outlook of modern Western man. Therein a placard declared that although all of his ideas have been shown to be inaccurate, he is still highly influential. Freud had some extremely strange ideas, such as the Oedipus complex – that every man is sexually attracted to his mother. However, Śrīla Prabhupāda said that Freud was correct inasmuch as he recognized that the intrinsic feature within human society is sex (as per *Śrīmad-Bhāgavatam* 5.5.8). But Freud's emphasis on sexuality in analyzing mental states gave rise to a widely held assumption that all psychological problems are caused by repression of sexual desires.[1]

---

1. See Śrīla Prabhupāda's discussion of Freud in *Beyond Illusion and Doubt*, ch. 13.

A contemporary proselyter of this theory is a doctor in Tamil Nadu, whose name (believe it or not) is Dr. Kamaraj.* He appears on television every Saturday morning and preaches that daily sex with one's wife is the only way to keep away both the doctor and the lawyer. Otherwise, a man will visit prostitutes and later need to be treated by a doctor; and the wife will not be carnally satisfied so will want a divorce.

However, until only recently throughout the world, marriage was understood to be an irrevocable religious commitment – "till death do us part" – whereby man and woman unite in the eyes of God. Sex is allowed only within marriage, and dovetailed for procreation. Sex is undeniably important within marriage, but marriage is not meant to be centered solely on sex. Without a religious commitment, there is no difference between the sexual behavior of humans and that of animals. There is no marriage among dogs and cats – only lust.

Sex, Dissatisfaction, and Family Decline

As previously quoted, Śrīla Prabhupāda writes that because demons do not follow Vedic injunctions, especially those stating that women should not be given independence, "the moral condition of women is not very good now" and "marriage is practically an imagination in human society."[1]

Clearly, a major factor in the decline of family stability is an inordinate emphasis on sex. Emphasis on sex is a symptom of the mode of passion, which by its very nature is dissatisfying, and dissatisfaction leads to instability. As Lord Kṛṣṇa states in the *Gītā:* "That happiness which is derived from contact of

* Kāmarāj(a) – (literally, "the king of lust") a name of the god of love. This name is well-known among Hindus.

1. Bg 16.7, ppt.

the senses with their objects and which appears like nectar at first but poison at the end is said to be of the nature of passion."[1] Actual family stability derives from a sense of duty, responsibility, and dharma, which are symptomatic of the mode of goodness: "That which in the beginning may be just like poison but at the end is just like nectar and which awakens one to self-realization is said to be happiness in the mode of goodness."[2] Even if in the beginning some difficulty is felt by maintaining the mode of goodness, actions in the mode of goodness must promote happiness, because such activity elevates one to the platform of renunciation. On the contrary, for those who do not cultivate the mode of goodness, lust can never be satisfied.[3] The ensuing dissatisfaction spawns strife between spouses, and eventually one or both of them may seek solace in illicit sexual partners.

Vaiṣṇava *gṛhasthas* must know that actual satisfaction lies only in surrender to Kṛṣṇa, and that indulgence in sex for any purpose other than procreation is a block to advancement in Kṛṣṇa consciousness.

Men and Women Are Different

As Śrīla Prabhupāda posited, "How can a man and woman be equal? The woman has to give birth, she has to become pregnant. Why can the man not become pregnant?"[4] *

Biologically and psychologically, men and women are different. A woman's body is quite different from a man's body, and

* Lecture: Equal Rights is Insanity <www.bvks.com/2263>

1. Bg 18.38.
2. Bg 18.37.
3. Bg 3.39.
4. Conversation, 29 May 1974.

her mentality is different from that of a man. Consequently, her social role must also be different. Śrīla Prabhupāda also pointed out: "[There] is a natural distinction between men and women. How can it be changed? Women are meant for certain activities, just as men are. You may try to change this artificially, but basically it cannot be changed."[1]

Sane civilizations recognize this and accordingly ascribe distinctive social functions to men and women. Particularly, *varṇāśrama-dharma* is based on the understanding that men and women are spiritually equal yet have different social duties (*sva-dharma*), which at once correspond to, and fulfill, their respective natures (*sva-bhāva*). *Varṇāśrama-dharma* is designed so that both men and women of all social classes are facilitated in fulfilling their various functions, so that all can advance toward spiritual perfection – although not all in the same way.

Previously throughout the world, it was unquestioned that men and women have particular roles according to their specific physical and psychological propensities and abilities. Generally, men take charge and women play a more subtle, subdued role. This is the natural order, as well as a defining feature of *varṇāśrama-dharma.* For instance, many great *kṣatriya* heroes fought in the Battle of Kurukṣetra, whereas their wives remained at home. "Ladies are not aggressors; they are sacrifice personified."[2]

Even today in countries wherein women are expected to work within the society, some occupations – such as secretaries, nurses, elementary and middle-school teachers, and cashiers – are dominated by women,[3] whereas others – including

---

1. From *Dialectic Spiritualism*, discussion of Auguste Comte.
2. B. R. Śrīdhara. *The Golden Staircase*, ch. 4.
3. jobs.aol.com/articles/2010/07/27/where-women-work/ (retrieved 12 Dec 2014).

welding, construction, sports commentary, and politics – are primarily male domains.[1] It should be simple to understand that certain tasks are better suited for women, and others for men. But feminists wish to override this natural order and try to make women exactly equal to men. Failure to recognize such differences, and attempting to make everything "all one" is akin to impersonalism. Śrīla Prabhupāda noted:

> The impersonalist philosophers have given indirect impetus to the abominable mundane sex life because they have overstressed the impersonality of the ultimate truth. Consequently, man without information of the actual spiritual form of sex has accepted perverted material sex life as the all in all.[2]

Feminist Folly

A major cause for the highly disturbed condition of the modern world is the selfish individualism whereby everyone wants to pursue his own interests, caring little for the wellbeing of others. The attitudes underlying feminism typify such selfishness: "What can I get for me? Shove the men out of the way, and to hell with the kids!"* Especially the more militant forms of feminism engender hatred of men, while accusing men of hatred of women.†

Along with the word "misogyny" (hatred of women), another prominent feminist buzzword is "sexism" – discrimination based on gender, especially discrimination against women; and the belief that one gender is superior to the other, especially

---

* See analysis of selfishness, p. 8.

† See comment re misandry, p. 67.

---

1. uk.askmen.com/top_10/entertainment/top-10-male-dominated-industries_1.html (retrieved 12 Dec 2014).

2. SB 1.1.1, ppt.

that men are superior to women. (Although feminists complain of male chauvinism, they nonetheless typically assert that women are morally superior to men. Illogically, they do not admit this to be sexism.)

Especially in the West, feminists have been so successful in promoting their propaganda that persons (especially men) who dare to disagree are labeled "misogynist" and "sexist."* For instance, if one says that women should not be allowed to wander alone at midnight, he is considered to be a woman-hater for advocating a curtailing of their freedom. But obviously, there is a problem with women being alone in public at midnight, obvious at least to anyone whose brain hasn't been addled by feminism.

Feminists maintain that women have long been mistreated and therefore the "emancipation" of women is the only way forward for a progressive society. "Now we are so advanced, we are rectifying the antiquated, unjust, stultifying attitudes of the primitive past." But that will not solve their problem. Rather, such thinking is itself a pernicious problem, for feminism has been a major factor in worsening the self-centeredness, immorality, psychological disturbances, and perversity in the materialistically developed countries, and increasingly all over the world. Particularly, so-called "free sex" and the commercialization of the female body are curses upon womanhood, ironically inflicted in the name of liberation and progress.

The concept of gender equality translates as "equality to enjoy the senses." Hence, "equal rights" is the notion that

* However, feminism could never have been "successful" had it been promoted only by women. Without the strong support of certain men, feminism could not have flourished. Hence, feminism is not the preserve of females. Many men are strident feminists (as indeed also a growing number of women are anti-feminist).

women should have at least the same opportunities for sense enjoyment as do men. The concept of individual constitutional rights is based on the presumption that sense gratification is the primary goal of life, and therefore the central goal of all of society's institutions, laws, and customs is to maximize the potential for each individual to obtain sense enjoyment. By extension, the central purpose of feminism, "equality," and "equal rights" is to maximize women's potential for obtaining sense enjoyment. Ongoing efforts to transform from a patriarchal to a feminist society are meant to transfer the privileges of the elite members (who possess the greatest facility for sense gratification) from men to women. Therefore feminism, like all other isms in this world, is founded on the useless pursuit of sense gratification – which cannot but result in misery, both individually and collectively.[1]

Gender equality is a mythical notion, and therefore all attempts to institute it simply result in various contrived, complicated stratagems to facilitate women's illusory independence. Because it is founded on a misunderstanding, feminism can do no good for the world. It is just another in the futile history of speculative ideologies that have been proposed as solutions within the material situation. However, the very nature of material existence is problematic, and all attempted solutions simply create more problems. Analogously, often the symptomatic treatments used in modern medicine not only fail to cure but also create undesirable side effects, whereas the ancient science of Ayurveda is based on deep understanding of human physiology and prescribes gradual treatments aimed at eradicating the root cause of any ailment. Similarly, Vedic knowledge of the human condition provides the ultimate spiritual solution to all material adversities.

---

1. See Bg 5.22.

Feminists claim that the feminist movement has much improved the position of women; formerly women were repressed, but now they are free to explore the opportunities of the world. However, the opportunity that most "liberated women" explore is sex, which animals also have full freedom to explore. Freedom for women has rendered them usable objects of others' gratification, "instruments of sense enjoyment,"[1] out in the marketplace offering their services for pay. So how are they better off? As Śrīla Prabhupāda observed, "Independence for a woman means miserable life. In this age, so many girls are unmarried and falsely imagining themselves free, but their life is miserable."[2]

Several studies indicate that women are now less happy than in previous times.[3] In the past, women would have one husband for their entire life; now they have gained an illusory independence yet have lost their innocence, purity, and dignity. But however much they may clamor for equality, their independence and self-assertion have not earned them respect. And why should anyone who doesn't act in a respectable manner expect to be respected?

Feminists would have us believe that the women who have bought into the perverse feminist propaganda are enjoying unprecedented freedom. But nowadays women are actually more exploited than at any previous time in history. Women today are incessantly depicted as sex objects, not only in hard pornography (a multi-billion dollar business) but even in regular movies and advertisements. Pretty women are converted into prostitutes, who simply for the sake of some

---

1. SB 4.26.6, ppt.
2. SB 9.9.32, ppt.
3. E.g., see www.youtube.com/watch?v=HXeszLlTX5E

money shamelessly reveal their body to millions of men.* This is extremely low-class and a most degrading insult to womankind, especially to the millions of women who prefer to lead a respectable, restrained, religious life.

Furthermore, the very notion of freedom is wholly absurd, being that each of us is controlled in so many ways by higher ordinance. No one chooses where to be born or in what circumstances. Everyone must receive the karmic results of previous actions.† Especially women, if they perform their natural function of bearing and caring for children, cannot be free. They must depend upon others (which in a sane society primarily means the husband) and must accept responsibility to nurture the children.

Sinfully, feminists discourage women from marrying and bearing children, instead promoting "opportunities for women" (opportunities to degrade themselves). Feminists have stigmatized the dignified, sheltered life of the religious wife and mother. They have brainwashed people to think it absurd that a girl should marry young, raise a family, and lovingly serve her husband and children as service to God.

The legacy of feminism is a disaster. No one is happy. Stable family life is almost nonexistent and family values have largely been lost. Many feminists consider this to be a sign of progress that has been effected by their efforts in undermining the

* Feminists are divided over whether or not such commodification of the female body is desirable. Some feminists uphold that women should have the freedom to choose whether or not to become involved in pornography, whereas other feminists oppose it on the grounds that such involvement means pandering to the desires of men and perpetuating the male-stereotyping of women as mere sex objects. But the latter camp is hardly likely to prevail, because feminism is indeed a ploy by powerful males for increasing the pool of available sex objects.

† Lecture: The Myth of Freedom <www.bvks.com/20578>

institution of family life, which they deem to be anachronistic, parochial, and restrictive of the human spirit. People are so messed up that they have redefined the concept of family to what they call homosexual and lesbian "families": two men, or two lesbians, "marry" (even in a church, if they so desire) and then adopt children. The children then have two mothers and no father, or two fathers and no mother. Or sometimes a lesbian "wife" will be artificially inseminated with some unknown man's semen, and the baby that she delivers is considered the child of the two lesbian mothers. This is cultural genocide, yet is applauded by feminists.*

"Women's liberation" is actually a very bad deal for women. Which is better: to have had more boyfriends than you can remember, or to be a respectable wife and mother? A girl whom I knew from childhood never married. She rejoiced in being "sexually liberated." But now she is over sixty, her good looks are gone, and nobody cares for her. She never cared enough for anyone to commit herself to marriage, so despite having had numerous sexual partners, she has no husband, no children, and no prospect for old age except loneliness and misery.†

No wonder then that Śrīla Prabhupāda pointed out how feminism, or the so-called independence of women, has been

* That the movements for "women's rights" and for "gay rights" are intimately linked is unsurprising, for both insist on redefinition of traditional gender roles. Almost invariably, religious denominations that accede to feminist claims (for instance, by rewriting scriptures to render them gender-neutral, and by admitting women as clergy) shortly thereafter also embrace the demands of homosexuals. It cannot be expected that ISKCON's capitulation to feminism will not also be followed by a "gay wave"; indeed, already the much-publicized blessing of a "gay union" by a prominent ISKCON leader has gone uncensured by the GBC. See "Hridayananda Das Goswami Blesses Gay Male Couple"; www.chakra.org/announcements/persFeb01_09.html (retrieved 16 Feb 2015).

† Lecture: Women's Liberation or Women's Bondage
<www.bvks.com/1782>

a major factor in the ongoing massive degradation of human society. The feminist call for individual fulfillment is a masked plea for selfishness and irresponsibility. Although freedom and equal opportunities and rights for women might sound very good, Śrīla Prabhupāda deemed it an "artificially devised puffed-up concept of womanly life" whereby "the moral condition of woman is not very good now."[1]

To be true to its name, feminism should make women more feminine, but the attempts of women to become equal to men have largely been through imitating masculine functions. After all, there are only two genders, and if women forswear the trappings of womanhood, then even while protesting their independence they become compelled to adopt male role models – to the extent that, in the name of "equal opportunity," they also join the military and fight in wars.

Put simply, women are not suited for warfare. Women on the front lines become a liability to the men. They cannot carry heavy weights like men, and they have lesser endurance. Furthermore, women are always a distraction for men, and in life-or-death circumstances any amount of distraction is highly dangerous. It is also horrible to think about what happens to women who are captured by the enemy. Even in their home barracks, military women are regularly subjected to sexual harassment by male soldiers.[2] Also, the nausea, easy fatigue, or sudden light-headedness that are typical of pregnancy, and the need for maternity leave, make women a liability, not an asset, to the military – or any other organization that requires its members to function at optimal efficiency.

Any sensible person can understand that women should be protected, and not sent into combat. Yet the political

---

1. Bg 16.7, ppt.

2. See for instance www.servicewomen.org/military-sexual-violence/ (retrieved 27 Jan 2015).

correctness of feminism trumps common sense to the extent of risking national security rather than admitting the obvious: women should be at home, and only men (if anyone) should be on the battlefields.

Not only is "gender equality" often ridiculously and dangerously impractical (another example being women firefighters who are not physically competent for the job), it can also be blatantly unfair. For instance, the electoral system in India reserves certain posts for women candidates, which thereby enforces undemocratic and unequal opportunities by disallowing those positions to men. In the name of eradicating inequality, another inequality is created.

Thanks to feminism, women have lost their femininity. "Anything you can do, I can do better" went the lines of a popular song of 1946, being a spoof of a woman taunting a man. Women seem to have taken this too seriously, judging by female boxing matches, body-building, and other grotesque imitations of men by women. (Naturally, respectable women, those who are not victims of feminism, are completely turned off by brash, macho women who try to imitate the worst kind of men.)*

And because women can never actually be the same as men, feminists try to make men more like women.† In so many ways,

---

* Lecture: Why Not Go Along with Feminism <www.bvks.com/10628>

† For instance, see: "Pyrrhic Victoria: Why Men Are Becoming More Like Women" www.huffingtonpost.com/marcus-buckingham/why-men-are-becoming-more_b_360349.html (retrieved 13 March 2015).

Two key quotes therefrom: "Men's attitudes more and more resemble women's attitudes" and "Men's behaviors are becoming more and more like women's."

See also a feminist's lament that "In Austria, less than 2 percent of kindergarten teachers are men" in.reuters.com/article/2015/03/12/us-un-men-genderequality-idINKBN0M80A720150312 (retrieved 13 March 2015).

feminism has simply exacerbated the madness of the totally confused, demonic, humanistic society. Śrīla Prabhupāda summarized the situation:

> Presently women are given full independence like men, but actually we can see that such independent women are no happier than those women who are placed under guardians. If people follow the injunctions given by the great sages, *śrutis,* and *smṛtis,* they can actually be happy in both this life and the next. Unfortunately rascals are manufacturing so many ways and means to be happy. Everyone is inventing so many methods. Consequently human society has lost the standard ways of life, both materially and spiritually, and as a result people are bewildered, and there is no peace or happiness in the world. Although they are trying to solve the problems of human society in the United Nations, they are still baffled. Because they do not follow the liberated instructions of the Vedas, they are unhappy.[1]

Demonic "Broad-mindedness"

Opponents of so-called women's liberation, whether within secular society or ISKCON, are liable to be criticized as not "broad-minded." The concept of broad-mindedness is generally understood to mean giving wide scope to everyone to do whatever he likes. But this is totally opposed to the message of *Bhagavad-gītā,* as is clear from multiple statements therein – for instance, "The demons do not know what is to be done and what is not to be done"[2] and "He who discards scriptural injunctions and acts according to his own whims attains neither perfection, nor happiness, nor the supreme destination."[3]

---

1. SB 4.18.3, ppt.
2. Bg 16.7 verse translation.
3. Bg 16.23 verse translation.

Devotees of Kṛṣṇa are supposed to accept all such statements of His, notwithstanding being scorned by persons sworn to egalitarianism. But even within ISKCON, certain members clearly have difficulty imbibing such instructions. They resemble secular feminists in criticizing devotees who follow Śrīla Prabhupāda's example of advocating the restriction of the "rights" and "privileges" of women. This is redolent of *ardha-kukkuṭī-nyāya* (half-hen logic). A farmer might like the half of his hen that lays eggs but not appreciate the half that must be fed, and therefore chop off the chicken's head in an attempt to keep only the egg-laying portion, thus killing the hen. Similarly, to accept only those statements of Śrīla Prabhupāda's that one likes – rejecting, ignoring, or imaginatively interpreting the others – is tantamount to invalidating (killing) his authority in its entirety, for if Śrīla Prabhupāda's commentaries were wrong or irrelevant regarding even one point of *śāstra*, then nothing else that he has said would be authoritative unless it were confirmed by some other authority. Devotees who adopt such a stance regarding Śrīla Prabhupāda's instructions have wittingly or unwittingly become enemies of those instructions. But to avoid the appearance of apostasy, they disguise their enmity by adopting a seemingly broad-minded or moderate position in contradistinction to those devotees who follow Śrīla Prabhupāda's example of opposing non-traditional gender roles – whom they (narrow-mindedly and immoderately) label as "fanatics,"* "misogynists,"[1] and even as "the Taliban."[2] It is true that the social aims of ISKCON's traditionalists are largely

* Misuse of the word "fanatic" and of similar terms is endemic within ISKCON. See "Fanaticism and Fundamentalism," ch. 11 of my book *On Speaking Strongly in Śrīla Prabhupāda's Service.*

1. www.chakra.org/2013articles/2013-01-18b.html, first comment by Niscala Devi Dasi. (retrieved 17 Dec 2014).

2. www.dandavats.com/?p=11120#comment-17118 (retrieved 17 Dec 2014).

the same as those of the Taliban – for instance, to institute the kind of gender differentiation that was almost universally accepted until the advent of liberal humanism. However, whereas the Taliban are truly malicious (their policy being to kill all who disagree with them), ISKCON's traditionalists simply refer to Śrīla Prabhupāda's instructions regarding the role of women in a civilized society. Fortunately, we have Śrīla Prabhupāda's books (including his purport to *Bhagavad-gītā* 16.7) by which to mold our lives.

Why Women Need Protection

A vital role of women is to not simply bear children but to themselves be religious and of pure consciousness, and to unite with their similarly virtuous husbands so as to bring forth good progeny that will enhance human society and help prevent it from degrading. As stated in the *Bhagavad-gītā* (1.40), unprotected women become victims of unscrupulous men, and thus *varṇa-saṅkara* (bad children) are born, and the whole civilization is spoiled. Śrīla Prabhupāda's purport to this verse is:

> Good population in human society is the basic principle for peace, prosperity, and spiritual progress in life. The *varṇāśrama* religion's principles were so designed that the good population would prevail in society for the general spiritual progress of state and community. Such population depends on the chastity and faithfulness of its womanhood. As children are very prone to be misled, women are similarly very prone to degradation. Therefore, both children and women require protection by the elder members of the family. By being engaged in various religious practices, women will not be misled into adultery. According to Cāṇakya Paṇḍita, women are generally not very intelligent and therefore not trustworthy. So the different family traditions of religious activities should always engage

> them, and thus their chastity and devotion will give birth to a good population eligible for participating in the *varṇāśrama* system. On the failure of such *varṇāśrama-dharma,* naturally the women become free to act and mix with men, and thus adultery is indulged in at the risk of unwanted population. Irresponsible men also provoke adultery in society, and thus unwanted children flood the human race at the risk of war and pestilence.

Śrīla Prabhupāda further elaborated on this theme in his purport to verse 5.2.21 of *Śrīmād-Bhāgavatam:*

> *Bhagavad-gītā* (1.40) declares, *strīṣu duṣṭāsu vārṣṇeya jāyate varṇa-saṅkaraḥ:* when women are polluted, *varṇa-saṅkara,* unqualified children, are generated, and when the *varṇa-saṅkara* population increases, the entire world becomes hellish. Therefore, according to *Manu-saṁhitā,* a woman needs a great deal of protection in order to remain pure and chaste so that her children can be fully engaged for the benefit of human society.

Śrīla Prabhupāda described how the policy of keeping girls unmarried leads to their exploitation:

> It is a regular policy that girls may remain unmarried, and the drunkards and the meat-eaters may take advantage of the prostitution. This is the policy. They have no sympathy. So many hundreds and thousands of innocent girls – they're like children. And they're exposed to prostitution. They have no shelter. Now these girls who are with us – they're feeling that we are giving some shelter.[1]

While presiding over a wedding, Śrīla Prabhupāda offered other reasons why women require protection:

> The whole idea is that woman requires protection. They are very innocent, the weaker sex. They should not be given freedom.

1. Conversation, 11 Dec 1973.

> That is very dangerous. Just like a child cannot be given freedom; it is dangerous. If I give a child freedom – "All right, you cross this road" – that means his life is at risk. Similarly, women are the weaker sex. Artificially, don't try to become one with man; that is not possible. That is not possible. Better to remain protected by man. In childhood a girl is protected by the father; in youth she is protected by the husband; and in old age she is protected by the elderly sons. This is the three stages of woman. There is no fourth stage. That is nice. So this system – the husband taking charge of the young girl, husband and wife in Kṛṣṇa consciousness – it is very nice life. Introduce this. Everyone will be happy.[1]

Also: "Women are self-interested by nature, and therefore they should be protected by all means so that their natural inclination to be too self-interested will not be manifested."[2] Nevertheless, being protected does not mean being micromanaged:

> No independence means they are well-protected. No independence does not meant that she has no independence to act. No, she has got, but under protection. Just like there are some nations still now – protectorate. America is protecting. America is a big nation, and protecting another, small nation. That does not mean they have no independence. They are also independent. They are acting like that. But because [they are] weaker, they should be given protection.[3]

Women are generally not only physically weaker than men but are also "very prone to be misled."[4] Once while lecturing in a university in Australia, I mentioned that women should be protected, and at the end a female student rather skeptically

1. Lecture, 9 July 1971.

2. SB 6.18.42 ppt.

3. Lecture, 23 Oct 1968.

4. Bg 1.40, ppt.

asked me, "Why do women need to be protected?" and I answered, "From lusty men." She got the point. As Śrīla Prabhupāda explained, a sixteen-year-old boy can travel all over the world, but it is very difficult for a sixteen-year-old girl to do so.[1]

Women complain about rape, but they will move about by themselves, and often dressed in a manner that is calculated specifically to attract men. Nowadays it is not uncommon in the big cities of India that unaccompanied women are on the streets in the middle of the night – which was unimaginable even only a few years ago. Nor are they likely to be prostitutes. For instance, they could be going to or returning from shift work in a call center or a hospital. But the freedom of women to wander alone in public at any time means that they cannot be properly protected, and an increase of rape is inevitable. And what to speak of kidnapping. The pronounced upsurge in human trafficking and sex slavery (both of which mainly victimize females) could be curbed immediately if women would submit to restrictions that proscribe their venturing alone outside the home. Indeed, such crimes are so widespread and so atrocious as to themselves warrant a serious case for the legal implementation of such restrictions. Better that women be controlled than be subject to such terrible risk.

Women especially need assistance and protection during the later stages of pregnancy, when they are physically hampered; during the great strain of childbirth and the required several weeks of recovery thereafter; and when they have young children, whom they must constantly care for. In traditional societies, wherein "the natural ambition of a girl to possess not only more than one child but at least half a dozen"[2] is not

---

1. Conversation, 5 Mar 1975.

2. Cc 1.14.55, ppt.

crushed by artificial propaganda, most of the life of a woman would be centered around child-bearing and rearing, and the question of her need to be protected does not arise.

And after her child-bearing period, a woman must undergo menopause, another potentially difficult time that can last several years. The body undergoes considerable hormonal changes and the mind can become quite disturbed. Women need help, care, and protection during this challenging period, which they can best negotiate within the shelter of a long-established marriage.

Another significant kind of protection that most women need is the emotional support of a man, without which they tend to feel insecure and thus dissatisfied or dysfunctional – even to the point of becoming a feminist. Often it is seen that women who are superficially renunciants try nevertheless to cozy up to a man (usually a renunciant) whom they admire; they cannot forswear their need for male shelter. Undoubtedly, this need for male protection is a major reason why formal renunciation for women is mostly discouraged within Vedic culture, wherein women are glorified for being chaste, not for being renounced. A man becomes glorious if he renounces family life for the sake of spiritual realization, and thus becomes a genuine sannyasi. But such renunciation is not meant for women. Śrīla Prabhupāda noted: "A female is never awarded the order of *sannyāsa.* Because a female is never considered independent and *sannyāsa* was never awarded to any female in the past by the great *ācāryas* like Śaṅkara, Rāmānuja, etc. The female sannyasis are to be immediately understood as pretenders or prostitutes."[1]

Yet feminist women absurdly oppose their need to be protected, considering it an offense, or as being "patronized" or "treated as

1. Letter, 14 Mar 1967.

a child." In so doing, they not only disconnect with reality, they also deny to men their natural role as protectors of women. By rejecting the good will of men, feminists inadvertently (and in contradiction to their stated aims) leave little but sexual attraction to factor in male-female relationships. They also contribute to the overall decreased safety even of women who do not agree with their theories.*

Independent Women Are Unprotected, Exploited, and Unhappy

Śrīla Prabhupāda noted, "In the name of freedom of woman, they are being exploited.... Foolish women are being cheated by intelligent men."[1] When asked, "How do you feel about women's liberation?" Śrīla Prabhupāda replied:

> So-called equal rights for women means that the men cheat the women. Suppose a woman and a man meet, they become lovers, they have sex, the woman becomes pregnant, and the man goes away. The woman has to take charge of the child and beg alms from the government, or else she kills the child by having an abortion. This is the woman's independence. In India, although a woman may be poverty-stricken, she stays under the care of her husband, and he takes responsibility for her. When she becomes pregnant, she is not forced to kill the child or maintain him by begging. So which is real independence: to remain under the care of the husband, or to be enjoyed by everyone?[2]

Women cannot demand both protection and independence. That would be analogous to the inverse correlation between fast driving and avoiding fatal accidents; as the incidence of either of these increases, the other must decrease. Protection

* Lecture: Why Five Classes Need Protection <www.bvks.com/945>

1. Conversation, 13 Jul 1975.

2. Conversation, 30 Jul 1975; *Science of Self-Realization*, ch. 1.

means inevitable restrictions. One who is under protection must voluntarily accept to be controlled, and must also be submissive and grateful, for no one will be inclined to protect someone who poses as an equal or competitor.

Śrīla Prabhupāda noted:

> *Mukti* means if you give up the artificial endeavor to become predominator and become situated in your original position: being predominated. Suppose a woman is trying to become man artificially – how long it will go on? How can she be happy? That is not possible. Actually, in the Western countries at least, we see that the woman class want equal rights with men. And there is no distinction. But it is my experience that the woman class are not happy in the Western countries. And still in our country, although we are so fallen [sarcasm], still our woman class remains satisfied. Being predominated, they are happy. That is my practical experience. According to our *Manu-saṁhitā,* women should not be free. *Na strī svātantryam arhati:* "*Svātantryam* is not allowed to the woman class." Actually, we have seen, and by experience, those who are under the domination of the father when still they are not married are happy, those who are under the domination of the husband after being married are happy, and those who are under the domination of elderly children are happy. Just like children should not be given freedom – similarly, woman should not be given freedom. They should be given all protection. That is our Vedic culture.[1]

The Vital Role of Gṛhasthas

Man and woman, as husband and wife and as father and mother, are complementary to each other, and when harmoniously combined they form an ideal family and thus contribute to the making of an ideal society.

---

1. Lecture, 8 Dec 1972.

Society is comprised mostly of *gṛhasthas,* and their role is essential, as it is they who give birth to, nourish, and sustain the members of all the *āśramas. Gṛhasthas* have the vital responsibility to bring forth good population by themselves being self-controlled and religious (Kṛṣṇa conscious). The alternative is children born of lust: "*varṇa-saṅkara,* unwanted population which disturbs the peace of the general society. In order to check this social disturbance, there are prescribed rules and regulations [of *varṇāśrama-dharma*] by which the population can automatically become peaceful and organized for spiritual progress in life."[1]

Due to propaganda against the respectable, dharmic way of living, as conducted by Dr. Kamaraj and his ilk, modern society casts everyone in unnatural roles. The traditional familial relationships of father, mother, husband, wife, and so on, are nowadays highly compromised and will gradually become practically unknown. In this chaotic situation, self-controlled *gṛhasthas* can perform important preaching by demonstrating that even today it is possible and desirable to live an ideal family life according to religious principles.*

Women Should Be Married (Gṛhasthas, Not Sannyasis, Should Protect Them)

The Vedic social institutions of *brahmacarya, gṛhastha, vānaprastha,* and *sannyāsa* are defined largely according to levels of interaction between male and female. Only in *gṛhastha* life is there some allowance for extended association between men and woman. In *gṛhamedhī* culture, which largely defines Western society today, there is no restriction regarding how much a husband and wife may interact. But among Vedic

* Seminar: Gṛhastha Life in Kṛṣṇa Consciousness <www.bvks.com/1833>

1. Bg 3.24, ppt.

gṛhasthas, even association between husband and wife was limited.* Traditionally, family elders would not allow the young married members to mix very much. Men and women did not go shopping, partying, playing, dating together, and even if they worked together (e.g., in agricultural fields), they would usually do so in separate groups.

Śrīla Prabhupāda said, "Woman is good, man is good; when they combine together, bad.[1] Nevertheless, we factually see that many householder couples are working together cooperatively in Kṛṣṇa consciousness, with the wife encouraging the husband spiritually – so under certain conditions the combination can be good. The first condition is that association with women is allowed only for *gṛhasthas.*[2] "When protected, women as a class remain an always auspicious source of energy to man."[3] "Therefore according to Vedic culture a girl must be married."[4]

A major reason why all women should become married is to afford their protection. Upon attaining puberty, a girl needs a mate. If females are not obliged to marry, and instead are misguidedly afforded the freedom to remain independent and unprotected, they thus become potential victims of exploitation, with the result that they will produce bad progeny. Vedic culture does not allow such freedom to women any more than it does to children, as both classes are incapable of properly utilizing it.†

---

* "There are two kinds of householders. One is called the *gṛhamedhī,* and the other is called the *gṛhastha.* The objective of the *gṛhamedhī* is sense gratification, and the objective of the *gṛhastha* is self-realization. (SB 3.32.1, ppt.)

† See Bg 1.40, ppt., quoted on p. 103.

1. Conversation, 31 Jul 1976.

1. SB 4.22.52, ppt.

3. SB 4.21.4, ppt.

4. SB 9.9.32, ppt.

Because only *gṛhasthas* are allowed to associate with women, protection of women is meant for *gṛhastha* men, not others. It is an abomination and a major embarrassment to ISKCON if any of its sannyasis keeps a woman as a constant companion, as a de facto wife.

Women in Bengal

Śrīla Prabhupāda was a leading proponent of Indian culture, which may also be called Hindu culture or Vedic culture. He particularly promoted the essence of that culture, which is spiritual knowledge and commensurate behavior. Yet, as with any major cultural genre, Indian culture is not uniform, and there are many variations according to region, caste, religious subsects, and so forth.

Gauḍīya culture, the form of Vaiṣṇavism that Śrī Caitanya Mahāprabhu inaugurated, has always encouraged spontaneity of expression, which is particularly evident when contrasted to the rather staid, ritualistic forms of Vaiṣṇavism of South India. Śrī Caitanya Mahāprabhu's movement is intimately linked with Bengali culture, and is thus undoubtedly a causative factor for the openness and liberality among Bengalis in their social dealings, as compared with other parts of India. Of course, it is not a general free-for-all; in Bengal, as in other parts of India, extramarital sexual relations are considered disgraceful.

Another major cultural influence in Bengal is the worship of Śakti, the primeval energy, in the form of Durgā or Kālī. In Śakti worship, all women are supposed to be seen as representatives of the Goddess and are themselves revered as goddesses. This is another important influence in attitudes toward and behavior of women in Bengal.

Women in Bengal traditionally have been considerably less restricted than, for instance, their counterparts in the Hindi-speaking belt of North India, where even today some families consider it respectable for the womenfolk to mostly stay at home and be soft spoken and demure – for instance, they avoid speaking in the presence of men. Although the role of traditional Bengali women is clearly as housewives and mothers, they tend to be less reserved and restricted than their sisters in other parts of India. Indeed, they can be very loud, especially when they ululate during religious functions – although they keep their heads covered and stand apart from the men.

Devotee women with a Western mindset and who are trying to make a transition to the more conservative and restrictive lifestyle within *varṇāśrama-dharma* would do well to study and attempt to emulate Bengali women, who can be both chaste and forthright, and effusive yet observant of *maryādā* (literally, "limit," translated as dignity, etiquette, etc.).

Illicit Sex in the Name of Religion

By misapplication of the Gauḍīya principles of spontaneity and liberality, several *apa-sampradāyas* have arisen, claiming allegiance to Śrī Caitanya Mahāprabhu while allowing or encouraging the mixing of men and women under the cover of religious activity.* Recently in South India, a bogus guru was exposed as being a pervert. He had told a group of schoolgirls, "I don't see any difference between male and female, so let's all dance together." This is typical of the reasoning of the *prākṛta-sahajiyās,* among whom are so-called gurus who keep *sevā-dāsīs,*† young widows who willingly become their sexual

* *Apa-sampradāya* – deviant religious sect.

† *Prākṛta-sahajiyās* – deviant devotees who "pose as followers of Śrī Caitanya Mahāprabhu although they indulge in lusty affairs with women." (Cc 1.17.276, ppt.)

Sevā-dāsī – a maidservant. In Gauḍīya usage, this term refers to the attendants of Śrīmatī Rādhārāṇī, and thus is grossly misused in connection with mistresses of pseudo gurus.

partners, in a travesty of the sacred relationship between guru and disciple.

We members of ISKCON should not think that we cannot fall into such degradation. Indeed, we may already be well on the way, for divorce and remarriage is now treated as normal, and even the stealing of others' wives, or sannyasis having de facto wives, seem to cause little consternation.*

To save ourselves from further disgrace, we must properly understand the teachings of Śrī Caitanya Mahāprabhu and Śrīla Prabhupāda and not misapply them in the name of imagined spiritual advancement. Remembering that the "big plan" of *varṇāśrama-dharma* is "to cut down this attraction between male and female… to train the candidates gradually to become free from this entanglement of man and woman,"[1] we should follow *varṇāśrama-dharma* rules, which restrict association between men and women, and not act beyond the parameters of our actual less-than-fully-realized status.

Fire and Butter

Śrīla Prabhupāda explained the principle of gender segregation:

> In the *Śrīmad-Bhāgavatam* it is stated that man is like butter and woman is like fire. As soon as there is fire and butter, the butter must melt. Therefore they should be kept aside. And the *śāstra* says that in a solitary place you should not remain even with your daughter, even with your sister, even with your mother.[2]

* Śrīla Prabhupāda equated remarriage by women to prostitution. For the quote (which has become nigh taboo in today's "politically correct" ISKCON), see SB 7.11.28, ppt.

1. Lecture, 30 Oct 1976.
2. Lecture, 28 Jul 1973.

The injunction restricting association with women is the basic principle of spiritual life. Associating or talking with women is never advised in any of the Vedic literatures.[1]

Women and men should live separately. That is essential. Butter and fire must be kept apart. Otherwise the butter will melt. You cannot stop it.[2]

Women should be taken care of, as daughter, as wife, as mother. No freedom. Then [there will be] prostitution. Then spoiled, the whole thing – unwanted children, contraceptive, abortion. Very dangerous. In our society there are girls; they should live separately. They should be given full engagement, taken care of. No mixing – then it will be spoiled. The example is given: fire and butter. You cannot say the butter will not melt even in fire. Woman is like fire, and man is like butter.[3]

Even Paramahaṁsas Are Cautious About Female Association

Varṇāśrama-dharma is to be observed by aspiring transcendentalists and even advanced transcendentalists. Only those devotees who are totally perfect need not adhere to *varṇāśrama-dharma. Avadhūtas* do not follow any rules or regulations even of *sādhana-bhakti,* what to speak of *varṇāśrama-dharma.* For instance, Śrīla Gaurakiśora Dāsa Bābājī did not use counting beads, and Vaṁśīdāsa Bābājī did not chant any rounds. But both strictly followed one regulation: to not mix intimately with women.*

* Lecture: Giving Up Female Association <www.bvks.com/20278>

1. SB 7.12.7, ppt.
2. Conversation, 10 Jul 1975.
3 Conversation, 30 Apr 1977.

Among our recent *ācāryas,* Śrīla Bhaktivinoda Ṭhākura much decried the sexual malpractices of certain supposed followers of Śrī Caitanya Mahāprabhu. And Śrīla Bhaktisiddhānta Sarasvatī was similarly extremely strict in such matters. Prior to establishing the Gauḍīya Maṭha, he had been active in the Navadvīpa-dhāma-pracāriṇī Sabhā, an association that had been founded by Śrīla Bhaktivinoda Ṭhākura. One of the rules of the Sabhā was that women were not allowed to take part in any way.

In one incident, Śrīla Prabhupāda, at that time well over seventy years old, refused to remain alone in a room with his own sister, who also was elderly and a pure devotee of Kṛṣṇa. After she left, Śrīla Prabhupāda quoted:

mātrā svasrā duhitrā vā nāviviktāsano bhavet
balavān indriya-grāmo vidvāṁsam api karṣati

> One should not allow oneself to sit on the same seat even with one's own mother, sister or daughter, for the senses are so strong that even though one is very advanced in knowledge, he may be attracted by sex.[1]

Although clearly on the highest platform of devotional service, for the benefit of his disciples Śrīla Prabhupāda showed the ideal example of precaution in dealing with women.[2] Apart from during the earliest days of ISKCON, Śrīla Prabhupāda mostly kept male disciples around him, not females. This can be attested from the many recordings of Śrīla Prabhupāda's conversations with others, wherein the vast majority of interactions are with men, both disciples and outsiders.*

* See also the first few paragraphs of "Feminism in ISKCON" (pp. 63–64).

1. SB 9.19.17.

2. From *Śrīla Prabhupāda Nectar.*

Devotees Must Reject Feminism

As anyone who reads his books cannot fail to note, Śrīla Prabhupāda advocated traditional Vedic roles and duties for women and was solidly opposed to the notion of women's independence. Although this stance is very difficult for many people to accept, it is fully in accord with *śāstra,* and was enshrined by Śrīla Prabhupāda in his *Bhagavad-gītā As It Is.* Those who claim to be followers of Śrīla Prabhupāda are obliged to embrace, preach, and live according to this and all other positions that he espoused.

Of course, feminism was not the only modern idea that Śrīla Prabhupāda opposed. According to the famous *Bhāgavatam* verse *tad-vāg-visargo janatāgha-viplavaḥ* ..., the broadcasting of the transcendental descriptions of the Supreme Lord are directed toward "bringing about a revolution in the impious lives of this world's misdirected civilization."[1] From the perspective of the *Bhāgavatam,* modern civilization is misdirected, and accordingly, all of its institutions, values, and customs must also be understood as misdirected. Hence it is no surprise that almost all of Śrīla Prabhupāda's social teachings militate against all that is considered politically correct by the regnant world order.

Indeed, Śrīla Prabhupāda's promotion of *varṇāśrama-dharma* is anathema to egalitarian humanists. According to their line of thought, which derives from the social theories of Rousseau, Hegel, and Marx, they believe that class difference is the cause of exploitation and therefore say that *varṇāśrama's* hierarchical structure will create social injustice and stifle individual progress. But in fact the opposite is true: without *varṇāśrama-dharma,* people (especially females) will find it nearly impossible to fulfill their natural duties

1. SB 1.5.11, verse translation.

and functions, because their minds will be too absorbed in sense gratification and material pursuits to make any serious spiritual advancement. Such absorption spawns persistent dissatisfaction, which cannot be mitigated by the thoroughly misguided ideas concerning gender roles, which typify mainstream, demonic society.

Feminism is motivated by two ideas that our *ācāryas* have identified as the most formidable obstacles to Kṛṣṇa consciousness. The first is impersonalism, for the impersonal denial of differences between the sexes is responsible for the proliferation of mundane sex life: "The impersonalist philosophers have given indirect impetus to the abominable mundane sex life because they have overstressed the impersonality of the ultimate truth."[1] * Of course, even the most hardened gender feminists do not dispute that there are important differences between the sexes, and they will agree that those differences are important enough to warrant asymmetrical laws. An example is menstrual leave, which is a concession for women but certainly not also for men, and which enjoys the support of nearly all feminists. But aside from provisions such as this, feminists believe that male and female roles are generally interchangeable due to having been "socially constructed" (which is a notion of human creation). They disbelieve that there is a natural order to human society, what to speak of a natural order sanctioned by God. (Indeed, the disestablishment of the concept of a fixed human nature is widely considered to be one of the seminal achievements of the Western Enlightenment.)

The second major fault of feminism is that it directly encourages *strī-saṅga* (the intermingling of men and women)

* Lecture: Feminism is Nirviśeṣa-vāda <www.bvks.com/1108>

1. SB 1.1.1 ppt.

in society at large. Since the goal of feminism is to afford equivalent social, political, and economic opportunities to women as are available to men, a primary objective of feminists is to secure equal access to the same resources that men use. And this means that men and women must intermingle even for trivial activities. But such intermingling is a great impediment for spiritual advancement, because the basis of material existence is the attraction between male and female: "The whole material creation is moving under the principle of sex life";[1] *tamo-dvāraṁ yoṣitāṁ saṅgi-saṅgam:* "the path to hell is wide open for those who associate with people fond of women and sex";[2] *puṁsaḥ striyā mithunī-bhāvam etam:* "The attraction between male and female is the basic principle of material existence."[3] *

Because feminism encourages social conduct that increases the prevalence of sex indulgence, it further implicates people in material life, thus making it more difficult for them to take up Kṛṣṇa consciousness even if they are able to associate with devotees. Western nations have instituted innumerable policies and laws whose purpose is to ensure that women are not subjected to sexual abuse, yet the deluge of sexual abuse continues. And other countries that have been aping the West are now also being plagued by sexual misconduct.

Feminism is an evil that devotees should determinedly oppose. Rather than imitating men's duties, women devotees can perform significant preaching by committing themselves to traditional roles as wives, mothers, grandmothers, daughters,

* Lecture: Why Men and Women Should Sit Separately <www.bvks.com/11110>

1. Ibid.
2. SB 5.5.2, verse translation.
3. SB 5.5.8.

sisters, and so forth, and by being prepared to forcefully defend their doing so if challenged.* Senior ISKCON women who act as wannabe men send the wrong message to younger female devotees, who will naturally try to emulate them. Women devotees who insist on performing male duties also indirectly declare to the public that our movement has bought into the perverse secular conception of gender equality. This is all the more absurd because many nondevotee women (even in the West) are articulately opposed to feminism.[1]

Opposition to feminism should not be misconstrued as opposition to females. Even thousands of years after their presence in the world, glorious women such as Sāvitrī, Damayantī, Devahūti, Kuntī, and Draupadī are still honored within Vedic culture. But even such exalted women observed social codes and remained in the background, consciously subordinate to and in the shelter of men. Undoubtedly, there are many advanced women devotees in ISKCON today, and as respectable ladies it behooves them to follow the role models of Kuntī and others.†

* Lecture: Grandmother Tattva <www.bvks.com/11109>

† Lecture: Great Ladies in Vedic History <www.bvks.com/1068>

1. See e.g. womenagainstfeminism.tumblr.com/

Section Two

Fulfilling Women's Potential – As Mothers

In every traditional culture in the world, it was axiomatically understood that a woman's primary role is that of mother (which should be obvious, because the female body is biologically made for giving birth). As stated in the *Manu-saṁhitā* (9.96), women were "created to be mothers." Yet feminists consider that to be a stay-at-home mother and housewife is the most absurd, demeaning, anti-female thing a woman could do. They insist that women should be ambitious to "achieve" and "do something," to "make their mark." They maintain that women should not be tied to hearth and home but should realize their full potential as politicians, soldiers, airline pilots, and so on.

Although a number of women have indeed achieved top-paying positions, most women, including some who are highly educated, end up in dull, low-paying jobs or cannot find work at all. But because of the deep materialism that has overtaken society, it has become a necessity for women to join the work force. They have been duped by impious feminists and greedy business magnates into believing they need more money, to maintain what Śrīla Prabhupāda called "unnecessary necessities."[1]

Women are exhorted to maximize their potential, but what about the natural potential of a woman's body for bearing children? Undeniably, the female psychophysical constitution is specialized for bearing and rearing children. And because these activities are natural for women, it follows that women are generally happy when they are able to engage in them and unhappy when they cannot.

1. SB 7.14.5, ppt.

Although feminists like to present women as being morally superior to men on account of women's natural propensity for nurturing, they nonetheless encourage women to engage in occupations for which that propensity has little or no advantage. For example, a nurturing and caring attitude in business, diplomacy, or politics is typically regarded as a weakness, as it invites opponents who are all too willing to take advantage of it. Better to let the men tend to those kinds of occupations, for which their psychophysical makeup is optimized.

In the natural course of life, the motherly nurturing spirit, which is so intrinsic to womanhood, manifests even in small girls from the youngest age. As I have seen in traditional villages of Bengal, young girls even from the age of four or five, without any training or inducement, automatically start caring for babies – picking them up, carrying them around, and soothing them when they cry.

But nowadays the motherly inclination is crushed at the outset by feminism. In the current demonic society, young girls are taught, "You should become a doctor or a lawyer, or a head of state, or a business magnate, or an airline pilot. Why do you want to be a housewife?" Feminists have labeled the natural female inclination for motherly affection as foolish. How horrible! Even if women do become corporate leaders, they will always remain frustrated, because such occupations transgress their natural psychology. After delivering a child, her duty is to actually *be* a mother – not in name only, while being out at work all day and largely unavailable to her children.

Recently, one woman at the top of her profession – the head of a corporate giant – created a stir by admitting that working women like to pretend that they can "have it all" (i.e., an intensive professional life and also being a dutiful parent) but the truth is that they cannot. She said that women cannot properly strike a work-home balance, and related how she would "die of guilt" for being a "bad mother."[1]

But modernized women would rather be busy pursuing a career, or watching TV, or doing something according to their own choice. I know of one man from South India whose wife refused to follow him when his company transferred him to a city in North India. She didn't want to relinquish her employment with a bank. So she divorced him and kept her job. Actually, there are many such cases. Indeed, numerous women nowadays do not want to marry at all, being more interested in money, ambition, and career. And if they can be persuaded to marry, they don't want to have children. But if they can be persuaded to have children, they do not want to look after them. They want to get back to work, to their career, which they value more than their family. It is an insane, unnatural, cruel society.

Materially ambitious women make trouble, both directly and indirectly, for others. They cannot be good wives, they cannot be truly happy, and they simply cause an imbalance and disharmony in society.

Undoubtedly, modern woman has proven herself capable in many areas that previously were all-male preserves. But at what cost? Family, the quintessential building block of a smoothly functioning society, has deteriorated rapidly since women turned their attention away from the home. Even if a woman is as talented and efficient as a man (or more so), is that really a legitimate reason for her to pursue a career over and above her duties at home? Not according to Kṛṣṇa, who states: "It is

---

1. www.theatlantic.com/business/archive/2014/07/why-pepsico-ceo-indra-k-nooyi-cant-have-it-all/373750/ (retrieved 22 Dec 2014).

See also: www.theatlantic.com/magazine/archive/2012/07/why-women-still-cant-have-it-all/309020/r (retrieved 22 Dec 2014).

better to engage in one's own occupation, even though one may perform it imperfectly, than to accept another's occupation and perform it perfectly. Duties prescribed according to one's nature are never affected by sinful reactions."[1] In this regard, Śrīla Prabhupāda has written:

> Everyone should think that he is engaged in a particular type of occupation by Hṛṣīkeśa, the master of the senses. And by the result of the work in which one is engaged, the Supreme Personality of Godhead, Śrī Kṛṣṇa, should be worshiped. If one thinks always in this way, in full Kṛṣṇa consciousness, then, by the grace of the Lord, he becomes fully aware of everything. That is the perfection of life. [2]

Everyone is obligated to perform specific duties for the sake of upholding peace and harmony in society – even if one feels more inclined to do the duty of another. Because failure of the *varṇāśrama* system results in an unwanted *varṇa-saṅkara* population, and since women are naturally more directly responsible for bearing and rearing new members of society than men are, women have a special obligation to dedicate themselves to their duties as a wives and mothers. This is a more important service to society than any other occupation they could possibly take up.[3]

By trying to compete with, dominate, and outdo men, women have simply exacerbated the confusion and imbalance in today's highly disturbed world. At home, the wife's feminine qualities are supposed to relieve the husband's stress, but in nuclear families there are often explosions after the husband and wife return from work, both with frazzled nerves. Women

---

1. Bg 18.47.
2. Bg 18.46, ppt.
3. Some of the previous four paragraphs is adapted from www.dandavats.com/?p=2438, comment by Campakalatā Devī Dāsī.

do the best service as loving homemakers who provide a haven of comfort for their husband and children. Their prime duty is to be a wife and mother.

"Mother" does not mean merely the biological function of giving birth, but an embodiment of self-sacrifice, nurturing, compassion, and comforting. To actually care for children is a full-time job, a twenty-four hour responsibility, and a major challenge. And babies require exclusive attention; both parents are permanently on call and may go days without proper sleep. Although many fathers also take much of the burden, still, the contribution of the mother is irreplaceable – for instance, only she can breastfeed. And actually a woman's innate psychology is to enjoy being a mother and sacrificing for her family. Mother's love – in abundance – is essential for raising good children. It is by doing their duty as wives and mothers that women realize their potential.

As exemplars of selflessness (which *varṇāśrama-dharma* is meant to inculcate*), mothers are vital in contributing to social stability, good population, family values, and religious culture. But feminism suppresses selfless, motherly tendencies: "You have to get a job and work hard, prove yourself, have a career, be a success." Brashness and aggressiveness are encouraged as better qualities for a career woman than shyness and respectability. Women are so cut off from reality that they think that any recommendation for a woman to do what is natural and best for her, what she instinctively wants to do, is misleading her into a life of exploitation.

At some point in time, humankind might wake up to the amazing discovery that it is natural for women to like being a mother. When this natural desire is curbed and women are misguided to not have children, or to have as few as possible

* See p. 24.

so that they can have the "freedom" to work like asses in the marketplace, then actual human society degrades to the level of *dvipada-paśu,* two-legged animals.[1]

Children Are the Victims

Feminists like to portray women as victims of chauvinistic men. But actually, the whole ethos of feminism and sexual emancipation creates a downward spiral, whereby especially children suffer:

> In this age illicit connection with women will render many women and children uncared for. Circumstantially, the women will try to become independent of the protection of men, and marriage will be performed as a matter of formal agreement between man and woman. In most cases, the children will not be taken care of properly.[2]

Children need parents who are physically present to care for them, who are willing to make the sacrifices that parenting entails – not that the parents are so busy working at their jobs that their children hardly see them. Śrīla Prabhupāda related:

> In big cities like Calcutta and Bombay, they are coming early in the morning from home, and going home at night – ten o'clock, eleven o'clock – and then sleep for two or three hours and again go to work. So there is a story that a little child, when his father comes back, he is asleep, and when the father goes out of home, he is asleep. So one night he saw one man is lying there. So he is asking his mother, "Who is this man?"[3]

The term "latchkey child" refers to those lonely souls who return from school to an empty home because their parent or

1. SB 5.9.9.
2. SB 1.16.21, ppt.
3. Lecture, 30 Aug 1975.

parents are away at work. It also refers to a child who is often left at home with little parental supervision. Similarly uncared for are children of devotee parents who are so preoccupied with devotional activities, such as outside preaching, that they don't give their children the attention they need. A basic duty of a mother is to feed her family, but neglected children have to get something from the fridge or from a fast-food joint or store. Their mother is absent, too busy to give them proper nourishing food served with love. But in any sane culture, it is the mother's life and pleasure to have children, look after them, cook for them, and feed them.

If at all there is to be consideration of rights, then women who out of selfishness pursue their own interests might consider their children's right to have a real mother. A part-time mother lets her children know that she has higher priorities than to care for them. Neglected children can intuitively understand that their mother considers them a nuisance. Similarly, if a woman goes through three or four husbands, then her children can palpably sense that she is more interested in her own happiness than in maintaining a stable family environ. Moreover, parents who do not care for their children will surely not be cared for in old age by their children.

Children who have not known love will have none in their heart. Feminism is breeding generations of children who, being angry at the whole society, become attracted to cruelty and to ideologies of violence. Severe psychological disorders, substance abuse, and criminality are rife among youth today. Is there any link between school shootings and the culture of selfishness whereby women are encouraged to neglect their offspring?*

---

* Lecture: Why School Shootings Will Continue <www.bvks.com/10274>

Frustration Due to Unrealistic Expectations

Increasingly common in the Western world are gangs of girls as young as twelve, who indiscriminately attack others with knives, rob them, then use the money for drinking, drugs, or other sinful purposes. Their prey may be women or men, old or young, and sometimes these vicious little girls even kill their victims. When I was growing up in Britain, armed gangs of boys were rare except in a few of the worst areas of the country, and juvenile violence would hardly go beyond fist-fights. Gangs of girls were unimaginable.

Some years ago, shortly after returning to India from the West, I related to a young American devotee-couple something that I had read in a London newspaper about girl-gangs. The couple was not at all surprised, explaining that they were from Detroit, where girl-gangs had been around for years.* In that news article, the reporter analyzed that one major reason that girls join gangs is out of frustration. From birth they are told, "You can do it! You can make it! Get out and conquer the world!" but not everyone can be a great material success; and these girls become increasingly frustrated due to unreal expectations.†

Early and Late Marriage

In a letter to a concerned parent, Śrīla Prabhupāda wrote:

> To protect them, woman must have husband. And it is recommended they should be married at very early age, then the wife will remain always chaste and devoted to her husband. At such young age, from the first night onwards, she can never for a moment forget him, being still child and unspoiled,

---

* Detroit is infamous for staggeringly high incidence of violent crime.

† See: www.cbsnews.com/news/girls-getting-increasingly-violent/

> therefore she becomes the perfect chaste wife, and in those times the wife was so much devoted to her husband that she would voluntarily die in the fire of his cremation, unable to live without him. Myself, I was very young when I got married, and my wife was 11 years only. But there is no question of separation in our marriage belief, neither your daughter will ever be separated from that boy, that is their vow. Rather, it is when people are a little grown-up, when they have got little independence and their own ways of doing things, then if they marry there is often difficulty to adjust, just as it is more difficult to bend the bamboo when it is yellow.[1]

Similarly, to an American female disciple, Śrīla Prabhupāda explained the Vedic principle of early marriage for girls:

> In Vedic society no girl was allowed to remain independent and unmarried. Independence for women means they become like prostitutes, struggling to capture some man who will take care of her. In this way the so-called independent woman has to work very hard to make herself attractive by artificially wearing cosmetics, mini-skirts, and so many other things. Formerly the girl would be married to a suitable boy at a very early age, say six years old. But although a girl was married early she did not stay with her husband immediately, but was gradually trained in so many ways how to cook, clean, and serve her husband in so many ways – up until the time of her puberty. So all the time there was no anxiety because a girl would know "I have got a husband" and the boy would know "I have got this girl as my wife." Therefore when the boy and girl would come of age, there was no chance of illicit sex-life. And the psychology is the first boy that a girl accepts in marriage, that girl will completely give her heart to, and this attachment on the girls side for her husband becomes more and more strong; thus if a girl gets a good husband – one who has accepted

---

1. Letter, 7 Nov 1972.

> a bona fide spiritual master and is firmly fixed up in his service – automatically the wife of such a good husband inherits all the benefits of his spiritual advancement. So you are fortunate. Go on in this present attitude, serve your husband always, and in this way your life will be perfect, and together husband and wife go back home, back to Godhead.[1]

Śrīla Prabhupāda pointed out that it is not beneficial for human society when women remain unmarried, because they will be exploited instead of protected. They will not be happy, and bad offspring will be produced.[2] So every woman should be married, and the sooner the better. This does not mean that an unmarried woman should rush into marrying. Marriage should be entered into carefully, but it should not be delayed.

In the West, however, it is still considered scandalous for unmarried girls in their early teens to have babies (unfortunately, such opprobrium nourishes the flourishing abortion industry). But Westerners consider it an even greater scandal when girls in their early teens get married before becoming pregnant. The idea is so repugnant to them that they establish non-profit organizations dedicated to "rescuing" young girls in other countries from arranged marriages at a young age. They are much more comfortable with the idea of girls getting pregnant prior to marriage or having abortions.

Now in India, child marriage, which previously was an intrinsic part of the culture, is literally a crime. Indian law bizarrely prohibits marriage for females before age eighteen, and for males before twenty-one, yet allows consensual sex from age sixteen. Hence it is legal for a sixteen-year-old girl to have sex and become pregnant, but illegal for her to marry!

---

1. Letter, 28 Jul 1973.
2. Bg 1.40, ppt.

With his typical pragmatic, *śāstra*-based reasoning, Śrīla Prabhupāda explained why especially girls should be married young:

> A young woman who has no husband is called *anātha,* meaning "one who is not protected." As soon as a woman attains the age of puberty, she immediately becomes very much agitated by sexual desire. It is therefore the duty of the father to get his daughter married before she attains puberty. Otherwise, she will be very much mortified by not having a husband.[1]

As described in the *Śrīla Prabhupāda-līlāmṛta:*

> According to the Vedic system, a marriage should be carefully arranged by the parents, and it should take place before the girl reaches puberty. Gour Mohan [Śrīla Prabhupāda's father] had gotten his first daughter married in her ninth year, his second daughter at twelve years, and his third daughter at eleven. When his second daughter was going on twelve, Rajani had said, "I shall go to the river and commit suicide if you don't get her married at once." In the Vedic system there was no courtship, nor was the couple allowed to live together during the first years of their marriage. The young girl would begin serving her husband by cooking for him at her parents' house and coming before him to serve him his meal or by taking part in some other formal exchange. Then as the boy and girl grew to physical maturity, they would become so lovable to one another that they would be inseparable. The girl would naturally remain faithful to her husband since she would have no association with any other boy as she grew to puberty.

A devotee from Europe told me that when his daughter was five years old she asked, "When am I going to get married?" As Śrīla Prabhupāda explained, a girl should be betrothed while she is still very young, so that she will not have any anxiety

1. SB 4.25.42, ppt.

in that regard. Only upon attaining puberty would a girl go to live in the husband's home. In some parts of India, this still goes on, but clandestinely. Some years ago, an Indian disciple of mine told me, "I want to get my daughter married." I said, "Well, traditionally she would be of marriageable age." He said, "Yes, that is what I am talking about. I am going to get her married within the next year." His daughter was five years old.

According to *Manu-saṁhitā* (9.90), if three years after her having attained puberty her father has not yet fulfilled his duty to give her away in marriage, she can independently find her own husband. Of course, that is not ideal.

Śrīla Prabhupāda dilated on the topic of early marriage for girls in a lecture that was titled "The Psychology of Chastity."[1] Late marriage contravenes the natural order. Late-marrying women often have problems in conceiving, and children born to them have a high likelihood of congenital, or of later developing, physical or mental defects. Furthermore, women who do not have children, or who put off bearing them, are more likely to suffer gynecological problems, including infertility and cancer, as well as breast cancer, because the function of the mammary gland is to produce milk. To suppress that function is unnatural, and the reaction is disease.*

Nowadays, because young women go to school and college and then pursue a career, often their marriage is delayed until around age thirty. But by that age, a woman should already have grownup children. Previously, as soon as a girl had reached puberty, she was sent to live with her husband, and

* See: iml.jou.ufl.edu/projects/spring03/soll/cons.htm

www.yourdiseaserisk.siteman.wustl.edu/YDRDefault.aspx?ScreenControl=YDRGeneral&ScreenName=YDRBreastRisk_List

1. Lecture on *Bhagavad-gītā* 1.40, 28 Jul 1973. https://prabhupadavani.org/main/Bhagavad-gita/GT025.html

soon after that would have her first child. And if her first child happened to be female, she could well become a grandmother before the age of thirty.

Career women consider early marriage to be a burden, and even more so, consider it a burden to have children. When they are young, they think "There are so many men. I can pick one up at any time." But it often happens that when they reach age thirty or so, they start to panic: "I'm getting old, my face has a few lines – I need to get married right now!" All along they were saying "I won't get married, I won't get married," and when they finally say "I want to be married" no one wants to marry them, because men prefer beautiful young girls, not worn out thirty-year-olds who have already been used so many times. So the aging women become desperate.

Another common scenario in India is that of parents unduly waiting to find the perfect match for their daughter (the main consideration being that the groom should earn big money) but when she becomes too old to compete with the younger belles, the parents become desperate and marry her off to anyone – rich, poor, ugly, whatever – whoever agrees to marry her.*

Arranged Marriage

For a girl to choose her own husband is very risky. Overcome by sentiment and infatuation (otherwise called lust), a young girl does not possess the sober discrimination to understand who is right for her. The traditional system is that the parents carefully arrange their child's marriage based on caste, astrological compatibility (taking into account mental, emotional, intellectual, and sexual matching), and other considerations. After marriage, the young couple are supported

* Lecture: Marriage and Guru-disciple Relationships <www.bvks.com/167>

by a social network of mothers, fathers, aunts, uncles, and siblings. And even before marriage, from the beginning of the child's life, there is training on how to remain chaste and dutiful in marriage.*

Still in India today, arranged marriages are the norm (although this is changing rapidly). The boy and the girl to be married are mutually selected by their parents. Or in the case of girls, often the girl's older brother (or sometimes younger brother) determines which boy she will marry, just as Lord Balarāma took up the task of arranging Subhadrā Devī's marriage.[1] Nonetheless, often the boy and girl do not choose their would-be spouse (although in many arranged marriages both are given the final say as to whether they will marry the other).

Liberal humanists deem all this to be inhumane. They insist that one must first love a person before marrying. But what is that so-called love? They love, marry, and later divorce; love, marry, divorce; love, marry, divorce... and thus the phenomenon known as "serial monogamy." It is considered a "human right" to revoke one's marriage contract at will. But in the traditional Indian system, even though the spouses don't know each other before being married, they remain married "until death do us part."

So which is better: the cycle of marriage and divorce, or indissoluble marriage irrespective of the perceived happiness within it? The answer that one will settle on depends on the predominant mode of nature (*guṇa*) that colors one's consciousness. If one is predominated by the mode of passion, then his interest is governed by the desire for sense gratification. As soon as trouble arises in their marriage, persons who are

* Lecture: Qualities of a Chaste Wife <www.bvks.com/877>

1. SB 10.86.3.

impelled by passion will naturally seek to abrogate their agreement.* Śrīla Prabhupāda wrote:

> A young man and a young woman meet, and the senses drive the young man to see her, to touch her, and to have sexual intercourse. In the beginning this may be very pleasing to the senses, but at the end, or after some time, it becomes just like poison. They are separated or there is divorce, there is lamentation, there is sorrow, etc. Such happiness is always in the mode of passion. Happiness derived from a combination of the senses and the sense objects is always a cause of distress and should be avoided by all means.[1]

But persons who are predominated by the mode of goodness will stay married even if the marriage produces little immediate happiness for them, because they understand that it is dharmic and pious to do so, and will ultimately yield a good result, even if not directly perceived in this lifetime. For countless generations in Hindu society, this attitude governed by the mode of goodness toward marriage ensured family stability, and thus was a major factor in the overall stability of Hindu culture and civilization. But now India is increasingly following the West and becoming predominated by the mode of passion. As Indians come to value personal sense satisfaction over social responsibility, infidelity and divorce naturally proliferate.

---

* In their paper titled "These Boots Are Made for Walking: Why Most Divorce Filers are Women," Margaret Brinig and Douglass Allen report that "throughout most of American history, wives rather than husbands have filed for divorce." They state that during most of the nineteenth century, around 60% of all divorces in America were filed by women; after the introduction of no-fault divorce [starting in 1969 in California], that percentage increased to 70% in some places; and as of 2000 it stabilized at about 66%, or about twice the number of divorces filed by men [American Law and Economics Review V2 N1 2000, (129 - 169)].

Brinig and Douglass also report that, for the sample they studied, only 6% of divorce filings by women were on grounds of cruelty. (149)

---

1. Bg 18.38, ppt.

Nonetheless, even today arranged marriages are the norm in several countries other than India. But how long this will last remains to be seen. Within living memory, in Ireland and in other parts of Europe, some parents still insisted that their children take their permission before marrying the spouse of their choice. But that culture is now completely lost. Everywhere, liberal humanists are forcefully eroding traditional values, with a resolve to forever rid the world of theism and theistic moral systems. As Śrīla Prabhupāda observed:

> At the present moment, father, mother, sends the daughter for prostitution: "Find out a suitable man. Attract a suitable man. Don't marry abruptly. Just test this man, this man, this man, this man, this man – then marry."[1]

Many parents allow or even encourage their daughters to wear revealing clothes (such as tight jeans and T-shirts), never imagining that anything untoward – such as rape – could result. Other parents, who want their daughters to have the best of both worlds, try to instill in them traditional values in regard to female chastity and demureness while simultaneously encouraging them to pursue "a good career." Such a balancing act often becomes tragically shattered when the parents learn that their daughter has become illegitimately pregnant, or when she insists on marrying a boy whom they disapprove of (in many cases even converting to Islam to do so). However well a girl has been groomed at home, in youth she will naturally hanker for a mate and be attractive to males; so to send her unchaperoned among young men runs the high risk that she will lose all sense of discrimination and become mad after a boy for whom she is not at all suitable. Hence the phenomenon of "love marriages."

---

1. Lecture, 3 Jan 1971.

"Love Marriage"

Modern psychologists stress emotional compatibility as the overriding factor to be considered for a good marriage. However, while emotional compatibility is of major importance in the Indian conjugal tradition as well, astrological compatibility is also indispensible: "Regardless of the affluence of the boy or the personal beauty of the girl, without this astrological compatibility the marriage would not take place."[1]

According to the Western conception of "falling in love," a boy and a girl should live together for some time to ascertain their mutual compatibility. But how they will relate in the long-term cannot be gauged in a mere few weeks or months. After two people have actually married, the initial euphoria recedes and the partners must face the reality of living with together day in and day out. Marriage is the school of hard knocks. As the joke goes: "First comes the engagement ring, then the wedding ring, and finally the boxing ring." And indeed, many love marriages end in acrimony due to unreal expectations of conjugal ecstasy, as typically portrayed in romantic movies that feature invisible orchestras striking up whenever the bliss overflows.

"Love marriage" (a term in Indian English) is based on infatuation, not love, and is therefore risky. If people "fall in love" and then "fall out of love," there never was any real love at all. It was simply an obsession caused by imagination, false expectations, and lust. As a young Bangladeshi described about his experiences in America:

> They make a big show of love. When a man drops his wife off to work, they do this big kiss. [Public kissing, even as an affectionate gesture between husband and wife, is unthinkable in Bangladesh.] But then they fight and divorce as easily as

---

1. SB 9.18.23, ppt.

they kiss. In our country we never even talk about love, and we certainly don't make a big show of it. There's no need. It's automatically there. There's no question of a wife not loving her husband. Naturally she loves her husband, because he's her husband. Many Americans asked me about arranged marriages. "How can you marry someone you never met? How can you love them?" I tell them, "Your system is to fall in love before marriage. We fall in love after marriage. The difference is that afterwards you fall out of love as easily as you fell into it. And you think nothing of falling out of marriage also. That we don't do."[1]

The Real Formula for Marital Success

Previously in high-class Hindu society, a boy and girl would not see each other or even know what each other looked like until their wedding ceremony. But nowadays, rather than being "made in heaven," marriages are more likely to be made over the internet. Even among ISKCON devotees, physical appearance can be a deciding factor in selecting a spouse. A young boy is given a photo of various devotee girls (or vice versa) so that he can decide which he likes best, simply based on looks – which ignores Śrīla Prabhupāda's admonition: "When the wife is accepted as a sense gratificatory agency, personal beauty is the main consideration."[2] The boys and girls meet, and may even date, to see if their "chemistry" is right. I know cases, and probably there are many more, of a boy rejecting a girl as being "not beautiful enough." Even if he himself is not particularly good-looking, he wants to marry a beauty queen.

But physical attractiveness is short-lived and illusory, just a covering of skin on blood, bones, mucus, and other nasty things. It is a trick of *māyā* to think that a beautiful face must

1. From *Glimpses of Traditional Indian Life*, p. 32.

2. SB 3.14.19, ppt.

indicate a beautiful personality, especially considering that in today's promiscuous society, sex appeal is often used to allure and exploit others. In the long run, it is far better to live with a sweet personality than a sweet face. After all, whatever the spouses may look like, they have to live with each other, and good looks cannot compensate for bad character. To have to live with an exquisitely beautiful person who is (for instance) selfish and arrogant is likely to be hellish. The real formula for marital success is that the husband should be responsible and the wife should be faithful and submissive, with both having Kṛṣṇa consciousness as their ultimate goal.

Homemakers and Working Wives

Should women work outside the home? Generally, the answer should be no.* Since the attraction between male and female is the basic principle of material existence, society should be arranged so as to minimize the possibility of sex indulgence. Hence, both for women living in cities as well as rural village women, association with men outside of their family should be strictly curtailed. A married woman who works outside the home usually spends more time around other men than she does with her husband; and she may also grow to like them more. Thus ensues adultery, the breakdown of marriages, and all of the misery that these two vices engender.

Another major point is that women are meant to look after their children, and women who are away working cannot give the children their full attention. In traditional societies, although women do not work for a paycheck, they still may contribute economically. If, for example, there are many women in the home, not every one of them will always be looking after children. Some may be engaged in weaving, basket-making,

* Lecture: Conversation with Young Girls <www.bvks.com/20272>

or helping in the fields. It is not that women cannot contribute toward the economy, but it is best done from the home. And apart from economic activities, housewives have various caste-specific services. For example, the wives of *brāhmaṇas* assist their husband in performing daily *yajñas* at home.

One devotee told me that his wife is highly qualified educationally – more so than he – but that on principle she does not go out to work. She understands that a woman's dharma is to serve in the home, and is happy with that. Fortunately, many other women think like her; not all are fooled by feminist propaganda.

But unfortunately, almost all young girls today are trained for and pushed into the workplace. This is touted as women's freedom, but the main beneficiaries of that so-called freedom are the employers, who thus acquire a larger labor force and can keep wages down.

The Scourge of Divorce

Divorce is not one of Kṛṣṇa's ideas. It is not mentioned in *śāstra*, and was not even imagined in traditional Indian or Hindu culture. There is no Sanskrit word for divorce, but recently one has been coined: *vivāha-viccheda* ("the breakup of marriage"). The common Hindi word for divorce is *talāk*, an Urdu term associated with Muslim culture. Divorce was nonexistent in Hindu culture until 1955, when Jawaharlal Nehru, Prime Minister of India, legalized it, thus shaking countless centuries of marital stability.

Previously even in the West, divorce was rare and widely considered sinful. Despite their being meat-eaters and wine-drinkers with not even a clue about the high philosophy of Kṛṣṇa consciousness, almost everyone stayed married to the same person throughout their life. But that rapidly changed in the 1960s, when, for example, popular songs such as "Please Release Me" (Engelbert Humperdinck, 1967) fanned the growing popular trend away from traditional restrictions:

> Please release me, let me go,
> For I don't love you anymore.
> To waste our lives would be a sin.
> So release me and let me love again.

The idea is that if one no longer feels attraction to someone whom he is married to (or is in a relationship with), he should be able to move on to another. Of course, this outlook is simply selfishness: "We are meant to enjoy life, and everyone should do so to their maximum potential; so if a husband becomes an obstacle, the wife should just kick him out – and vice versa – and if they don't like one another, they should simply divorce." Such reasoning encourages competition, rather than cooperation, between spouses. It is based neither on dharma nor on consideration of the purpose of human life.

> Divorce has now become a common affair, although formerly one's marriage would continue lifelong, and the affection between husband and wife was so great that the wife would voluntarily die when her husband died or would remain a faithful widow throughout her entire life. Now, of course, this is no longer possible, for human society has fallen to the level of animal society. Marriage now takes place simply by agreement. *Dāmpatye 'bhirucir hetuḥ* (SB 12.2.3). The word *abhiruci* means "agreement." If the boy and girl simply agree to marry, the marriage takes place. But when the Vedic system is not rigidly observed, marriage frequently ends in divorce.[1]

Throughout the history of Ireland, which (until only recently) was an overwhelmingly Catholic country, divorce was illegal (prior to 1996). Many years ago on Irish television, I saw several women being interviewed about their married life. They were

1. SB 9.18.23, ppt.

making comments such as "My husband gets drunk and beats me. All I want is to divorce him." The implied message was: "My life is being spoiled by this man, so I should just dump him and find my real Prince Charming. Then I will have no more problems." And now that the divorce law has been introduced, people are taking undue advantage of it. They demand more, compromise less often, and are quick to take the easy escape route out of marriage.*

Nowadays in the West, divorce is considered almost inevitable – unfortunately, even among our devotees. I was present at a lecture in Germany wherein a godbrother of mine stated that he had been married to the same wife for thirty years – then paused for the expected, and forthcoming, applause, because for a devotee nowadays to have had the same wife for thirty years is considered a great achievement.

A few years ago at a gathering of devotees in the Czech Republic, I gave a lecture that later came to be known as "the revolutionary lecture about divorce."[1] The audience found it revolutionary that I had pressed the subject of "no divorce."

From these few anecdotes, one can understand how deeply sick the Western world is, and how deeply affected by it is our ostensibly spiritual movement.

Some devotees conjecture that divorce is more common throughout worldwide ISKCON than in the broader society, but no statistical analysis has been undertaken to either support or refute this claim. And by all reports, the use of contraception by ISKCON members is widespread, notwithstanding Śrīla Prabhupāda's having described it as a "most sinful activity."[2]

* Lecture: Even Hiraṇyakaśipu Didn't Divorce His Wife <www.bvks.com/1635>

1. Included on accompanying DVD. Also available at: http://bvks.com/516/

2. Conversation, 10 Aug 1975.

Most painfully and shamefully, even abortion is not unknown among ISKCON devotees.*

The ultimate aim of the Kṛṣṇa consciousness movement – to spread Kṛṣṇa-*prema* – will remain far distant as long as such abominations continue.

Discouraging of Divorce Among Devotees

The endeavors of certain well-meaning devotees who attempt to stem the tide of divorce within ISKCON might actually be worsening matters, because their methodology is based on pragmatic or phenomenological concepts of psychological compatibility. As has been related to me, such devotee counselors have advised quarreling couples to first try to adjust; then after some time, if there is no significant improvement, they may recommend divorce. But far better would be to advise devotees to adhere to dharma, even if the going is rough, because the alternative is *adharma,* or sin. Devotees who are embarking upon marriage should know that between husband and wife there will always be some problems, and that, especially in the modern age, it is increasingly rare to find a good relationship between any two people, but that devotee couples should nonetheless remain together and perform their respective duties in Kṛṣṇa consciousness.

Śrīla Prabhupāda wrote: "Formerly husband and wife used to live together peacefully throughout their whole lives, but nowadays it is a very difficult task."[1] The basis of family life is duty (dharma), so even if a husband and wife do not always like each other, once they have married they must adhere to their religious commitment and somehow or other learn to adjust.

* Lecture: Abortion, Gayrights, and Brussels Sprouts <www.bvks.com/10759>

1. SB 3.21.15, ppt.

Divorce is no silver bullet for marital problems. By *māyā's* illusion, conditioned souls presume that simply changing their situation will improve it, but there is no guarantee. In fact, the very process of divorce is often a prolonged nightmare that engenders long-standing bitterness.

Divorce is also often a form of child abuse, because children are generally the worst affected by the scourge of divorce.

Divorce Can Be Averted

Some years ago in Russia, a young couple visited me along with their young daughter. I had never seen or heard of them before, yet they came to ask my blessings for divorce! I responded, "Definitely not! I am completely against it!" And they said, "But we have so many problems and cannot get along. How can we live with each other?" I told them, "Look: you got married, and you have a daughter, and you have to stick with it." Fortunately, they were submissive enough to comply. And by resigning themselves to living together, they soon discovered that there really weren't any serious problems between them. But simply by entertaining the possibility of divorce, their mutual commitment had become undermined, and therefore they did not hesitate to neglect and hurt each other. Yet as soon as they recommitted to persevere, they knew that they must adjust and be considerate of the other's needs, personality, and so on. And now, fifteen years later, they are still together and are more or less content. The proposed "solution" of divorce was just *manasijam* (created in the mind).[1] *

Family Planning and Big Families

India's most famous propaganda slogan for family planning is *ham do hamāre do* – "We are two (husband and wife) and we

* Lecture: Divorce is Inevitable <www.bvks.com/1924>

1. See SB 7.9.45.

have two (children)" – or the variant *ham do hamārā ek*: "We are two and we have one." The idea is to limit births by utilizing contraception and abortion, both of which are very sinful and were disapproved by Śrīla Prabhupāda: "Now because society has deteriorated there is propaganda to have one or two children and kill the rest by contraceptive methods."[1] On this topic, Śrīla Prabhupāda noted: "In the absence of voluntary restraint, there is propaganda for family planning, but foolish men do not know that family planning is automatically executed as soon as there is search after the Absolute Truth."[2] * And he elaborated:

> A responsible father never begets children like cats and dogs. Instead of being encouraged to adopt artificial means of birth control, people should be educated in Kṛṣṇa consciousness because only then will they understand their responsibility to their children. If one can beget children who will be devotees and be taught to turn aside from the path of birth and death (*mṛtyu-saṁsāra-vartmani*[3]), there is no need of birth control. Rather, one should be encouraged to beget children.[4]

With the understanding that "many Kṛṣṇa conscious children are required,"[5] Śrīla Prabhupāda encouraged his married disciples to beget offspring:

> All our children born of the Kṛṣṇa conscious parents are welcome and I want hundreds of children like that. Because in future we expect to change the face of the whole world, because child is the father of man.[6]

---

* Lecture: Spiritual Family Planning <www.bvks.com/504>

1. Cc 1.14.55, ppt.
2. SB 1.2.10, ppt.
3. Bg. 9.3.
4. SB 10.3.33, ppt.
5. *Nectar of Instruction* 1, ppt.
6. Letter, 21 Aug 1968.

> Even the generative organ can be used for Kṛṣṇa. If you can beget children who will be Kṛṣṇa conscious, then produce one hundred children. Otherwise, stop producing cats and dogs.[1]

Speaking at a wedding, Śrīla Prabhupāda said:

> The aim of married life is to produce nice children, Kṛṣṇa conscious children. That is the best service to the human society – produce nice children.[2]

On another note, Śrīla Prabhupāda encouraged restraint:

> If one does not want more than one or two children, he should voluntarily stop sex life. But one should not strictly use any contraceptive method and at the same time indulge in sex life. That is very much sinful. If the husband and wife can voluntarily restrain by powerful advancement of Kṛṣṇa consciousness, that is the best method. It is not necessary that because one has got wife, therefore you must have sex life. The whole scheme is to avoid sex life as far as possible. And if one can avoid it completely then it is a great victory for him.[3]

Śrīla Prabhupāda recognized that "the natural ambition of a girl is to possess not only more than one child but at least half a dozen."[4] Notably, Śrī Kṛṣṇa Himself begot ten sons and one daughter in each of his wives. Unfortunately, nowadays many women feel that to have multiple children is too costly and bothersome – more children means more work.

One advantage of having many children is that those children usually learn to adjust and share with each other (including sharing the parents' attention) and thus are less likely to become self-centered. On the contrary, single children, because their

---

1. Lecture, 1 Mar 1967.
2. Lecture at wedding – 22 Jul 1968.
3. Letter, 20 Sep 1968.
4. Cc 1.14.55, ppt.

parents' affection is lavished on them alone, often turn out to be egoistic, with little consideration for others and assuming that everything is meant for them only.*

Joint Families

The joint family entails five or six generations (up to great-great-grandparents) living together, all brothers and sons with their wives and children. And if each brother has more than one wife, a joint family can be like a community in itself.

Whereas the nuclear family places all the burden of motherhood and wifehood on one lone and lonely woman, the joint family provides a supportive group of women sharing the tasks of cooking, cleaning, and looking after all the children, and also keeping each other company. Joint families provide children with many siblings and many mothers, both of which is psychologically better for the children.

The joint family system is practically a necessity in non-mechanized agrarian societies, for it provides many workers to help produce food and tend cows. Similarly, joint families are practical for those who run family businesses.

Polygamy

As a principle, Śrīla Prabhupāda advocated polygamy (more precisely, polygyny).†

> Generally in every society the female population is greater in number than the male population. Therefore if it is a principle

* Lecture: To Have Many Children or Not <www.bvks.com/10954>

† Polygamy is the practice of marrying more than one partner. There are two types of polygamy: polygyny (wherein a man has more than one wife) and polyandry (wherein a woman has more than one husband). In common usage, polygamy generally refers to polygyny.

> in the society that all girls should be married, unless polygamy is allowed it will not be possible. If all the girls are not married there is a good chance of adultery, and a society in which adultery is allowed cannot be very peaceful or pure. In our Kṛṣṇa consciousness society we have restricted illicit sex. The practical difficulty is to find a husband for each and every girl. We are therefore in favor of polygamy, provided, of course, that the husband is able to maintain more than one wife.[1]

> People have become so degraded in this age that on the one hand they restrict polygamy and on the other hand they hunt for women in so many ways. Many business concerns publicly advertise that topless girls are available in this club or in that shop. Thus women have become instruments of sense enjoyment in modern society. The Vedas enjoin, however, that if a man has the propensity to enjoy more than one wife – as is sometimes the propensity for men in the higher social order, such as the *brāhmaṇas, kṣatriyas,* and *vaiśyas,* and even sometimes the *śūdras* – he is allowed to marry more than one wife. Marriage means taking complete charge of a woman and living peacefully without debauchery. At the present moment, however, debauchery is unrestricted. Nonetheless, society makes a law that one should not marry more than one wife. This is typical of a demoniac society.[2]

However, although Śrīla Prabhupāda was overall "in favor of polygamy,"[3] he forbade it within ISKCON for several reasons, including "the possibility of becoming scandalized in the public for breaking their laws in this way; and in future also the devotees who are neophyte may not understand our policy in this connection, and we gradually could wind up attracting only a class of men who are very eager for unlimited sex life only."[4]

1. Cc 1.14.58, ppt.
2. SB 4.26.6, ppt.
3. Cc 1.14.58, ppt.
4. Letter, 9 Jan 1973.

Śrīla Prabhupāda also wrote: "In India ... even until fifty years ago, polygamy was freely allowed. Any man, especially of the higher castes – the *brāhmaṇas*, the *vaiśyas*, and particularly the *kṣatriyas* – could marry more than one wife."[1] However, polygamy is now illegal in India (except for Muslims).

Although it is generally supposed that women do not like the idea of having to share their husband with co-wives, for some it may be an attractive proposition. For example, if given a choice between having all to one's self a husband who is an ordinary clerk or of being a co-wife of a wealthy celebrity, many women would prefer the latter. In economic terms, it would be something like the difference between owning one hundred percent of your personal slum tenement or owning a portion of a timeshare in an exclusive location. And factually, polygamy has traditionally been practiced mostly by men of above-average means.

As a family institution, polygamy has further benefits. As in the joint family, polygamy provides a support system for women and children. It also provides the means and facility for all women of society to physically and legitimately become mothers, and for them and their children to subsequently be maintained and protected.

It is also well known (and supported in scientific literature) that women are hypergamous, which means they have a general and observable tendency to "marry upwards," i.e., to desire a man of higher social status – superior wealth, power, intelligence, physical attractiveness, and so forth. This is evidenced by patronage of modern commercial reproductive clinics, wherein women unfailingly prefer donors who have superior physical and social characteristics. In fact, certain characteristics are in such demand that the clinics will not accept donors who do not possess them. For example, no

1. Cc 1.14.58, ppt.

commercial clinic will accept a donor who is not at least 5' 8" (172 cm) tall, because clients simply will not purchase their semen. Donors who have had psychological problems or other inheritable, physical ailments are also routinely excluded.

Because desirable male attributes are not all "socially constructed," and therefore can be passed on by means of reproduction, polygamy affords a built-in program of social eugenics. In other words, men of superior nature are given more opportunity to distribute their physical and psychological traits throughout society. In a Kṛṣṇa conscious society, value is placed on characteristics such as self-control and religiousness; so polygamy would facilitate the production of children who have an advantage in their ability for sense control. This is certainly a much better proposition for society than the questionable commercial reproductive clinics.*

Polygamy was traditionally well-accepted in Hinduism, Buddhism, and Islam. And even some Christians contest that the insistence on monogamy is not supported by their scriptures; indeed, the Old Testament clearly mentions instances of polygamy. But although polygamy is an ancient and very practical feature of human civilization, due to the influence of Christian morality it has greatly declined throughout the world.

In Vedic culture, Śrī Rāma is the supreme exemplar of *eka-patnī vrata* (the vow to have only one wife). Śrī Kṛṣṇa showed another ideal by very kindly marrying 16,100 women, none of whom could otherwise have gotten a husband, for they had already been kept by another man.

According to one of my godbrothers, Śrīla Prabhupāda's statement that we cannot allow polygamy within ISKCON

* To fully appreciate the perniciousness of commercial reproductive services, one need only read stories of persons who were conceived through these technologies – for example, at: www.anonymousus.org/.

means that if a man is being maintained by our institution, he should not have more than one wife.[1] Why should ISKCON, as a religious and charitable institution, financially support such an arrangement? "He may not live off temple funds."[2] Śrīla Prabhupāda further stated: "If they want to marry more than one wife, they must live outside our temples in their own arrangements. We have no objection if he does it, but it must be done outside the temple."[3] In other words, if a man has sufficient economic capability, if he is not maintained by ISKCON but is generating his livelihood independently, and if he is prepared to maintain and protect more than one wife, then that might be acceptable. However, polygamy is illegal in most Western countries, so for the sake of advancing Śrīla Prabhupāda's mission, that illegality alone could be sufficient reason for disallowing polygamy within ISKCON (even if according to the laws of *śāstra* it should be allowed).

But many young women who come to Kṛṣṇa consciousness via ISKCON do not get a husband. So the reasoning that Śrīla Prabhupāda has given for sanctioning polygamy in general society applies also to this situation in ISKCON. Of course, polygamy is not mandatory for anyone; it is elective. Hopefully, at some time in the future it will be more viable for devotees to incorporate polygamy within their social policy; and for the sake of guiding society, they will then need comprehensive understanding of this issue.*

* An unintended consequence of the success of the gay marriage movement in the West is that it has become increasingly difficult for the status quo to fend off moral objections and legal challenges from Western proponents of polygamy. Possibly, polygamy in the Western countries may become legal soon and in an unexpected manner.

1. www.16108.com/dharma/polygamy_devotees_online/lectures_tapes.htm (retrieved 28 Dec 2014).

2. Letter, 8 Nov 1976.

3. Letter, 7 Sep 1975.

Education for Girls: Chastity and Cooking

Another revolutionary instruction by Śrīla Prabhupāda concerned the education of girls:

> We shall teach the girls two things: one thing is how to become chaste and faithful to their husband, and [the other is] how to cook nicely. If these two qualifications they have, I'll take guarantee to get for them good husband – I'll personally. Only these two qualification required. Then her life is successful. Ordinary education is sufficient – a, b, c, d. This is all nonsense: so big, big, sound education and later on become a prostitute.
>
> Let them learn varieties of cooking. These two qualifications, apart from Kṛṣṇa consciousness, materially they should learn. There are many stories – Nala-Damayantī, then Pārvatī, Sītā – five chaste women in the history. They should read their life. And by fifteenth, sixteenth year, they should be married. And if they are qualified, it will be not difficult to find out a nice husband. Here, the boys do not want to marry because they are not very much inclined to marry an unchaste wife. They know that "I shall marry a girl, [but] she is unchaste." This is psychology: if woman is chaste, even though she is not very beautiful, she will be liked by the husband. So train them in that way – very chaste, faithful wife, and knows how to cook very nicely. Other qualification, even they haven't, that's all right. And Kṛṣṇa consciousness is being trained up. And boys should be first-class man.
>
> In India still, eighty percent, ninety percent, are very happy in their family life, never mind one is poor or rich, because the wife knows these things.[1]

But nowadays just the opposite has become the norm. Girls may have a PhD but have no idea how to cook even a chapati!

---

1. Conversation, 10 Jul 1975.

Some years ago, shortly after one devotee had married, he found out that his wife didn't know how to cook *anything*. He knew how to cook one item – *kicharī* – so he taught her how to prepare that. So one day he would cook *kicharī*, and the next day she would cook. How miserable – he couldn't even get decent food.

"The way to a man's heart is through his stomach" is as true today as it ever was. A man whose palate and belly are satisfied is much more likely to be overall content than one who cannot even get something pleasing to eat. Hence, simply by performing her natural duty of regularly preparing tasty meals, a wife does much toward keeping her marriage intact.

Formerly, young girls at home would naturally learn how to cook and keep house. But nowadays, in the name of progress, girls are expected to go to school and eventually get a degree, so they do not have the opportunity to imbibe domestic arts as did their mothers and grandmothers. However, considering that many girls will become housewives, one of the subjects offered in Indian colleges is "home science" – how to cook and keep house. It is simply insane that girls are sent to college to imbibe what they could and should learn much better within the home.

The second point that Śrīla Prabhupāda stressed in regard to girls' education was the inculcation of chastity. Indeed, chastity is central to Vedic civilization, being "very, very important for producing good population."[1] The quality of chastity is summarized by Nārada Muni:

> To render service to the husband, to be always favorably disposed toward the husband, to be equally well disposed toward the husband's relatives and friends, and to follow

1. Lecture, 28 Jul 1973.

> the vows of the husband – these are the four principles to be followed by women described as chaste. A chaste woman must dress nicely and decorate herself with golden ornaments for the pleasure of her husband. Always wearing clean and attractive garments, she should sweep and clean the household with water and other liquids so that the entire house is always pure and clean. She should collect the household paraphernalia and keep the house always aromatic with incense and flowers and must be ready to execute the desires of her husband. Being modest and truthful, controlling her senses, and speaking in sweet words, a chaste woman should engage in the service of her husband with love, according to time and circumstances. A chaste woman should not be greedy, but satisfied in all circumstances. She must be very expert in handling household affairs and should be fully conversant with religious principles. She should speak pleasingly and truthfully and should be very careful and always clean and pure. Thus a chaste woman should engage with affection in the service of a husband who is not fallen. The woman who engages in the service of her husband, following strictly in the footsteps of the goddess of fortune, surely returns home, back to Godhead, with her devotee husband, and lives very happily in the Vaikuṇṭha planets.[1]

Śrīla Prabhupāda once recalled an incident from his college days: While at the home of a friend, he noticed a sweeper woman standing outside of the room. She was holding a bucket and broom, and her head was covered – she was too shy to enter while the men were inside. So he and the friend left the room so that she could enter to clean. Although that woman was superficially uneducated and low-class, her shyness made an impression upon Śrīla Prabhupāda that he would remember throughout his life:[2]

---

1. SB 7.11.25–29.

2. Mentioned in lectures, 28 Jul 1973 and 26 Nov 1976.

> Shyness is a gift of nature to the fair sex, and it enhances their beauty and prestige, even if they are of a less important family or even if they are less attractive. We have practical experience of this fact. A sweeper woman commanded the respect of many respectable gentlemen simply by manifesting a lady's shyness. Half-naked ladies in the street do not command any respect, but a shy sweeper's wife commands respect from all.[1]

On the other hand, Śrīla Prabhupāda further observed: "Modern girls are all rubbish; therefore they are simply used for sex satisfaction."[2] No one cares for unchaste women. Like snot tissues, they are simply "use and throw." A young woman cedes her virginity to a boy in expectation that he will marry her, but then he says, "Okay, thanks. It was fun while we were together, but now I have to move on."

What is to her benefit if a girl is highly educated but loses her chastity and dignity? What is the value of colleges if they are also places for picking up and using girls? "Topless, bottomless – there is regular business in India also. In the hotels, there is a regular business to pick up college girls to be enjoyed by the guests. So many things are going on on this basis of sinful activity, all over the world."[3] Śrīla Prabhupāda further commented: "The basic flaw in modern civilization is that boys and girls are given freedom during school and college to enjoy sex life"[4] and "Modern educated girl means how to become unfaithful to the husband, how to divorce, and how to kill child. The uneducated girls do not do this."[5]

---

1. SB 1.10.16, ppt.
2. Conversation, 27 May 1974.
3. Conversation, 13 Mar 1974.
4. SB 4.31.1, ppt.
5. Conversation, 26 Nov 1975.

Victory for a Woman

From *Śrīmad-Bhāgavatam* (9.3.10):

> Cyavana Muni was very irritable, but since Sukanyā had gotten him as her husband, she dealt with him carefully, according to his mood. Knowing his mind, she performed service to him without being bewildered.

Śrīla Prabhupāda's purport:

> This is an indication of the relationship between husband and wife. A great personality like Cyavana Muni has the temperament of always wanting to be in a superior position. Such a person cannot submit to anyone. Therefore, Cyavana Muni had an irritable temperament. His wife, Sukanyā, could understand his attitude, and under the circumstances she treated him accordingly. If any wife wants to be happy with her husband, she must try to understand her husband's temperament and please him. This is victory for a woman. Even in the dealings of Lord Kṛṣṇa with His different queens, it has been seen that although the queens were the daughters of great kings, they placed themselves before Lord Kṛṣṇa as His maidservants. However great a woman may be, she must place herself before her husband in this way; that is to say, she must be ready to carry out her husband's orders and please him in all circumstances. Then her life will be successful. When the wife becomes as irritable as the husband, their life at home is sure to be disturbed or ultimately completely broken. In the modern day, the wife is never submissive, and therefore home life is broken even by slight incidents. Either the wife or the husband may take advantage of the divorce laws. According to the Vedic law, however, there is no such thing as divorce laws, and a woman must be trained to be submissive to the will of her husband. Westerners contend that this is a slave mentality for the wife, but factually it is not; it is the tactic by which a

woman can conquer the heart of her husband, however irritable or cruel he may be. In this case we clearly see that although Cyavana Muni was not young but indeed old enough to be Sukanyā's grandfather and was also very irritable, Sukanyā, the beautiful young daughter of a king, submitted herself to her old husband and tried to please him in all respects. Thus she was a faithful and chaste wife.

Hopeless Women Become Feminists – Men Should Become First-class

Śrīla Prabhupāda analyzed that a woman's desire for social emancipation arises because of feeling hopeless at the prospect of getting a good husband:

> Śrīla Prabhupāda: In the Western countries they don't think there is need of husband – but they feel. I have seen one girl, she saw another friend: "Oh, she has got a husband," whispering. So I can understand that everyone aspires after husband, but there is no hope – hopelessness. This is the position. Every woman wants a good husband, good home, good children, little ornaments, nice food. That is the ambition of every woman. But they are hopeless. Although they are well qualified – European, American girls – they are hopeless, not to get any husband, not to get any home. This is their position. I have studied thoroughly. Hopelessness. When we see in our association [of devotees] all these girls – they are so nicely, well qualified. Whatever they are taught, they immediately pick up.
>
> Indian man: In America they were asking my wife how Indian women are able to keep such devotion for their husbands. So they are actually very much interested and envious of this situation in India.
>
> Śrīla Prabhupāda: Yes, that is the nature. They want to be a faithful wife, but there is no husband. Where to become faithful?

Harikeśa: So then they want to become liberated.

Śrīla Prabhupāda: Yes. Being hopeless repeatedly, now they want liberation.[1]

The cause of feminism being the frustration of women with inadequate or exploitive men, the solution is that men should become first-class:

Śrīla Prabhupāda: These instances are in the Vedic literature, that the wife remains always faithful and subservient to the husband. That is their perfection. Now the Americans may not like this idea. That is a different thing. But we are speaking of the Vedic culture.

Brahmānanda: Actually, they are just feeling frustrated, because it is a fact that woman has been exploited by the men. So now they want to counteract this.

Śrīla Prabhupāda: No, we don't say that woman should be exploited by men. We say the man should be responsible and give protection to woman.

Brahmānanda: But they feel so angry from the exploitation that they cannot accept that actually a man could protect them.

Śrīla Prabhupāda: That is bad experience. But the ideal is different. Ideal is that man must be first class and he must be responsible to take care of the woman, and she should be given all protection, all necessities. That is the duty of man. Just like father takes the charge of his daughter, similarly, husband should take charge of the woman. And similarly, elderly sons also took charge of the woman. The father never exploits the daughter. He gives all protection. That is the duty of the husband also. When she is grown up, she cannot remain under the protection of father. She is given, therefore, to a suitable boy

1. Conversation, 27 Sep 1975.

to take charge. But the charge is the same – to give protection, all comforts. And because there is no first-class man to take charge of the woman, they are declaring independence. All the men are doing that. They keep a girlfriend, make her pregnant and go away.

Brahmānanda: In that sense we can say that the women are inferior, but the men also, they are not first class.

Śrīla Prabhupāda: That we also said, that there is no first-class men. So if there is first-class men, then whole question is solved.[1]

Of course, first-class men are rare to find in an age wherein everyone is born as a *śūdra*.[2] Thus Śrīla Prabhupāda wanted to institute *gurukula* education, to train boys to become first-class.[3] The shortage of well-qualified husbands and wives does not, however, mean that spouses should en masse reject their partners. Preferably, everyone should tolerate and do the best they can within a marital situation even if it is not fully to their liking, just as in the example of Sukanyā (related above) or of Śrīla Prabhupāda himself, who wrote: "I never liked my wife, but I knew it was my duty to stick until my sons were grown-up, then I left."[4]

Some Misconceptions of Men

Proponents of traditional gender roles are often charged with particularly stressing the duties of women over those of men. However, the reason for particularly emphasizing women's duties is that a major disparity in modern society is that of women trying to be like men – not vice versa. Of course, it is

1. Conversation, 9 July 1975.
2. See Cc 1.7.67, ppt.
3. E.g., see lecture of 5 Nov 1976.
4. Letter, 17 December, 1972.

also essential that men know how to relate properly both with their wives and with other women.

An essential principle that Śrīla Prabhupāda often quoted (from Cāṇakya Paṇḍita) is *mātṛvat para-dāreṣu:* "One should consider another's wife to be one's mother."[1]

Some men wrongly think that because women are meant to be submissive, a man therefore has license to slap women around, mistreat them, and have little consideration for them. But Śrīla Prabhupāda warned us:

> Girls should not be taken as inferior. Sometimes we say from scripture that woman is the cause of bondage. That should not be aggravated – that "woman is inferior," or something like that. The girls who come – you should treat them nicely. After all, anyone who is coming to Kṛṣṇa consciousness, man or woman, boys or girls, they are welcome. They are very fortunate.[2]

Another misunderstanding is to think "I am married with three kids, but it's a hell of a burden; and my wife is no longer beautiful. Actually, it's better for my spiritual life to renounce. I think it's time to take *sannyāsa*." (Of course, some exalted devotees of the past did renounce family life at a young age. Famous examples are Śrī Rāmānujācārya, who left his wife because she was offensive to his guru, and Śrī Rāghavendra Swami was also young when he abandoned his wife. Yet what these two outstanding devotees did for the world was remarkable.) This kind of "renunciation" is actually irresponsibility. Instead of falsely renouncing their family, men should adhere to their duty.* Even if a man dislikes his wife, he should nonetheless maintain his marriage vow and remain faithful and responsible. As stated in the *Bhagavad-gītā* (18.8):

* Lecture: Duties of Men <www.bvks.com/7327>

1. See e.g. SB 8.9.4, ppt.
2. Conversation, 24 Sep 1968.

> Anyone who gives up prescribed duties as troublesome or out of fear of bodily discomfort is said to have renounced in the mode of passion. Such action never leads to the elevation of renunciation.

In his purport to this verse, Śrīla Prabhupāda wrote:

> Such renunciation is in the mode of passion. The result of passionate work is always miserable. If a person renounces work in that spirit, he never gets the result of renunciation.

Duties of Married Men

In a lengthy letter to a recently married man who wished to leave his wife, Śrīla Prabhupāda offered important instructions regarding duty, divorce, the protection of women, and related topics:

> You are requesting me to leave your wife and take the *vānaprastha* order of life. I know your wife Līlā-śakti, and I know that she is [a] very serious and advanced disciple. But now you are married to her, [so] there is some obligation according to our Kṛṣṇa consciousness or Vedic system. These things cannot be taken so lightly, otherwise the whole thing will become a farce. Simply get married without considering what is the serious nature of married life, then if there is little disturbance, or if I do not like my wife or my husband, let me go away, everyone else is doing like that. So in this way the whole thing is becoming a farce. You say that your "association together was hindering your advancement." But Kṛṣṇa consciousness marriage system should not be taken in that way, that if there is any botheration that means something is hindering my spiritual progress, no. Once it is adopted, the *gṛhastha* life, even it may be troublesome at times, it must be fulfilled as my occupational duty. Of course, it is better to remain unmarried, celibate. But so many women are coming, we cannot

reject them. If someone comes to Kṛṣṇa it is our duty to give them protection. Kṛṣṇa has informed us in *Bhagavad-gītā* that even women and *śūdras* and other inferior classes of men can take refuge in Him. So the problem is there, the women must have a husband to give protection. Of course, if the women can remain unmarried, and if there is suitable arrangement for the temple to protect them, just like in the Christian Church there is nunnery for systematic program of engaging the ladies and protecting them, that is also nice. But if there is sex desire, how to control it? Women are normally very lusty, more lusty than men, and they are weaker sex; it is difficult for them to make spiritual advancement without the help of husband. For so many reasons, our women must have husband. That's all right, but if once they have got a husband he goes away so quickly, that will not be very much happy for them.

Now I do not know the situation in your particular case. I am simply giving you the general policy or background understanding. We should never think of our so-called advancement as being conditioned by or dependent upon some set of material circumstances such as marriage, *vānaprastha*, or this or that. Mature understanding of Kṛṣṇa consciousness means that whatever condition of life I am in at present, that is Kṛṣṇa's special mercy upon me, therefore let me take advantage in the best way possible to spread this Kṛṣṇa consciousness movement and conduct my spiritual master's mission. If I consider my own personal progress or happiness or any other thing personal, that is material consideration. If there was unhappy adjustment for becoming married, why you got married at all? Whatever is done is done, that is a fact, but I am only pointing out that once before you did something without proper study of your real responsibility, [and] now you are contemplating again some drastic action in a similar manner. Therefore consider it carefully in this light. There is one verse from *Bhagavad-gītā: yasmān nodvijate loko lokān nodvijate ca yaḥ/ harṣāmarṣa-bhayodvegair mukto yaḥ sa ca me priyaḥ,* "He for whom no one is put into difficulty and who is not disturbed by anxiety, who is steady in happiness and distress, is very dear to Me." (12.15) One mistake of judgment often made by the neophyte devotees is that any time there is some disturbance or some difficulty they are considering that the conditions or the external circumstances under which the difficulty took place are the cause of the difficulty itself. That is not the fact. In this material world there is always some difficulty, no matter in this situation or that situation. Therefore simply by changing my status of occupation or my status of life, that will not help anything. Because the real fact is that if there is any difficulty with others, that is my lack of Kṛṣṇa consciousness, not theirs. Is this clear? Kṛṣṇa says that His dearest devotee is one who does not put others into difficulty, in fact, who puts no one other into difficulty. So try to judge the matter on these points, whether or not you are putting either your wife or yourself into some difficulty. The right understanding of *Bhagavad-gītā* is Arjuna's understanding. In other words, Arjuna came to the conclusion that he must perform his occupational duty, not as a material obligation, for reasons of wife, family, friends, reputation, professional integrity, like that – no. Rather, he must conduct the functions of his station of life only as a devotional service performed for Kṛṣṇa. That means that devotional service is what is important, not my occupational duty. But it does not mean that because occupation duty is not the real consideration, that I should give it up and do something else, thinking that devotional service may be carried on under whatever circumstances which I may whimsically decide. Kṛṣṇa recommended Arjuna to remain as he was, not to disrupt the order of society and go against his own nature just for convenience sake. Our occupational duty is not arbitrary; that means once we have taken up some field of action, if we are advanced in our understanding, then we shall not change it for another. Rather, our devotion is the important factor, so what does it matter what I am doing so long [as] my work and energy are completely devoted to Kṛṣṇa? Just like Kṛṣṇa, He is the Supreme Personality of Godhead, He has no work, neither He has anything to do, still He comes here to teach us this lesson. He accepts not only His occupational duty as cowherd boy, royal prince, but also He accepts married life, He enters politics, He is philosopher, He is even chariot driver during a great battle. He does not give example of Himself avoiding His occupational duty. So if Kṛṣṇa Himself is exhibiting by His own conduct what is the perfection of existence, then we should heed such example if we are intelligent. Even supposing there is wife at home, with children, that does not matter, that is no hindrance to our spiritual life. And once we have accepted these things, occupational duties, we should not lightly give them up. That is the point. Of course, our occupational duty is as preachers of Kṛṣṇa consciousness. So we must stick to that business under all circumstances; that is the main thing. Therefore married, unmarried, divorced, whatever condition of life, my preaching mission does not depend on these things. The *varṇāśrama-dharma* system is scientifically arranged by Kṛṣṇa to provide facility for delivering the fallen souls back to home, back to Godhead. And if we make a mockery of this system by whimsically disrupting the order, that we must consider. That will not be a very good example if so many young boys and girls so casually become married and then go away from each other, and the wife is little unhappy, the husband is neglecting her in so many ways, like that. If we set this example, then how the thing will go on properly? Householder life means wife, children, home; these things are understood by everyone, why our devotees have taken it as something different? They simply have some sex desire, get themselves married, and when the matter does not fulfill their expectations, immediately there is separation – these things are just like material activities, prostitution. The wife is left without husband, and sometimes there is child to be raised; in so many ways the proposition that you, and some others also, are making becomes distasteful. We cannot expect that our temples will become places of shelter for so many widows and rejected wives; that will be a great burden and we shall become the laughing stock in the society. There will be unwanted progeny also. And there will be illicit sex life; that we are seeing already. And being the weaker sex, women require to have a husband who is strong in Kṛṣṇa consciousness so that they may take advantage and make progress by sticking tightly to his feet. If their husband goes away from them, what will they do? So many instances are already there in our society, so many frustrated girls and boys.

So I have introduced this marriage system in your Western countries because there is custom of freely intermingling [of] male and female. Therefore marriage [is] required just to engage the boys and girls in devotional service, never mind distinction of living status. But our marriage system is [a] little different than in your country; we do not sanction the policy of quick divorce. We are supposed to take husband or wife as eternal companion or assistant in Kṛṣṇa consciousness service, and there is promise never to separate. Of course if there is any instance of very advanced disciples, married couple, and they have agreed that the husband shall now take *sannyāsa* or renounced order of life, being mutually very happy by that arrangement, then there is ground for such separation. But even in those cases there is no question of separation; the husband, even if he is a *sannyāsī,* he must be certain his wife will be taken care of nicely and protected in his absence. Now so many cases are there of unhappiness by the wife who has been abandoned by her husband against her wishes. So how can I sanction such thing? I want to avoid setting any bad example for future generations, therefore I am so much cautiously considering your request. But if it becomes so easy for me to get married and then leave my wife, under excuse of married life being an impediment to my own spiritual progress, that will not be very good at all. That is misunderstanding of what is advancement in spiritual life. Occupational duty must be there, either this one or that one, but once I am engaged in something occupational duty, then I should not change that or give it up; that is the worst mistake. Devotional service is not bound up by such designations. Therefore once I have chosen, it is better to stick in that way and develop my devotional attitude into full-blown love of Godhead. That is Arjuna's understanding.[1]

1. Letter, 4 Jan 1973.

Section Three

Women As Leaders

Should women be leaders? In one sense they are automatically leaders, because although the father is the "head of the family,"[1] "it is the duty of the wife to take charge of household affairs."[2] Practically, the woman is the queen of the home – because she orchestrates everything therein. Śrīmatī Draupadī, the chaste and devoted wife of the Pāṇḍavas, managed the entirety of the palace affairs – which would be akin to running a major modern-day commercial enterprise – with people continually coming and going, appointments to be fixed, and properly feeding everyone at all different times. And even to manage an ordinary home is no small job – hence the common saying: "A woman's work is never done." Leadership implies responsibility and control. It is never easy, whether one is the leader of a nation or the organizer of a home.

Everyone in this material world has the propensity to control, and women can best exercise this inclination within the sphere of the home, especially by controlling their children. When women aspire or demand to control everyone else, that becomes intolerable, whereas women who devotedly control and guide their children are respected and loved for doing so.

Even in the management of universal affairs, the departmental heads are mostly men. And the few important demigoddesses (among whom Durgā and Sarasvatī are prominent) discharge their duties within the context of being a faithful and subordinate servant of their respective husband.

---

1. SB 2.6.6, ppt.
2. SB 3.22.11, ppt.

In one sense, women can be "more powerful than men" – in a subtle way, "as a power of inspiration for men."[1]

Śrīla Prabhupāda was not in favor of women occupying public leadership positions:

> It is most regrettable when a woman becomes the executive head instead of a lionlike king. In such a situation the people are considered very unfortunate.[2]

> As we learn from the history of the *Mahābhārata,* or "Greater India," the wives and daughters of the ruling class, the *kṣatriyas,* knew the political game, but we never find that a woman was given the post of chief executive. This is in accordance with the injunctions of *Manu-saṁhitā.*[3]

> According to the Vedic conception, woman is never offered leadership. Experience has shown that woman's leadership has not been successful. I do not say of any particular woman. But according to Vedic civilization, we have never seen in the history that woman has become a leader.[4]

In a list of proposals that Śrīla Prabhupāda planned to present to Indira Gandhi, then prime minister of India, one was that she should become "Mother Queen," and her son the king.[5] So it appears that Śrīla Prabhupāda wanted to effectively transfer power to her son.

In 1973, Śrīla Prabhupāda wrote: "We especially have to try to attract the educated young men and women in your country so that in future there will be many strong leaders to keep our

---

1. SB 1.9.27, ppt.
2. SB 4.16.23, ppt.
3. SB 10.4.5, ppt.
4. Television interview, 9 July 1975.
5. *A Transcendental Diary,* vol. 5, entry for 26 Nov 1976.

Kṛṣṇa consciousness movement strong."[1] And indeed, in the early days of ISKCON in the West, women were raised in many ways as equal to their male counterparts.[2] Nevertheless, it is a historical fact that, from the beginning, Śrīla Prabhupāda did not appoint female disciples to crucial leadership positions – neither as GBC members nor as temple presidents.* He often referred to his "GBC men." When asked if a woman could become a temple president, Śrīla Prabhupāda replied, "Yes, why not?" and then explained that a woman should remain dependent on either her first-class father, first-class husband, or first-class son.[3] The apparent contradiction of a woman being both in charge (as a temple president) and dependent is resolved in another statement by Śrīla Prabhupāda – that a *gṛhastha* temple president should be like a father to the devotees, and his wife should be like their mother.[4] A woman whose husband is a temple president shares in his role by being "a devoted wife, who is according to revealed scripture the better half of her husband."[5] "The wife is accepted as the better half of a man's body because she is supposed to be responsible for discharging half of the duties of the husband."[6]

---

* Briefly, under unusual circumstances, a female devotee was in charge of a center in 1968. See VedaBase 1968 entries re Krishna Devi.

---

1. Letter, 7 April 1973.
2. See *Yamuna Devi – A Life of Unalloyed Devotion*, vol. 2, p. 58, a portion of which is paraphrased herein.
3. Conversation, 5 Jul 1975.
4. Told by Guru Dāsa.
5. SB 1.7.45, ppt.
6. SB 3.14.19.

Women As Gurus

In all the ancient Vedic literature, there is no reference to even one woman who acted as an initiating guru.* That the role of guru is intrinsically male is inherent in the concept of initiation as a second birth, wherein "Vedic knowledge is the mother, and the spiritual master is the father."[1] Yet in another sense, the biological mother is considered to be the first guru of the child – not in the same way as an initiating guru, but because she teaches her children the basic principles of human behavior and instills in them the primary principles of dharma, which is later solidified by formal gurus. Mothers and grandmothers tell children stories of Rāma and Kṛṣṇa, and of other outstanding personalities described in the Vedic literature. But a woman's main method of instruction to her children is through her personal example of self-sacrifice, that most noble virtue for which motherhood is universally glorified.

By being chaste and submissive to her husband, a woman teaches her children how to respect superiors. If a woman disagrees with her husband, she may express herself privately to him only, or in the presence of family elders, but not in the presence of children, for that would set a bad example. As I remember, even one generation ago in India, children were mostly sweet-natured and well-behaved, because they were so carefully protected and nurtured. But nowadays, many children are raised more by television, video games, and the internet than by their mothers – with profoundly negative effects both for those unfortunate children and for the overall society that they becomes constituents of.

---

* This chapter does not attempt to minutely examine the various positions regarding the institution of women as gurus, but simply argues against it from the perspective that a woman's natural role is to be a mother.

1. Commentary on verse one of *Teachings of Lord Kapila.*

Although there are indications that Śrīla Prabhupāda wanted his spiritual daughters to formally accept the role of guru,[1] the norm in Vedic culture is that women should follow *strī-dharma,* and that formal leadership roles, such as that of guruship, is restricted to men. In Vaiṣṇava history there have been some rare exceptions wherein a woman acted as a formal guru, which Śrīla Prabhupāda acknowledged: "It is not that woman cannot be *ācārya.* Generally, they do not become – in very special case."[2]

In the Gauḍīya tradition, exceptional cases of women as guru were Jāhnavā Mātā (one of the two wives of Nityānanda Prabhu), Gaṅgāmātā Gosvāminī, and Hemalatā Ṭhākurāṇī (a daughter of Śrīnivāsa Ācārya). However, all of them largely observed *strī-dharma.* For instance, at the famous Kheturi festival, Jāhnavā Mātā took charge of the kitchen and cooked for the attending devotees. These few "very special cases" of lady gurus are accepted within the Gauḍīya tradition as having been liberated souls situated on the topmost platform of devotional service.

Śrīla Prabhupāda's statement "Sunīti, however, being a woman, and specifically his mother, could not become Dhruva Mahārāja's *dīkṣā-guru*"[3] has been the subject of considerable speculative analysis in attempts to explain it away, yet at the very least it stands as a powerful indication that women are not meant to initiate.

Consider this: should a *brahmacārī* who does not adhere to the principles of *brahmacarya* be accepted as a spiritual guide? Or a *gṛhastha* man who does not fulfill his duties? Or a sannyasi who is a renunciant in name only? In each case: obviously not.

1. E.g. letter, 3 Jan 1969.

2. Conversation, 29 Jun 1972.

3. SB 4.12.32, ppt.

So why should a woman be accepted as a spiritual guide unless she properly observes *strī-dharma?* Surely, a chaste woman who is committed to *strī-dharma* would not be eager to take a public role and instruct men. Indeed, that just a few women within ISKCON are vocal about their "rights" suggests a vast majority who prefer to remain modestly in the background, as per their natural role.

The primary purpose of *varṇāśrama-dharma* – to overcome the sexual impulse – can hardly be effected by the social intermingling of men and women, not to speak of allowing women to hold prominent roles. Better that we first institute *varṇāśrama-dharma* and get society in order, with everyone understanding and acting in their proper position. Later on, we may consider exceptions such as women accepting the service of guruship. Rather than laboriously seeking novel ways to justify an unconventional idea that Śrīla Prabhupāda only rarely mentioned (that of female *dīkṣā-gurus*), it would be more chaste to Śrīla Prabhupāda's instructions to sincerely invest our efforts in *varṇāśrama-dharma,* which he repeatedly emphasized with increasing urgency.

In writing to a female disciple, Śrīla Prabhupāda suggested how women can be gurus within the home and by instructing other local women:

> If you can induce all the women of Los Angeles to place an altar in their homes and help their husbands have peaceful, happy home life in Kṛṣṇa consciousness, that will be [a] very great service for you. The actual system is that the husband is spiritual master to his wife, but if the wife can bring her husband into practicing this process, then it is all right that the husband accepts wife as spiritual master. Caitanya Mahāprabhu has said that anyone who knows the science of Kṛṣṇa, that person should be accepted as spiritual master,

> regardless of any material so-called qualifications, such as rich or poor, man or woman, or *brāhmaṇa* or *śūdra.* So if you can show the women of the community how to help their husbands and children to perfect their home life, and all aspects of life in Kṛṣṇa consciousness, by chanting, *ārati* ceremonies, and eating Kṛṣṇa *prasāda,* then you will improve the conditions of the neighboring communities to an incalculable extent.[1]

These directions for how women can be gurus are clearly in regard to their giving spiritual guidance, with no mention whatsoever of conferring formal initiation.*

Women Giving Classes and Leading Kīrtanas

> Materially a woman may be less intelligent than a man, but spiritually everyone is pure soul. In the absolute plane there is no gradation of higher and lower. If a woman can lecture nicely and to the point, we should hear carefully. That is our philosophy. But if a man can speak better than a woman, the man should be given first preference. But even though a woman is less intelligent, a sincere soul should be given proper chance to speak, because we want so many preachers, both men and women.[2] †

Although Śrīla Prabhupāda sometimes had his female disciples speak publicly in his presence, overall within ISKCON it was quite rare that women would give lectures. For instance, during the four annual Māyāpur festivals during which Śrīla Prabhupāda was present (1974–1977), there was not a single

* Lecture: Can Women be Dīkṣā-gurus? <www.bvks.com/10568>

† Feminists within ISKCON sometimes mendaciously promote this quote sans the caveat that men be given first preference. See e.g. www.dandavats.com/?p=14535 (first slideshow, 2 minutes). Retrieved 5 Jan 2015.

1. Letter, 14 Jun 1969.
2. Letter, 8 Feb 1968.

instance of any woman lecturing, whereas dozens of talks were given by men. Yaśomatīnandana Dāsa recalls that from the time that he joined ISKCON in 1972 onward until Śrīla Prabhupāda's departure in 1977, he never saw a woman giving class.

Śrīla Bhaktivinoda Ṭhākura indicated that women may teach and preach, but only among other women.[1] And this is the standard still today in many Hindu institutions. (Of course, women may also teach young children.) For instance, every afternoon at the ISKCON temple in Baroda, Gujarat, a group of local housewives assemble to chant *bhajanas.* As they are not working women, they have time daily to attend *sat-saṅga.** And the resident female devotees at ISKCON Baroda assemble twice weekly for a *sat-saṅga* comprised of singing, reading, and chanting scriptural verses.

Women who want to lead *kīrtanas* may best do so in all-women *kīrtanas,* and maybe also among *gṛhasthas.* Women should not teach courses or seminars to men. In this way, the principles of shyness and chastity will be upheld, without which "women will create devastation."[2]

Dancing

Śrīla Prabhupāda did not encourage his female Indian disciples to become like Westerners. Although he appreciated that his Western women disciples would enthusiastically dance during *kīrtana,* he never instructed his Indian lady disciples to do the same. They would stand at the back and hardly move. Śrīla Prabhupāda explained that in Indian culture, respectable

* *Sat-saṅga* – religious gathering.

1. As described in *Jaiva Dharma* and *Prema Pradīpa.*
2. Conversation, 29 Dec 1976.

women do not dance in public, although low-class women may do so.[1] He actually wanted that his disciples adopt the culture of *brāhmaṇas*, the highest class of people in India.

A woman's dancing can be very enticing to men, even if she is not overtly trying to attract them. Spirited jumping up and down is certainly fine for men, but hardly so for women, because of their bodily construction. If a young woman regularly dances vigorously in view of men, it is clear that she wants to attract them, that she wants a mate. Even to publicly raise the arms, as men do while dancing, was never done by traditional shy women, so as to always keep their breasts fully covered.

In Los Angeles, which at that time was the world headquarters of ISKCON, Śrīla Prabhupāda originally instructed that men should dance on one side and women on the other. Later on, he said that the women should be on the balcony. Dānavīra Goswami recalls:

> The men occupy the front space and the ladies are occupying the rear of the temple room as well as the balcony. Smiling, Śrīla Prabhupāda glances up at his female disciples gathered in the balcony. Perhaps he remembers how in the original Dvārakā city, respectable ladies used to go up upon their palace rooftops to have a look at Lord Dvārakādhīśa. Then the beloved spiritual master and spiritual father began to speak so that the ladies might not feel minimized in their new balcony station, "Yes, this is very nice," he says approvingly. "Now the ladies can dance on the heads of the men." Everyone laughs.[2]

Some recent anecdotes related by a godbrother in India:

> Around 2008 in Delhi during a Sunday evening *kīrtana*, one twenty-something *mātājī* visitor was becoming very

1. Conversation, 27 Jul 1976.

2. Dānavīra Goswami (ch. 7 of *His Divine Grace*).

enthusiastic because of the *kīrtana* and she wanted to dance. She looked around and saw the *brahmacārīs* dancing, jumping up and down. So not having any ladies to emulate, she also started jumping up and down. This lady had traditional Vedic proportions in the breast department, and her breasts were bouncing up and down in a very noticeable way. From the back of the room, an older woman came to the front of the temple, where this young woman was bouncing up and down, forcibly grabbed her and pushed her to the ground, and stopped her from dancing. Then she pulled up the girl (obviously her daughter) and took her out of the temple. All the *brahmacārīs* appreciated the mother protecting her daughter from the vulgar display that she was doing out of innocence. Any cultured woman would not want her daughter to dance like that. Another thing is that the daughter obeyed her.

I was once in Māyāpur for Gaura-pūrṇimā. At *sandhyā-ārati,* two Indian women, who seemed to be mother and daughter, were dancing in front of the Deities in a very crude and vulgar manner, bumping and grinding their hips around like there were doing the hoochi-coochi [a sexually provocative belly dance]. I went up to one of the Bengali ladies in the security force and indicated to stop them. She pounced on them and shut them down immediately. I got the impression that she was furious with them and was just waiting for someone like me to tell her to shut that show down.

Menstruation

In this very strange age, I (a sannyasi) am sometimes asked what women should do during menstruation. The question arises because in Vedic culture (as in most other traditional cultures) there are special restrictions for women during their monthly cycle. *Śāstra* describes that to touch or even see a woman during menses can destroy a man's knowledge and strength and decrease the duration of his life. Anything touched by her becomes impure. Among the offenses in Deity worship is to touch a woman during her menstrual period.[1] And, "a woman is considered contaminated just after childbirth or during her menstrual period. She cannot perform ordinary religious activities at such times, which [for her] are therefore inauspicious and impure."[2]

There is an argument that *bhakti* overrides all such considerations, which therefore need not be observed. But this notion is in the category of innovative theology, for no *śāstra* or *ācārya* to date has floated such a theory. The *bhakti* of a woman certainly renders her inherently auspicious, but that doesn't mean that she is eligible to worship Deities when in an impure state, any more than a male devotee can waive bathing before worshiping Deities. During menstruation, due to the continual discharge, bathing does not relieve ritual impurity, so at that time women should not worship Deities or perform other activities that require ritual purity.

But such rules are hardly followed in today's world. Daily life must go on, with girls going to school and women to work. Just a few countries, and some individual companies, have instituted "menstrual leave," in recognition of the physical pain and mental and emotional difficulties that menstruating women often undergo (which modern science explains in terms of hormonal disturbances).*

Traditionally in India, during menstruation women would suspend all regular activities (except breast-feeding) and stay in a separate cottage until the flow stopped. When one Western devotee woman first heard of this practice, she

* See: en.wikipedia.org/wiki/Menstrual_leave

1. SB 7.5.23–24, ppt.

2. SB 11.21.9, ppt.

responded, "Oh, what a wonderful idea – to take a break and be peaceful for three or four days." Indeed, for women who are busy serving others all day every day, menstruation is Kṛṣṇa's kind arrangement for them to have a few days each month for recuperation. And this is especially possible in joint families, wherein there are many women to cover all the required duties, even if one or two of them are temporarily sequestered.

Regarding Deity worship, Śrīla Prabhupāda wrote:

> According to the *smārta-vidhi,* women cannot touch deity during menstrual period but the *gosvāmī-vidhi* allows. But it is better not to do it. One thing is that the *sevā** can never be stopped for any reason. This also for the cooking.[1]

The essential point is that the Deity worship should not be stopped. Although if no one else is available then a menstruating woman may perform *pūjā,* this situation should be avoided. Of course, in the modern nuclear family, some concessions may be necessary for home Deity worship during such times,† but such concessions should never have to be made in public temples, wherein menstruating women should strictly be prohibited from engaging in Deity worship. After all, it is an offense to worship Deities after having touched a menstruating women, so what to speak of a menstruating woman personally engaging in Deity worship?

So what advice should be given to women regarding their activities during menses? In India, I generally recommend: "The ideal is to do as your grandmother, your great-

* *Sevā* – (Deity) service.

† This is one of several reasons why Deity worship generally cannot be very properly performed within nuclear families. It is hardly advisable to undertake worship in a situation wherein service by a menstruating woman will be a regular necessity.

1. Letter, 13 Aug 1974.

grandmother, and your great-great-grandmother did. But for today's situation, suggested minimum restrictions are to not cook, engage in sex, visit temples, or perform Deity worship. And as far as is practical, they may stay home and relax – even remaining out of sight if possible."

Many women today are so accustomed to doing everything else during their monthly period that they consider it acceptable even to enter a temple during that time. But the grandmothers of such women would surely severely berate them for that. It seems that while Śrīla Prabhupāda was in the West, he never discussed this issue. But he is reported as having ceded to the desire of his Western female disciples who were serving in Māyāpur in 1976, by allowing them to attend the temple wearing a silk sari when "off the altar" (ISKCON terminology for being in menses), but not to perform Deity worship.[1] This concession did not at all please the local Bengali woman devotees.[2] As a consequence of this allowance given to the Western women, some devotees have incited Indian women of ISKCON to do likewise. Accordingly, in some ISKCON centers in India, it can be understood that a woman is in menses by her sitting just outside the temple during programs. And some have gone further, by sitting inside but at the very back. Maybe already some menstruating women simply mix with all the other females in the temple, as they do at work – thus exercising their freedom to flout *śāstric* rules and traditions.

Even in a nuclear family, it is best that someone else, whether the husband or a sufficiently grown child, cook when the lady of the house is ritually unclean. Other possible alternatives during those days are to eat only temple *prasāda,* or that devotee families who reside proximately arrange to help each other when needed.

1. *Śrīla Prabhupāda is Coming* (Mahāmāyā Devī Dāsī), ch. 15.

2. Ibid. ch. 16.

Calling Women "Prabhu"

More evidence of the influence of feminism within ISKCON is the controversy over whether women devotees should be addressed as *prabhu* (master) or *mātā* (mother). Although this issue might seem trivial, the symbolism involved is significant, for these two terms of address connote widely differing outlooks regarding social norms for women, which again spring from widely differing outlooks concerning the practice of Kṛṣṇa consciousness in today's ethos. Clearly, those who advocate that women devotees be called *prabhu* are influenced by the insistent feminism that is nigh ubiquitous in the Western world.

The theory behind this practice is that men and women are equal on the spiritual platform. And evidence is offered from Śrīla Prabhupāda's teachings: "Initiated Vaiṣṇavas are addressed as *prabhu*."[1] But clearly, this statement is qualified by Śrīla Prabhupāda's oft-repeated instruction that women should be addressed as "Mother."

There is some evidence that during the beginning days of ISKCON, Śrīla Prabhupāda would sometimes address the devotee women as *prabhu*. My understanding is that he did so in accord with his "early days" policy of giving whatever Kṛṣṇa consciousness he could inculcate to newcomers in America, who were mostly completely ignorant of Vedic culture. Nonetheless, also during those early days, Śrīla Prabhupāda advised that male devotees address women as "my dear mother" and women devotees address males "my dear son."[2]

Mukunda Goswami, who has been with ISKCON since day one, stated that, until recently, he had never heard devotee women

---

1. Cc 2.10.23, ppt.

2. Told by Jadurāṇī Devī Dāsī.

being called *prabhu,* and that, as far as he remembered, the staple form of address for female devotees in ISKCON had always been *mātājī* or "Mother."[1] Similarly, Hari-śauri Dāsa, who lived day and night with Śrīla Prabhupāda from November 1975 to March 1977, said, "During all the time I was with Śrīla Prabhupāda, I never heard him call women *prabhu.*"[2]

Some years ago, while giving a lecture in an ISKCON center in Russia, I mentioned how in the West many devotees call women *prabhu* – whereupon the more than one hundred devotees present, both men and women, spontaneously laughed. To them it seemed absurd. And indeed it is.

Proponents of addressing women as *prabhu* maintain that those who don't do so still have material attachments and thus see only the bodies of women, rather than their spiritual identity. Of course, this idea is further speculation, considering that no one in Vedic culture – none of the great liberated *ācāryas,* nor even Śrī Kṛṣṇa or Śrī Caitanya Mahāprabhu – ever set the example of addressing women as *prabhu.* Are the demigods' wives addressed as *prabhu?* Mother Yaśodā? Lakṣmīdevī? Sītādevī? Śrīmatī Rādhārāṇī is the "master" of the Supreme Master, yet even She is not addressed as *prabhu!*[3]

Prabhu is a masculine term. To call women *prabhu* is similar to calling them "mister." Who would say "Mr. Sonia Gandhi"? To circumvent this obvious absurdity, some devotees invented the term *prabhvī,* the feminine form of (the masculine word) *prabhu.* However, that it is grammatically possible to coin such a neologism as *prabhvī* does not confer upon it any imprimatur

1. Recounted by his disciple Madana-mohana Dāsa, correspondence, 11 May 2008.

2. Confirmed by Hari-śauri Dāsa, personal correspondence, 14 Jan 2015.

3. The last four sentences of this paragraph are derived from Devakī Devī Dāsī, www.dandavats.com/? p=12806 (retrieved 15 Sep 2014).

of *ārṣa-prayoga* (irregular but accepted usage). The word *prabhvī* is not found in Sanskrit literature, for the simple reason that in Vedic culture women do not assume the role of master.

Responding to the statement "Śrīla Prabhupāda never said *prabhvī*, the female word for *prabhu*," a godbrother of mine wrote:

> Saying "the female word for *prabhu*" implies that anyone already accepts it as some sort of recognized usage, at least as we would have it – which is doubtful. Just because somebody decided to derive a feminization of the word *prabhu*, that alone cannot establish it as a lexical norm – much less the preferred usage of our *ācāryas* – or anyone else's.
>
> Where does this current fashion actually come from?
>
> It would be more responsible to demonstrate some substantial attestation for such novel use for *prabhvī*, by which I mean some clear attestation in Vaiṣṇava-*paramparā;* I don't think Monier-Williams* fits this description, since lexicographers themselves merely depend on the kind of attestation I'm also suggesting. Without doing so, our current notion of *prabhvī* remains more or less a neologism, and looks very much like a mere tool in the hands of the fairly passionate agenda-mongers of the day.
>
> My own admittedly limited experience with the Sanskrit and vernacular *bhakti* literatures of the last thousand or so years (including many of the verses Śrīla Prabhupāda quoted himself), leads me to the impression that the word *mātājī* is

* "Monier-Williams" refers to the Sanskrit-English dictionary compiled by Sir Monier Monier-Williams. The first edition was published in 1872 and the revised edition, completed in 1899, is still a standard reference work. However, its authority is questionable, especially because it was compiled by an outsider to Vedic culture whose openly stated mission in life was to contribute to the destruction of that culture.

used to fulfil the sense for which some now prefer *prabhvī* instead. The novel usage of *prabhvī* thus seems fairly skewed to me, as if external (and largely nonspiritual) influences were actually operating here far more than its advocates would care to recognize.

However, this is primarily a linguistic approach. Given what *Śrīmad-Bhāgavatam* suggests about epistemology (cf. *aitihya,* in 11.19.17), it might be more realistic (for those so inclined) to look for historical precedents involving the use of gendered terms of address among any bona fide Vaiṣṇavas.

Overall, the introduction of the word *prabhvī* was simply a creative cultural speculation, and is so awkward that it has largely been abandoned. Feminists are now back to calling women *prabhu.*

Yet those who insist on addressing devotees strictly from the spiritual perspective should consider both males or females as *prakṛti* (female) and thus refer neither to men nor women as *prabhu.* According to this logic, men also could be called Mātājī (for instance, Praghoṣa Mātājī) – and perhaps also wear saris.

The concept that women must be addressed as *prabhu* is yet another pseudo-egalitarian contamination that has entered ISKCON via the influence of modern feminism. It does not derive from the spiritual platform, and certainly not from *śāstra* or Vedic tradition.

Traditional Culture Is Still Appreciated

Fortunately, secularists and humanists have still not wreaked their full havoc in those large portions of the world wherein traditional culture is still widely appreciated. One such place is Bosnia, a Muslim-dominated country in Europe. One of my female disciples there comes from a Muslim family. Her late mother was an initiated devotee, and her sister also is a devotee. She opted to wed a man from a largely secular Muslim family that nonetheless still maintains many traditional Islamic principles, and her husband is agreeable to her being a devotee. She considered that she would have a better chance of securing a responsible, steady husband by marrying a man who adheres to Muslim values, rather than a Western-mentality ISKCON devotee. Notwithstanding various difficulties that she has undergone, overall the wisdom of her decision has been validated by a twelve-year-long marriage.

This devotee is a housewife as well as an architect who works from home. Her husband also is an architect. They have two sons and live a fairly simple, non-extravagant life, as is usual in Bosnia. She writes a blog in her native language to share her life as a devotee, and has earned acclaim from her readers, most of whom are young Muslim girls who appreciate how she is balancing her family and religious commitments. She has made friendships with several Muslim girls who, influenced by her writings, have come to respect Kṛṣṇa consciousness as a cultured religious process wherein women live a dignified life of devotion to God.

This particular example indicates that traditionalism, not liberalism and feminism, is clearly the best cultural approach for reaching the many people who wish to maintain traditional morals – which includes more than one billion Muslims. Of course, the Islamic world is not without problems, but the liberalized West (if it could muster up sufficient humility) could learn much from Islam. Certainly, gender roles within Islam are closer to the Vedic than are Western gender roles, and closer even than those in today's ISKCON in the Western world.

The Way Forward

Because sexual attraction will always be the basic principle of material existence, *varṇāśrama-dharma* is also called *sanātana-dharma*,[1] for it is specifically meant to facilitate the overcoming of sex desire. In this and many other important ways, Vedic culture helps to foster Kṛṣṇa consciousness. And also for the sake of societal peace and harmony, it is better that women stick to their natural duties and men to theirs.

Realistically, to transplant the Vedic culture into the demonic "civilization" will necessitate much intelligence, dedication, and patience. It won't happen overnight. Most devotees still struggle with their bad habits and misconceptions. And even those who fully acquiesce with Śrīla Prabhupāda's teachings regarding Vedic culture generally find themselves to be so conditioned that, although they know what is right, they still feel driven by the modes of nature to maintain their habitual contrary ways.

A practical beginning would be to impart systematic education and training in *varṇāśrama* principles, as Śrīla Prabhupāda ordered to do via *varṇāśrama* colleges.[2] Furthermore, we need to see examples of devotees engaged in *varṇāśrama-dharma*. Already there are some temple and farm communities progressing in the right direction. And several young adults who were raised as devotees from childhood are now, of their own accord, sincerely committed to Kṛṣṇa consciousness and family duties and thus becoming excellent examples for the rest of our society. These are all promising signs. But to effectively promote *varṇāśrama-dharma* within ISKCON requires that the institutional leaders take it seriously. Today's ISKCON cannot fully and properly satisfy Śrīla Prabhupāda if

1. SB 7.11.2, ppt.

2. Conversation, 12 Mar 1974.

its leaders remain in denial of this major mandate set by its founder-*ācārya*. Ultimately we have to choose to accept either the social values and gender roles of a society based on sexual indulgence, or to endeavor to establish a society based on curbing sexual fascination and developing pure love of God.

PART THREE

Gurudevis and Grandmothers

A posting on the Sampradaya Sun website (2 November 2012)

Undoubtedly, several senior women devotees in our movement are as learned, dedicated, and in other ways spiritually qualified as many of their godbrothers. Why then should there be any hesitation to induct them as diksa-gurus?

An important consideration is that the role of a guru, although wholly spiritual by nature, also has an inescapable social dimension. No one can live in any society without having a social role, which is determined by various factors including gender. For instance, only women can be mothers, and motherhood is much more than merely a biological function.

Among all possible forms of social organization, followers of Krsna's Vedic culture accept varnasrama-dharma as being axiomatically the best. In varnasrama-dharma, a specific, subtle, and subdued role is the norm for women, and men are accorded a more dominant role. From the beginning, Gaudiya Vaisnavas have largely accepted these gender roles, as is apparent in the sparse references to females among the associates of Lord Caitanya. More recently, Srila Bhaktisiddhanta Sarasvati's Gaudiya Matha was clearly a male-dominated institution.

Yet Lord Caitanya declared Himself to be not a member of any varna or asrama, and Gaudiya Vaisnavism aims to transcend all bodily designations and social roles. Lord Caitanya accepted among His topmost devotees Rupa, Sanatana, Haridasa, and others who were unacceptable to the social orthodoxy. Srila Prabhupada took this principle much further by inducting as brahmanas persons of wholly mleccha stock.

However, in accord with previous acaryas, Srila Prabhupada also wanted to reintroduce varnasrama-dharma. ("Varnasrama-dharma should be established to become a Vaisnava," said Srila Prabhupada in 1977. "It is not so easy to become a Vaisnava.") Varnasrama-dharma being a social arrangement and Vaisnavism a spiritual endeavor, there is a natural tension between the two. If devotees become overly concerned with the procedures of varnasrama-dharma, they risk subordinating its spiritual purpose and becoming dully ritualistic. Yet without varnasrama-dharma, aspiring Vaisnavas risk becoming sahajiyas, or losing Krsna consciousness altogether.

Why at all varnasrama-dharma is required, when Vaisnavism is meant to help its practitioners transcend all social considerations, was several times explained by Srila Prabhupada (e.g. in a conversation in Mayapur on 14 February 1977). Indeed, Srila Prabhupada stated that 50% of his mission was yet to be established, in the form of varnasrama-dharma. If we consider what Srila Prabhupada actually did, we can perceive a little of the massive task that Srila Prabhupada has left us. Just as spreading Krsna consciousness worldwide and compiling volumes of lawbooks for the next ten thousand years was an unprecedented and seemingly impossible achievement, so is the reestablishment of varnasrama-dharma.

Unfortunately we as an institution have opted to acquiesce with a misguided civilization that is collapsing all around us, rather than implementing varnasrama-dharma as the literally God-given remedy for all social ills. We have found it easier to be content with urban properties and followers rather than taking Srila Prabhupada's revolution to the next level by living on the land, protecting cows, producing our own food, and being happy by chanting Hare Krsna. For several years the GBC has been conducting strategic planning, but varnasrama-dharma is not on the agenda, even as a long-term project.

There is ample evidence of ISKCON's becoming increasingly compromised – in fact that is the subject of a whole book by

Professor E. Burke Rochford ("Hare Krishna Transformed"). That we have converted the gurukulas started by Srila Prabhupada into schools that teach government syllabi (in contravention of Srila Prabhupada's express order), and that we increasingly present our movement as being Hindu, are just two examples of our pronounced "mission drift." (See: www.harekrsna.com/sun/editorials/10-11/editorials7883.htm)

The non-implementation of varnasrama-dharma should be considered in light of the following grave words (Cc Adi 12.10):

acaryera mata yei, sei mata sara
tanra ajna langhi' cale, sei ta' asara

TRANSLATION

The order of the spiritual master is the active principle in spiritual life. Anyone who disobeys the order of the spiritual master immediately becomes useless.

PURPORT

Here is the opinion of Srila Krsnadasa Kaviraja Gosvami. Persons who strictly follow the orders of the spiritual master are useful in executing the will of the Supreme, whereas persons who deviate from the strict order of the spiritual master are useless.

Just as Srila Prabhupada criticized his godbrothers as being useless (see Cc Adi 12.8 purport) for not having fulfilled their guru's open order to preach Krsna consciousness, so future generations might well criticize us as being useless for having deviated from Srila Prabhupada's open order to establish varnasrama-dharma.

Therefore I suggest that the issue of female diksa-gurus be considered in relation to the whole direction of our movement. If we wish to continue neglecting Srila Prabhupada's order to institute varnasrama-dharma, then introducing female diksa-gurus is the logical next step in our pandering to the egalitarian fantasy that is intrinsic to modern so-called civilization.

But if somehow we get back to what Srila Prabhupada so much wanted and we decide to implement varnasrama-dharma, then we will have to put much energy into community development, starting at the family level. If husbands and wives cannot live happily together, there cannot be stable families, without which there cannot be stable communities, without which there cannot be varnasrama-dharma.

Sannyasis tend to get all the name, fame, and glory, but it is a great mistake to underestimate the importance of mothers and grandmothers. The body and psychology of women are designed to perform an essential function that men simply cannot do, which is to be mothers. Without the total giving of themselves to their children that is the natural characteristic of motherhood, we cannot expect children to develop into emotionally secure adults. In the modern world, females are unnaturally drafted into go-getter male roles, and not encouraged to develop their innate feminine tendencies toward motherly affection and selflessness. This is undoubtedly a major unseen factor in the discontent and psychological imbalance of innumerable individuals today. People can suffer lifelong if they do not grow up being soaked in mother's love.

ISKCON already has many devotees competent to deliver learned lectures, but we have yet to demonstrate to the world a better way of life based on stable, happy families. Because we have not developed a family culture, it might seem that that the only way that senior Vaisnavis can share their years of experience in Krsna consciousness is by traveling around giving lectures. No doubt some of our exalted godsisters can lecture as well as the best sannyasis in our movement. Yet by adopting a sannyasi-like lifestyle, they are inadvertently sending a message to junior matajis that the topmost aspiration for a woman in Krsna consciousness is to be an independent preacher – and now maybe a guru also. (However, guruship in ISKCON means a lot more than just big seats and flowers, and would-be gurudevis might have second thoughts if they knew what they were getting into.)

I respectfully submit that our senior Vaisnavis can better serve Srila Prabhupada's mission, not by trying to emulate sannyasis, but by serving as ideal grandmothers, helping to guide young mothers in how to manage households expertly, with unlimited warmth and affection, and in an exemplary Krsna conscious manner. By acting as home-based guides within small communities, senior Vaisnavis can perform a vital role in establishing Krsna conscious culture at grassroots level in a way that sannyasis cannot. Although in emergencies anything can be done, if we are to demonstrate to the world that varnasrama-dharma is the most stable, satisfying, and enlightened form of social organization, then we shall have to train our men as responsible husbands and fathers, and our women as devoted wives and affectionate mothers. Trying to cast everyone into male roles simply underlines our failure to institute varnasrama-dharma, and our unwillingness to reverse this trend.

We cannot browbeat lady devotees to adopt stri-dharma, and to attempt to do so would likely result in offenses. Yet if we are to establish that traditional household roles for women, although scorned by feminists, are indeed what Krsna has prescribed for them and is what works best for them and for the world, then first we as a society will have to understand and emphasize this point. We shall also have to praise and adore chaste women, as sastra teaches us to do, rather than simply neglect them.

The present controversy about female diksa-gurus is a symptom of the cultural rift that has been widening within ISKCON for at least fifteen years, and that if not resolved can only result in a distinct schism. It all centers on the question of the cultural orientation of our movement.

Over the years, the leadership of ISKCON has quietly, without consulting the wider body of devotees, promoted assimilation with the broader society rather than conquest of it by varnasrama-dharma. Hopefully, this current standoff concerning female gurus will lead to a society-wide reassessment of our cultural values and of the whole direction of our organization.

If that discussion were to result in a commitment to establish varnasrama-dharma, it would be a great step forward for our movement. By continuing to neglect this order of Srila Prabhupada, we risk being gradually cut off from his full mercy, as is manifest even today in our increasing adoption of secular and mundane traits.

(For a detailed discussion of the need for stri-dharma in ISKCON today, please listen to: www.bvks.com/1244)

Feminist Rhetoric on Dandavats

A posting on the Sampradaya Sun website (7 Jan 2013)

Disputes over gender roles are, of course, not unique to ISKCON. For several decades, certain Christian denominations have been racked and rent by gender wars, and sections of Islam and Judaism have also been affected.

What is perhaps unique in ISKCON, however, is a nigh taboo on the term "feminism" – maybe because Srila Prabhupada was so clearly against "women's liberation," or maybe because we consider ourselves to be too spiritual to be influenced by such mundane ideologies.

But let's be clear what the issue is: feminism, the doctrine that human history has been unjustly dominated by men and that now women should get their fair rights, or more. Feminists particularly contend that religious tradition has upheld gender exploitation, and religious feminists seek to reinterpret scripture and tradition in light of feminist ideology.

Within Vaisnavism, feminists have discovered that, because the souls in the bodies of men and women are equal, there should be no social differences between them – even though generations of devotees before them understood that the souls in the bodies of men and women are equal but that indeed there should be social differences between them. It is not simply coincidental that this new perspective has arisen in tandem with secular feminism.

Feminists everywhere are busy and effective in changing every facet of civilization to fit their belief. Intrinsic to their politics is the gross condemnation of anyone who wishes to uphold traditional values. Feminists presume that male traditionalists simply wish to manipulate women, and that female traditionalists are dupes; both are enemies of humanity and deserve to be denigrated in the most graphic terms.

It might have been hoped that such rhetoric would not enter Vaisnava discourse on gender issues. But alas, it is not below the dignity of even the Dandavats website to publish the terms "Taliban" and "patriarch" in relation to devotees who argue, with reference to guru, sadhu, and sastra, for traditional gender roles in Vaisnava society. (www.dandavats.com/?p=11120#comment-17118)*

Such pejoratives more reflect Western conditioning than the sastra-caksu through which devotees are meant to see the world. Although to Westerners "Taliban" might seem a natural metaphor for "terrorist," in certain countries there are many ordinary citizens who feel a comparable abhorrence toward Western governments who have devastated their homeland. Similarly, the scornful use of the term "patriarch" is loaded with the feminist ideology that is inculcated by the Western media.

Admittedly, the values of ISKCON's traditionalists are extremely different from those of modern Western society. However, to therefore insinuate that such traditionalists are dangerous, nasty extremists (like the Taliban) is to assume a position closer to that of the modern West than to that of Srila Prabhupada, from whom ISKCON's traditionalists imbibe what others see as their extremism. It is undeniable that Srila Prabhupada's outlook on almost all social issues is extremely different to that which is widely accepted in Western society.

---

* Where is the concession or compromise from the side of "conservatives" here? "Get educated but only be a mother and sister" – how is that different from the taliban/syrian type "She can own a car but cannot publicly drive it?"

And it is not that many women wouldn't like to be protected and stay home, but protection is not their responsibility – putting the onus on them is very effeminate from the side of 'patriarchs'...

As Dr. J. Stillson Judah wrote in his 1974 book "Hare Krishna and the Counterculture":

> "The position of women in the Society may not appeal to Americans interested in women's liberation. Swami Bhaktivedanta says that all women other than one's wife are to be considered as one's mother, and yet he regards them as prone to degradation, of little intelligence, and untrustworthy. They should not be given as much freedom as men, but should be treated like children; they should be protected all during their lives, by their fathers when young, later by their husbands, and in their old age, by their sons ... This view is largely consonant with the traditional one found in the ancient Indian law books. Females may not become presidents of any temple, nor occupy positions of authority. They may do the cooking, help with the devotional services and maintenance of the temple and prepare the flower offerings for Krishna." (Judah, 1974:86)

How is it that Dr. Judah, who was a friend of Srila Prabhupada's and of our movement, made such observations if they were not accurate? Moreover, Srila Prabhupada stated that he had read and approved of Judah's book (see conversation, June 20, 1975). No doubt Srila Prabhupada would have expressed concern if he had felt misrepresented by Dr. Judah.

Srila Prabhupada made literally dozens of non-PC statements. For instance in the following conversation:

> Prabhupada: So far gurukula is concerned, that also, I have given program. They have given the name of "girls." We are not going to do that.
>
> Tamala Krsna: What is that?
>
> Prabhupada: Girls. Boys and girls. That is dangerous. Girls should be completely separated from the very beginning. They are very dangerous.

Tamala Krsna: So we're... I thought there were girls in Vrndavana now. They said that they're going to have the girls' gurukula behind the boys' gurukula. Gopala was talking about that.

Prabhupada: No, no, no. No girls.

Tamala Krsna: It should be in another city or somewhere else.

Prabhupada: Yes. They should be taught how to sweep, how to stitch, clean, cook, to be faithful to the husband.

Tamala Krsna: They don't require a big school.

Prabhupada: No, no. That is mistake. They should be taught how to become obedient to the husband.

Tamala Krsna: Yeah, you won't learn that in school.

Prabhupada: Little education, they can...

Tamala Krsna: Yeah. That they can get at home also.

Prabhupada: They should be stopped, this practice of prostitution. This is a very bad system in Europe and America. The boys and girls, they are educated, coeducation. From the very beginning of their life they become prostitutes. And they encourage. They distribute pills. I have seen the boys and girls dancing together, embracing, in the school film. That ruins the career. Both of them are ruined. That is very regrettable. Then you shall require this sterilization, pills, another big program. They are creating animal civilization, and when the animals are disturbing, they are trying to find out some other means. This is their program. First of all create animals. Then, when the animals behave like animals, then another program. Why do you create animal? Woman brahmacarini, this is artificial.

Tamala Krsna: In our centers, though, there are so many brahmacarinis, and even sometimes they're encouraged to remain brahmacarini.

> Prabhupada: That they cannot. As soon as they will find opportunity, they will become vyabhicarini [sexually deviated]. For woman, protection.
>
> Tamala Krsna: So you don't advocate this remaining sing..., these women remaining brahmacarinis.
>
> Prabhupada: Therefore polygamy was allowed. Let them be taken care of, one husband, three wives. (April 29, 1977)

Mainstream Western thought would classify such statements of Srila Prabhupada as extremist, sexist, or maybe Talibanist. And it appears that members of ISKCON who acquiesce with mainstream Western thought think similarly about those devotees who maintain faith in such words of Srila Prabhupada.

What should we do with such statements? Expunge them from the Vedabase? Explain them as the eccentricity of an elderly Bengali gentleman? Or that they are merely the material, not spiritual, teachings of Srila Prabhupada and thus invalid? To simply ignore such statements is not an option because there are followers of Srila Prabhupada who take very seriously the principle "guru-mukha-padma-vakya cittete kariya aikya ara na kariha mane asa" and who will not very easily allow Srila Prabhupada's words to be forgotten or recast in the light of various popular theories.

Undoubtedly, we have to consider carefully how to present and apply Srila Prabhupada's teachings to a world that is not very open to them. But we are in danger of losing our connection with Srila Prabhupada if members of our own ranks adopt the prevailing dogmas of the misled civilization and employ them to attack those followers of Srila Prabhupada who are trying to uphold his message in its most pristine form.

“Sannyasinis”

A posting on the Sampradaya Sun website (22 Feb 2013)

Sannyasa for women is prohibited. Srila Prabhupada wrote:

> A woman is not supposed to take sannyasa. So-called spiritual societies concocted in modern times give sannyasa even to women, although there is no sanction in the Vedic literature for a woman’s accepting sannyasa. ... The woman must remain at home. She has only three stages of life: dependency on the father in childhood, dependency on the husband in youth and, in old age, dependency on the grown-up son... (From the purport to SB 3.24.40)

Srila Prabhupada also stated:

> Just like our women, Krsna conscious, they are working. They don’t want equal rights with men. It is due to Krsna consciousness. They are cleansing the temple, they are cooking very nicely. They are satisfied. They never say that “I have to go to Japan for preaching like Prabhupada.” They never say. This is artificial. So Krsna consciousness means work in his constitutional position. The women, men, when they remain in their constitutional position, there will be no artificial... (Morning Walk -- May 27, 1974, Rome)

However, ISKCON today encourages independent women preachers who roam alone around the world without protection. What is the meaning to the rule that women should not take sannyasa if some of them act as de facto sannyasis?

Of course, this raises the question of how otherwise to engage those senior female devotees in ISKCON who come from a decidedly Western background and who never made the cultural transition to the kind of social role exemplified by Kunti, Saci, and others in their old age.

Yet unfortunately by their being independent, itinerant, and female, ISKCON's traveling women preachers embody the feministic ideal: that the biggest, best women are out in the world doing what the men do, with no family connections or responsibilities. This is the same message that has destroyed the social fabric in karmi society in the West, that feminists worldwide are foisting everywhere, and that is now firmly accepted within ISKCON.

On the Subject of Female Diksha Gurus

By Phalini Devi Dasi

A posting on the Dandavats website (5 December 2012)

Dear Respected Vaisnavas,

Please accept my humble pranams. All glories to Srila Prabhupada and the great acaryas in our line.

Thanks to all who have posted thoughtful, articulate papers and comments on the topic of female diksha gurus. I have been in India preaching with my husband for the last six weeks and during that time was not able to keep up with the back-and-forth as the various comments emerged. But now after reaching USA I have found the time to read and re-read many articles and commentaries by devotees on both sides of the issue.

After traveling back and forth to India many times, living among the villagers and also interacting with high-class, educated, cultured, chaste ladies, observing them in their homes and temples as well as in public, I am further convinced that our Srila Prabhupada wanted us western women to learn how to behave like those women. Over the last thirty+ years of visiting India, I have seen powerful, effulgent women who use their native feminine power to uplift and promote their husbands. Such women are not only an inspiration to their husbands and families, but to men, women and children outside their families as well.

Women used to be satisfied remaining out of the spotlight. Remember back in the seventies how in every shop in Loi Bazaar you could not find one woman making sales or even assisting the merchant? They were nowhere to be seen. They were not even to be found serving Limcas to shoppers! Of course, just down the road in Delhi you could find women working in banks and cloth stores, but in small towns and villages, the ladies were in their homes, cooking, cleaning, taking care of the children. They did not clamor to be seen. They were content to remain hidden.

Nowadays, though, as we walk the streets of Vrndavana, we see huge, loud, garish posters plastered on the sides of buildings advertising loose-haired, imposing, scary-looking female so-called gurus. Such women are not content to remain hidden, to quietly share the wisdom they have earned by their many years of selfless service as wives, mothers and grandmothers with their daughters, nieces, granddaughters and other lady friends and acquaintances. Those unattractive billboard gurudevis are a far cry from such cultured ladies as those I have mentioned above.

Now I'm not implying that there are any *matajis* in our ISKCON who, if appointed as diksha gurus, would succumb to the temptation to wear their hair loose while sporting long, flowing orange robes and posing for photo ops. Allowing their faces to be blown up into larger-than-life-size to be forced upon every passer-by in the Holy Dhama is surely not likely to be tolerated by any proposed female diksha guru that the GBC might elect. They would surely present themselves more tastefully if chosen for the job.

Nonetheless, if FDG-ship becomes an institutional law in ISKCON, I recoil in apprehension at the thought of the can of worms that a generation of ISKCON gurudevis could open up for far-down-the-road future generations of not-so-carefully chosen candidates for female diksha-guruship. What if in some future decade, some attractive young woman decides that she doesn't want to bother with the hassle of being married (after all, even though Srila Prabhupada wanted all the ladies to be married, marriage is no doubt rife with difficulties), but would rather take on the service of diksha guru? One can just imagine what might happen if such a young gurudevi finds herself approached by a male disciple who is desperately trying to remain celibate but is having emotional difficulties due to overpowering sex drive. The wise men in our Movement who are practicing celibacy know what would happen. They know how difficult it is for men to remain celibate in this day and age, and how gullible and soft-hearted-to-a-fault a young woman can be.

Better that such a young woman surrender to Srila Prabhupada's desire that all women be married. She can purify her heart by the method given by Lord Sri Krsna Himself: to serve her husband according to stri-dharma and bear children according to the process of garbhadhana-samskara, raising them as Vaisnavas. Her husband can become the guru for that struggling brahmacari, and she can assist her husband as his disciple's guru-mata. But if we create a precedent for future young women that diksha guruship is another choice for those women who are not satisfied to perform stri-dharma, there will be confusion in the minds of those women as to what their duties are.

I have personally found that if a woman is actually doing her duty, she has little time for anything outside her *stri-dharma*. "A man, he works from sun to sun, but a woman's work is never done." The fact that women always have too much to do is the expert arrangement of the Lord, who planned it that way. We women, although expert at a lot of tasks, are sometimes lacking in discrimination and weak in our resolve. We can easily fall prey to temptations and bad association, and be led astray. We require not only protection (which means protection from danger as well as control and direction) from our fathers, husbands and sons, but also full-time engagement. Busy women, happily engaged in the service of their husbands and families in Krsna consciousness, have little chance to get into trouble. In fact, they find their feminine power and loveliness as well as blessings from above increasing as they remain devoted to their protectors. If a woman follows her *stri-dharma* dutifully for the pleasure of the Lord, she is kept fully engaged, occupied in positive tasks, for her entire life up until the point of death. Again, this is the expert arrangement of the Lord for souls in women's bodies, and when women follow their dharma properly, the good effects of this perfect arrangement of the Lord are felt throughout human society.

If, by chance, a Vaisnavi finds that she does have extra time beyond her normal duties, then she can engage in other services that support the strengthening of Krsna consciousness among her family members, friends and others. If she feels inspired to do so, she can preach, distribute books, do public kirtan and perform temple and deity services, as long as her outreach endeavors are authorized by her protector.

Conversely, women who wander outside the jurisdiction of their male protectors – even in thought and even with the best of intentions – can easily find their feminine power, effulgence, influence and chastity beginning to wane like the waning moon which gradually becomes totally dark at amavasya.

A diksha guru has to be powerful and independent. Women are empowered by Krsna when they are devoted and obedient to their male protectors. If they remain dependent on their protectors in Krsna consciousness, Krsna is so pleased with such women that He bestows great power on them (See: stories of Shubha and Shaibya in Five Divine Abodes by Jayadayal Goyandka, taken from Padma Purana).

When women act independently, they become a source of trouble to their husbands and others, and their shakti dwindles. (Ibid.)

Srila Prabhupada made it clear in the Bhagavatam how he wanted us women to behave. (For some basics, see SB 3.23.2, 7.11.25-29, and 9.3.10) We lady followers of Srila Prabhupada need to apply ourselves to learning how to behave properly until proper behavior becomes second-nature. This takes a lifetime of practice. Everything else will fall into place in the coming generations if we pioneers continue to strive toward LIVING our stri-dharma in Krsna consciousness. This is how we women can do our part in promoting daiva-varnasrama-dharma.

If, on the other hand, we introduce practices which are unprecedented in Vedic culture and in our sampradaya, we are indulging in risky business. There have been a few initiating gurudevis in our line. I recognize that fact. Those female initiating gurus gave harinam initiation under the auspices of our guru-parampara during and around the time of Lord Caitanya. All but one of those ladies were acting under the protection and direction of their husbands or fathers, who were either Visnu-tattva or, as in Srinivasa Acarya's case, empowered representatives of Lord Caitanya.

As I have said before, more than female diksha gurus, the world desperately needs to see examples of ladies who are actually following the instructions for chaste women that Srila Prabhupada labored night after night to give us. If we refuse to perform our own duty according to the body we have earned by our very own prarabdha karma, if we think that the duties Lord Krsna has prescribed for us are somehow not sufficient preaching to bring souls to Krsna consciousness, if we feel that the different kinds of mentalities found in male and female genders and the duties ascribed to each are somehow irrelevant, outdated or inconsequential, if we feel that it is not enough to preach by example as a Krsna conscious wife, mother and grandmother, and if we choose instead to do another's duty, neglecting the intended social paradigm of the Lord, we take a risk, as Srila Prabhupada explains below.

> "So you have to study first of all what is nature's law. You cannot surpass the nature's law. That is not possible. Prakrteh kriyamanani gunaih karmani sarvasah [Bg. 3.27]. Nature's law will go on. Best thing is, let the hand... the hand can typewrite, but if you say "No, the leg will typewrite," that is not possible. Take hand's business, take leg's business, and combine them cooperatively. Then the body will be nice. If the leg says "Why hand will type? I shall type," that's not possible. "Legs, all right, you walk, and hands that you type." Then combine together. Then it will be nice. You cannot change the different capacities. There is God's law, nature's law. Let the man and woman combine together, live peacefully. The woman takes charge of the household affairs, the man may take charge of bringing money, and they meet together, have Deity at home, together chant Hare Krsna. Where is the difficulty? That is unity. Combine together, working differently but for the same purpose, for pleasing Krsna, then you will become happy. **That is equality**. (emphasis mine) Unity in variety. That is wanted. Variety is enjoyment. Variety is not disturbing. Just like Krsna gave, all of them fruits, but variety. They are coming from the same source, earth, but Krsna is so intelligent – varieties of fruit, varieties of flowers, varieties of grain, varieties of brain. That is enjoyment. So, take instruction from Krsna. Why He is sending so many varieties? He could have given one fruit, the coconut. With great difficulty to chop it you can get out the water, no? There are so many nice fruits. Just see Krsna's intelligence. So Krsna has made the varieties. Why should you disturb? Let the variety be united, just like these varieties are united, and it looks nice, and if you eat that will be nice. Why you want to stop the variety? That is Mayavadi. Equality does not mean to stop variety. All the varieties combine together for the same purpose. **That is required.** (emphasis mine) Is it not?

> One must know how to put the variety to look very (indistinct). If all the vases have only rose flowers it would not have been so beautiful. Rose is costly, but the leaves are not costly. But the leaves and the rose fit together, it becomes very good variety. That art is required, how to keep varieties together for Krsna consciousness, and look very beautiful. This art is known to the Krsna conscious person, not to the fools and rascals. Why Krsna has made varieties? Why you should try to change? That is lack of Krsna consciousness. When Krsna has made so many varieties there is some purpose. That one should understand. That is intelligence. You can organize these farms very nicely. Then this devil's workshop will stop." (Room conversation, 31/7/1975, New Orleans)

In the above quote, Srila Prabhupada says, "Equality does not mean to stop variety." We men and women are equal spiritually, but materially, we are not equal. According to the body we have earned by our karma, we are given prescribed duties. That is Krsna's expert arrangement. He has created the varieties of brains, bodies, mentalities and abilities within human society, and He has also created the relative varieties of work within human society. Let us learn what those prescribed duties are for each of the varnas and for women as a separate group, and let us perform those duties as perfectly as possible for the pleasure of Lord Sri Krsna who created varieties of brain, varieties of mentality, varieties of ability and varieties of work. In this way, we will feel equal and we will feel happy as well. "Combine together, working differently but for the same purpose, for pleasing Krsna, then you will become happy."

To fail to accept the varieties of engagement that Lord Krsna has given mankind based on the varieties of gender that Lord Krsna has created is dangerous, and can lead to offenses. It can even subtly pull us toward impersonalism. Maya can then cover our intelligence, with the unfortunate consequence that we may never understand Lord Krsna's and Srila Prabhupada's plan for human society.

Over the last few years since this topic of female diksha guruship came up, although we do have a few female gurus in our line in past history, I have leaned toward the side of avoiding institutionalizing diksha guruship for women. My attitude is based on five objections:

1. A diksha guru needs to possess a measure of independence in order to perform his service nicely. Women are never to be given independence. They are meant to be always dependent, always protected. Consequently, they can't effectively perform the necessarily independent duties of a diksha guru.

2. The diksha guru takes on the karmic reactions of his disciples. Husbands have to suffer the results of their wives' sins, therefore how can a woman take on the karmic reactions of someone else (a disciple) without passing them on to her husband?

3. Institutionalizing diksha guruship, even for males, what to speak of for females, is not shastric.

4. Traditionally, we see only male gurus giving diksha. The women in our line who initiated others during the time of Lord Caitanya were most likely giving harinam initiation, which is not actually diksha.

5. A woman cannot receive a sacred thread, so how can she give a sacred thread?

Someone objected to my stance, saying, "Well, not all elderly women in ISKCON have husbands or sons who can protect them, so what are they then to do? Who will protect them?" My answer is that instead of desiring or clamoring to take on a recognized position of leadership within ISKCON–which diksha guruship within ISKCON has come to denote–they should instead find a way to live quietly with other women, in a secluded place, as Srila Prabhupada recommended to Yamuna and Dinatarini to do, producing their own food and keeping a cow or two.

If they prefer not to live on a farm, then they should find someone, a Godbrother, a Godnephew, or a sadhu who is sympathetic with and supportive of Srila Prabhupada's teachings, who is willing to protect them and engage them in devotional service that is appropriate for ladies. Engagements that are compatible with the psycho-physical nature of women are many. Some of the services ladies can render are: teaching girls how to cook, sew, spin, weave, clean, decorate, care for babies and small children, perform deity seva, sing, dance and play musical instruments and serve a husband. Such women can also render many other services, including match-making, astrological, medical, counseling or child-care services.

For the rest of us who have husbands to protect us, we should submit ourselves to their leadership and promote them, encouraging them to become pure devotees. If they are brahminically inclined, we should encourage them to eventually take on the heavy responsibility of accepting disciples. After all, the wife benefits through the husband's spiritual progress. To be the wife of an initiating guru is a great privilege and heavy burden of love. It bestows auspiciousness on a woman by conferring yet another type of motherhood on her (guru-patni is one of the seven mothers). In this way, we not only invite great blessings upon ourselves and our husbands, but also upon our husband's disciples, our children, grandchildren and other Vaisnavas in our sphere of influence.

I have said it many times before, but I'll say it again: the world desperately needs to see Krsna conscious couples who are solid in their commitment to each other and to following their respective roles according to shastra. Srila Prabhupada's mission will be strengthened by the example of long-standing devotee marriages, especially those couples who follow their dharma as laid out by our founder-acarya. Most of the people in the world are householders, and they need to see that we Hare Krishnas follow our dharma, that we are still chanting Hare Krishna after many decades and that we couples are still together after all the challenges that Maya devi and the Personality of Kali have thrown at us.

"It is not that woman cannot be ācārya. Generally, they do not become. In very special case. But Jāhnavā-devi was accepted as, but she did not declare." (Room Conversation, 29/6/72 San Diego) Srimati Jahnava devi's service as successor to Her Lord is time and time again cited as reasonable evidence that ISKCON should adopt the practice of naming women as diksha gurus. Two important points are made by Srila Prabhupada in regard to Srimati Jahnava devi:

1. One point is that "She did not declare." I repeat, "SHE DID NOT DECLARE." The quiet service of Srimati Jahnava devi is a far cry from the billboard gurudevis plastered all over Vrndavana who have no qualms about declaring that they are quite available for darshan and, by the way, looking for followers. Jahnava Mata bore the cross of carrying on Her Husband's preaching mission because She was intended to do so by Sri Nityananda Rama, the Supreme Lord, not because She desired to enjoy the name, fame and the perks of being a declared gurudevi. She is simply Lord Nitai's fully surrendered maidservant and that is why He chose Her to do the job. She is an expansion of Sri Laksmi-devi Herself.

2. The other point Srila Prabhupada made in regard to Srimati Jahnava devi being the acarya for our sampradaya is that

lady acaryas are VERY RARE. So we should keep it that way. We should not bring criticism upon our ISKCON Movement by institutionalizing female diksha guruship, nor should we create artificial adhikara for our ladies by pronouncing them fit to offer diksha.

Srila Prabhupada observed that his female followers were happy because they were cleansing the temple and cooking very nicely. When confronted with the question, "Women today want the same rights as men. How can they be satisfied?" Srila Prabhupada replied:

> "Everything will be satisfied. Just like our women, Krsna conscious, they are working. They don't want equal rights with men. It is due to Krsna consciousness. They are cleansing the temple, they are cooking very nicely. They are satisfied. They never say that "I have to go to Japan for preaching like Prabhupāda." They never say. **This is artificial.** (emphasis mine) So Krsna consciousness means work in his constitutional position. The women, men, when they remain in their constitutional position, there will be no artificial..." (indistinct) (loud traffic noises) (Morning walk, 27/5/74, Rome)

Pranams and gratitude again to all those who have so far contributed to the discussion.

Your aspiring servant,

Phalini Devi Dasi (ACBSP)

Krsna Conscious Motherhood

A posting on the Dandavats website (19 February 2015) and Sampradaya Sun website (23 February 2015)

(An expectant mother, who is also a devotee book distributor, submits a question to H.H. Bhakti Vikasa Swami. He gave a short answer and asked one of his female disciples to give further advice.)

Questions

Dear Guru Maharaja

Please accept my humble obeisances. All glories to Srila Prabhupada.

My name is ***. I have a question to ask you.

I joined ISKCON five years ago. For the last four years my sole service has been to distribute the books of His Divine Grace Srila Prabhupada. During that time, due to both the mercy of Srila Prabhupada and the inspiration I received from the devotees here, I was able to distribute more than twenty thousand books.

Currently I am not able to be so active in book distribution because my husband and I are expecting a child. I was very upset due to not to being able to take part in the most recent December marathon.

Some time ago, a sankirtana department was created in our yatra. I was asked by senior devotees to take charge of all the matajis involved in book distribution. My service involves inspiring the other matajis, organizing traveling sankirtana, and cooperating with other departments of the yatra involved in preaching.

I really need your blessings. I am worried that I am not as busy and active in this service as before. Guru Maharaja, please tell me how else I can be useful to Srila Prabhupada's mission in my current situation. I am worried that I have nothing to offer to your feet and to the feet of Srila Prabhupada.

If you so desire, I would like to eventually return to the ranks of the book distributors and continue my service, having accepted your blessings to do so.

Your servant, ***

Answer From H.H. Bhakti Vikasa Swami

Sri Guru Gaurangau Jayatah

Respected Mataji ***,

Asirvada. All glory to Srila Prabhupada and his faithful followers!

Congratulation on your outstanding service in distributing Srila Prabhupada's books. Now you will give birth and you will have to concentrate on caring for your child. Raising children in Krsna consciousness is an important service that must not be neglected. I will ask one of my senior female disciples to advise you further in this matter.

Hari-guru-vaisnava dasa, Bhakti Vikasa Swami

Further Advice

Dear Godsister ***

Please accept my humble obeisances.

Jaya Srila Prabhupada. Jaya Guru Maharaja.

Our Guru Maharaja has asked me to advise you about your motherhood and devotional service.

(To begin with let me introduce myself. I am a thirty seven year old mother of two boys, aged nine and six. I have been married for twelve years to a supportive non-devotee. We live in Sarajevo, Bosnia. Our Guru Maharaja, H.H. Bhakti Vikasa Swami gave me initiation fifteen years ago and named me Revati Devi Dasi. When I am not chanting my rounds, taking care of my family, cooking, or cleaning, I do some services for the local temple and preaching - both from home.)

First of all let me congratulate you and express my admiration for your glorious book distribution service. The last four years of your life must have been filled with the ecstasy of sankirtana, encompassing many adventures and realizations. You and your husband were lucky to be part of the sankirtana mission. You distributed so many books!

Now your life is changing. As a couple you are expecting a baby and you yourself are wondering how you can contribute to Srila Prabhupada's mission in that position.

You can be useful to Srila Prabhupada's mission. Simply by serving as a Krsna conscious mother and wife you can help Srila Prabhupada and our Guru Maharaja establish varnasrama dharma.

Mother As the First Guru

In the Vedic scriptures the position of mother is very much respected. The first of the seven different kinds of guru is the mother. You have been preaching to thousands of people. Now you will be preaching to and caring for one who appeared in your womb. (Maybe more will also appear there in your family later.) Your baby is a lucky soul who is now for a short time under your influence only. Hearing what you hear and speak, experiencing your feelings, and eating whatever you eat. You are already preaching to that fortunate soul!

You can read in the Srimad-Bhagavatam how Prahlada Maharaja received spiritual knowledge while in the womb and how the soul in the womb is conscious as described by Lord Kapiladeva. Therefore many mothers read Srimad-Bhagavatam aloud to their unborn children. One can also chant prayers or bhajanas, play Srila Prabhupada lectures or bhajanas etc. for the benefit of one's baby.

You probably know from Srimad-Bhagavatam that Dhruva Maharaja's mother advised him to worship the Supreme Personality of Godhead. When Dhruva subsequently attained spiritual success, the Visnudutas came to take him to Vaikunthaloka and he saw his mother also going, being carried in a second airplane. Srila Prabhupada writes,

> "The conclusion is that a disciple or an offspring who is a very strong devotee can carry with him to Vaikunthaloka either his father, mother or siksa- or diksa-guru. Srila Bhaktisiddhanta Sarasvati Thakura used to say, "If I could perfectly deliver even one soul back home, back to Godhead, I would think my mission – propagating Krsna consciousness – to be successful." The Krsna consciousness movement is spreading now all over the world, and sometimes I think that even though I am crippled in many ways, if one of my disciples becomes as strong as Dhruva Maharaja, then he will be able to carry me with him to Vaikunthaloka."

Krsna Conscious Motherhood Is a Service and Also Preaching

> To raise one soul to Krsna consciousness is counted by Krsna as a very great service, so you do this duty very carefully and Krsna will certainly bestow His blessings upon you. (Srila Prabhupada letter to Krsna dasi November 2, 1969)

"Raising children in Krsna consciousness is an important service that must not be neglected." (as Guru Maharaja wrote to you in his letter above)

"Varnasrama-dharma should be established to become a Vaisnava," said Srila Prabhupada in 1977. "It is not so easy to become a Vaisnava." Srila Prabhupada wanted his disciples to establish varnasrama dharma. So, his female followers can help in this mission by following great women from sastra - many chaste and caring and loving mothers and wives. The family is the main cell for the structure of human society and as women we are keeping families united and raising future generations. In this chaotic and miserable world, people will also see examples of nice Krsna conscious families, devoted mothers who raise their happy and healthy and Krsna conscious children, so it is also preaching how this utmost knowledge functions in practice.

> We require so many householders to set the example for others, how in Krsna consciousness we can live peacefully, even in married life. Also we require so many Krsna conscious children to show how nicely and beautifully a child can develop when he is following the principles of God consciousness. (Srila Prabhupada Letter to Upendra dasa, December 8, 1968)

When I was a young student of architecture I asked Guru Maharaja whether I should put more energy into my studies because one day I would be designing temples for Krsna. His answer was as follows:

> I don't advise my young lady disciples to be career oriented. Nature has given you a body for bearing children and it is a mother's duty to spend time with and properly look after her offspring. Big preaching at grassroots level will be if our grhastha devotees take up responsibility of showing an ideal example to the world. (H.H. Bhakti Vikasa Swami letter to me Oct 6, 1999)

So, being a devotee mother, a mother who practices Krsna consciousness and who is giving motherly care to one or more spirit souls is a very important service in Srila Prabhupada's mission.

Great Mothers in Sastra

We can also learn how to be Krsna conscious mothers by reading how great women from sastra served their transcendental children with utmost care and love. Women described in sastra never felt they are "just mothers," who are "missing something more important." We can see, and get inspired by, the examples of Srila Prabhupada's mother, mother Saci, mothers Yasoda, Rohini, Kunti devi, etc.

As mothers we start to learn to be selfless personal servants adjusting ourselves totally to our children's needs. Therefore mothers are known as the best servants and are respected among mature Vaisnavas for their service rendered to their families. It is said that motherly love is the most selfless love in this material world. Srila Prabhupada insisted that every woman in our society should be respected as a mother, mataji. It is a honorary title, better that any Ph.D.!

Please don't feel that you will be missing something now when you will serve your child. Devotees will always push and ask for different services, but your most important service will be your baby and family. I've seen so many times how young mothers (including myself) have been praised for their services in the temple while they were neglecting their children, but it is completely wrong. I will never forget one cake I made for Radhastami, while my one year old son was crying. I will never do that again, no matter how many devotees call me and tell me that there is a festival and there is important service.

Living Stri-Dharma

Please be happy as a mother and enjoy spending time caring for your baby. Now you are wondering how to render book distribution service, but soon you will find yourself lacking sleep and chanting while breastfeeding, and your priorities will change. Please don't allow anybody make you feel guilty for serving your child in Krsna consciousness, no matter what may be going on regarding other important services. You may find many different lectures and seminars about this topic on the website www.bvks.com, and the most important seminar (now also available as a book) is "Women, masters or mothers" – which is highly recommended for all female devotees.

Many devotee mothers also experience troubles in chanting sixteen rounds, so chanting and taking care of your baby will take most of your time at first, and it is completely bona fide and natural. There is our godsister from Croatia who never missed to chant sixteen rounds daily - it is the most important instruction from a guru. She is a housewife and her three children are very nice and exemplary devotees.

Another godsister, from Czech Republic, was a book distributor for seven years. And now she has a baby boy. I was really inspired watching her spending all morning caring for his needs. She wasn't even a little bit frustrated (as I used to be) because she was missing the morning program, or a lecture because her son needed one hour to poop. She patiently and happily sat there with him. She told me how now she has a morning program a little bit later in the morning because she adjusted her sadhana to her baby's routine. She understood that it will not be like that forever, just while he is a baby. She is such an inspiration!

There is one poem "If I had my child to raise over again" which laments over all the mistakes we make when we are not fully dedicated to our children... With all spiritual knowledge and examples from sastra, we should not make mistakes in the future by neglecting our children, neglecting our motherly nature, and thus neglecting our guru's instructions. Our children will be with us for such a short time and they grow up so fast, we must utilize that time the best way we can. It may seem that we will change diapers and have sleepless nights forever, that we will be constantly interrupted while chanting or even sleeping... but after a few years our babies will grow and we shouldn't find ourselves lamenting that we could have been with them more, raised them better, loved them more, spent more time with them, taught them more about Krsna etc.

Even non-devotee materialistic women take maternity leave for a few years, why shouldn't you do the same for your baby? And why not a maternity leave for a lifetime? Therefore, I would advise you to tell the senior leaders of your yatra that you will be on maternity leave and that you will not be able to continue on with such responsibilities as organizing traveling sankirtana etc.

> Child-worship is more important than deity-worship. If you cannot spend time with him, then stop the duties of pujari. At least you must take good care of your son until he is four years old, and if after that time you are unable any more to take care of him then I shall take care. These children are given to us by Krsna, they are Vaisnavas and we must be very careful to protect them. These are not ordinary children, they are Vaikuntha children, and we are very fortunate we can give them chance to advance further in Krsna consciousness. That is very great responsibility, do not neglect it or be confused. (Srila Prabhupada's Letter to Arundhati dasi, July 30, 1972)

Motherhood Comes First

First things first. When our babies have grown up a little bit, are satisfied and taken care of, when our minimum 16 rounds are completed, when our house is clean, prasadam is served... we will find some time to do some service, too! (And we must accept that brahmacarini life is over and that motherhood is just as adventurous and fulfilling).

I know matajis who go out sometimes to distribute books with babies on their back. It is not that they keep their children hungry, without their daily routine, that they say to their husband that there will be no lunch because they are off on a sankirtana mission. Our godsister from Ireland is distributing books a few hours a week while her children are at school. Another mataji used to distribute books at public programs accompanied by her pre-school age son.

You may also try to distribute books online later. But please let the whole world stop for now and just be there for your baby. Establish that important and strong emotional bond between you. By loving you, trusting you, and seeing your example, your child will be attracted to Krsna as well.

There are many book distributors in ISKCON, but we also need loving mothers of future book distributors. And if you neglect your baby because of other services, your baby will feel that, too. We have had many examples of how devotee children are not interested in Krsna consciousness because they were disappointed with the parenting they received. Even now, while still in your womb the baby may feel that you consider him/her as an obstacle to your service. Be assured that by becoming a mother you are still advancing spiritually and serving Guru Maharaja.

Conclusion

You asked our Guru Maharaja what you can offer to his lotus feet. You can offer him your child raised, nurtured, cared for and loved as a spirit soul, eternal servant of Lord Krsna, growing in a Vaikuntha home, in a Vaikuntha family where you and your husband cooperate nicely. You can serve Guru

Maharaja simply by being a strict and sincere devotee, through stri-dharma, being a chaste wife and loving mother. I assure you that you are not missing or losing anything by serving in this way.

If you have any further questions or doubts, please feel free to write to me whenever you like. This is a big, important subject, but I will stop here. You can stay in contact and ask me further questions if you like.

I can also send you links to other important lectures by Guru Maharaja about stri-dharma, family life, and raising children in Krsna consciousness... as well as some other helpful and inspiring websites and blogs.

I wish you a happy delivery, Krsna conscious family life, and motherhood.

Your humble servant and sister, Revati d.d.

Time for a Revolution

A posting on the Dandavats website (25 November 2011)

(Based on a talk given by Bhakti Vikasa Swami – see accompanying DVD)

If you really want to see ISKCON a lot stronger than it is at present, and if you are ready to take part in a grassroots revolution, here is a program for you. It is non-political and non-controversial, easy to implement, and with negligible cost, yet it will benefit the whole society of devotees worldwide. The program is that all members of the Krsna consciousness movement should read all of Srila Prabhupada's books.

Of course, many devotees are already reading Prabhupada's books, but still, far too many are not. Numerous devotees who have been initiated for ten years or more, and are even brahmana-initiated, have not read all of Srila Prabhupada's books, and apparently have never thought of doing so. They are depriving themselves of the nectar of Srila Prabhupada's association and guidance – maybe due to lack of time, a sudra-like mentality (being preoccupied with working hard and earning money), having little interest in philosophy, wasting their life watching TV or on the internet, or reading other books apart from Srila Prabhupada's. Not that going to websites or reading other books apart from Srila Prabhupada's is necessarily wrong, but the focus should be on Srila Prabhupada's books.

It is Srila Prabhupada's books that will change the world, and it is Srila Prabhupada's books that give solid understanding of Krsna consciousness. It is particularly through Srila Prabhupada's books that we can make positive advancement and gain the strength to overcome maya. Srila Prabhupada's books tell us how maya works, and give practical advice for overcoming maya. For instance, it seems that nowadays many devotees do not even know that they should not eat food cooked by nondevotees. But by reading Srila Prabhupada's books, they will come to know.

Dear devotees, by reading Srila Prabhupada's books you will get spiritual strength and a clear understanding of the mission and philosophy of Sri Caitanya Mahaprabhu and Srila Prabhupada. If you are not feeling inspired in spiritual life, you will definitely gain inspiration by reading the books of Srila Prabhupada. You will also get inspiration to distribute those books and to preach Krsna consciousness.

Devotees enjoy hearing stories about Srila Prabhupada from his disciples, about how those disciples personally interacted with him. By reading Srila Prabhupada's books you will feel intimacy with him, like that which comes from a mother reading to her child. Srila Prabhupada said, "If you want to know me, read my books." By doing so, you will feel closeness to Srila Prabhupada, how he is personally speaking to you through his books.

Make Srila Prabhupada happy! He becomes pleased if you read his books. Here are just a few of the many quotes from his letters that confirm this:

> I am glad to see how nicely you are reading my books. Please continue to do this. We need so many preachers who are soundly versed in the scriptures to convince the world to take to Krsna consciousness. (9 November 1970)

> I request you to thoroughly study all of our literatures very thoughtfully and try to understand the sublime import of this Krsna consciousness philosophy. (4 January 1971)

> I am very pleased that you are inclined to read and study our books with seriousness. Thank you very much. So continue it wholeheartedly. We want good preachers also. Preaching shouldn't depend on me only. My disciples should become all good preachers, and that depends on studying the books nicely so that you can arrive at the right conclusion. (5 July 1971)

A commitment to reading Srila Prabhupada's books will not only impart strength to the individual members of ISKCON but will also give the whole movement the knowledge and potency to withstand maya and to take on the demonic atheistic civilization. (And if you didn't know that this civilization is demonic and atheistic and that we are supposed to be taking it on, then you should read Srila Prabhupada's books.)

Reading Srila Prabhupada's books will also give devotees the insight to recognize deviations when they (inevitably) arise within ISKCON and to not become bewildered by them. Or better still, if all devotees were fixed in the knowledge in Srila Prabhupada's books, then deviations could not arise.

A campaign for getting all devotees to read Srila Prabhupada's books is the best way to keep Srila Prabhupada in the center of ISKCON. We could put Srila Prabhupada's vyasasana in the middle of the temple room and dance around it – which would be very good – but to put his instructions (as given in his books) as central to all that we do is the very best way to keep Srila Prabhupada in the center of his movement.

Encouraging all devotees to read all of Srila Prabhupada's books is a very simple program.

Individuals can take it up, and leaders can encourage their followers to do so.

Gurus, those who are awarding initiation, can instruct those who (having endured the horrors of mundane education) have learned how to read that they should read Srila Prabhupada's books. Gurus could stipulate that before approving any candidate for initiation, the prospective disciple should have read a certain number of Srila Prabhupada's books.

Parents can teach their children how to read by reading with them from Srila Prabhupada's books.

Other obvious leaders, such as temple presidents and congregational preachers, can best benefit their wards by urging, coaxing, cajoling, or doing whatever is necessary to get them to read Srila Prabhupada's books.

Indeed, anyone who speaks about Krsna and Krsna consciousness to others can encourage everyone else to read Srila Prabhupada's books.

As more and more devotees read Srila Prabhupada's books, it will have a snowball effect. It is just a matter of resolving to do so and then making a habit of it. Reading should be done prayerfully, in a submissive mood of wanting to learn and to be purified. It should be done daily, and preferably a devotee should fix a time period within which to have read all of Srila Prabhupada's books. Maya always provides something seemingly more important to do, but actually there is nothing as important as reading Srila Prabhupada's books. And when you begin reading them, you will understand that all topics in the universe other than Krsna-katha, as delineated in Srila Prabhupada's books, is simply superficial.

Once you start, you won't want to stop. Careful regular reading of Srila Prabhupada's books elevates us to an entirely different dimension in spiritual life. On the other hand, if we do not read – if we do not know why we are doing what we are doing – then our devotional practice is probably on the basis of sentiment, which is insubstantial and means that we cannot advance properly. Srila Prabhupada wrote:

> All the devotees connected with the Krsna consciousness movement must read all the books that have been translated (the Caitanya-caritamrta, Srimad-Bhagavatam, Bhagavad-gita and others); otherwise, after some time, they will simply eat, sleep and fall down from their position. Thus they will miss the opportunity to attain an eternal, blissful life of transcendental pleasure. (Cc *Madhya* 25.278, purport)

Most of Srila Prabhupada's disciples will not be in this world much longer, which means that soon the whole responsibility to transmit the teachings of the parampara will be with the next generation. If you have not gone very deeply into those teachings as received through Srila Prabhupada, then what will you give to others? If you have not immersed yourself in Srila Prabhupada's teachings, if you do not have profound faith in them, then you will not be a strong link in the parampara; and many weak links makes for a weak movement.

As previously stated, the cost of this program would be negligible. All one has to do is purchase Srila Prabhupada's books. Every initiated devotee who lives in a home should have at least one full set of Srila Prabhupada's books. If you do not, then get them.

This program can only be auspicious. Nothing bad can come from it.

Listening to Srila Prabhupada's lectures is also a must for those who claim to be his followers. You can get all of Srila Prabhupada's recorded lectures, conversations, and also kirtanas, in a set of DVDs. Absorb the pure sound of Srila Prabhupada's Vaikuntha voice, from far beyond the realm of mundane illusion. Allow him to cut through all your anxiety, attachments, and misconceptions and to deliver to you what he came to give: Krsna. Hear how Srila Prabhupada preached – his clear delineation of the truth, piercing straightforwardness, transcendental humor, and sense of urgency to communicate Krsna consciousness.

Hare Krsna!

Playing The Hindu Card

Introduction

Śrīla Prabhupāda on Kṛṣṇa Consciousness and Hinduism

In an article called "Kṛṣṇa Consciousness – Hindu Cult or Divine Culture?" published in The Science of Self-Realization, Śrīla Prabhupāda wrote:

> There is a misconception that the Kṛṣṇa consciousness movement represents the Hindu religion. In fact, however, Kṛṣṇa consciousness is in no way a faith or religion that seeks to defeat other faiths or religions. Rather, it is an essential cultural movement for the entire human society and does not consider any particular sectarian faith. This cultural movement is especially meant to educate people in how they can love God. Sometimes Indians both inside and outside of India think that we are preaching the Hindu religion, but actually we are not.

Śrīla Prabhupāda then further discussed how the main traits of modern Hinduism are Māyāvāda and *karma-kāṇḍa* (supplicating God with the idea of getting something in return, with no motive to understand or please Him, but just to get something from Him). Śrīla Prabhupāda also stated that our social system is *varṇāśrama-dharma,* which he distinguished from the perverse caste system, and said that one will not find the word Hindu in the *śāstra,* for it is a relatively recent term. Hinduism is conceived of as a sectarian religion, whereas Kṛṣṇa consciousness is the ultimate truth.

Poster at Bhaktivedanta Manor

With that brief quotation from The Science of Self-Realization, I will develop the theme of this lecture. A few days ago, I saw on a website by the name of the Sampradaya Sun – which some devotees consider to be off grounds or unsuitable – I saw a photo of a poster from Bhaktivedanta Manor (the ISKCON center just outside London, UK). The poster featured a devotee and the large words "Hindu priest." It was an advertisement for the services of a Hindu priest, offered by Bhaktivedanta Manor. The devotee who had posted the photo on the website, one of my godbrothers, didn't give much explanation as to why he had done so. It seems that he didn't feel a need to explain how or why it was outrageous. His implicit message was: "How can we, as followers of Śrīla Prabhupāda, who clearly states that we are not preaching Hinduism, advertise our devotees to act as Hindu priests?" But obviously, the authorities at Bhaktivedanta Manor didn't consider it to be wrong. They have this poster at the Manor and maybe in other places also. Devotees who regularly frequent Bhaktivedanta Manor might initially have been surprised at seeing this poster; but when we repeatedly experience something, even if we feel that it is wrong, we gradually come to accept it as normal. And in fact, a whole generation of devotees at Bhaktivedanta Manor now consider normal an official ISKCON that is very much aligned with Hinduism.

Brief History of Bhaktivedanta Manor

1970s – Devotees Viewed as Hippies

From my vantage point, several thousand kilometers away, where I have been over the years, and having been allowed to join this movement at Bhaktivedanta Manor, I want to reconstruct a history – of course simplified and generalized – of how this happened. Why was it that my godbrother, who was raised in Kṛṣṇa consciousness to understand that we are not Hindus, became outraged (it seems) that nowadays devotees identify and indeed promote themselves as Hindus?

When I joined ISKCON in 1975, devotees were, in the eyes of the public, identified as disreputable hippies. And actually, most devotees had formerly been hippies and still maintained a hippielike attitude of rebelliousness against mainstream society. In my early days in Kṛṣṇa consciousness, it was common for devotees to get arrested for chanting in the streets and for distributing books. I once got arrested while just walking down the street! I hadn't even started my book distribution, but I was arrested because I had a bag full of books and clearly intended to distribute them.

Gujarati and Hindu Influx

From the inauguration of the Manor in 1973, it became a focal point for Hindus, especially Gujarati Hindus from the London area. At that time, there were maybe no other temples for Hindus in that locale, and a large Gujarati community had recently come to England. They had been booted out of Uganda by Idi Amin, who was kind enough not to eat them. (He used to eat his enemies.) The Gujaratis arrived in England with nothing but the clothes that they wore; even the gold nose-rings of the women had been taken from them in Uganda. The British government and people were kind enough to allow the Gujaratis in – Kṛṣṇa's plan, you could say. Many of them took up residence in Wembley, an area in London that is close to the Manor. By cultural background, most of those Gujarati Hindus were devotees of Kṛṣṇa, and the Manor became a temple and cultural center for them. Apart from Wembley, Hindu visitors started to come from as far away as Preston, Bolton, Wolverhampton, Coventry, Leicester – all places of major concentrations of Hindus. On festival days, many busloads would come.

Locals Demand Closure of Manor

But the villagers in Letchmore Heath were not much pleased with this Hindu influx. They had been enjoying the best of both worlds – going to work in London and returning to an idyllic village atmosphere. But they found their nice peaceful village overrun by these "damn Hindus" – brown skins and all. Of course, they didn't complain on racial grounds, and probably that wasn't their main concern. They wanted to maintain tranquility in their village, which was not an unreasonable concern. So they took action to try to close the Manor.

Hindus Support Manor, Gain Prominence

The Manor devotees, headed by Akhaṇḍadhī Dāsa, the long-serving temple president, orchestrated a campaign to keep the Manor open, taking help from Hindus all over Britain. Finally, after several years of struggle, the campaign was successful. And it further brought to the notice of British politicians that the Hindus were an emerging and important constituency. Although the Hindus had arrived with nothing, most of them, being more enterprising than the average Britisher, had within a short time become businessmen, and many of their children were qualifying for careers in medicine, dentistry, and other above-average professions. These Hindus were hardworking and family oriented – in many ways ideal citizens – not the type whose children were likely to become hooligans or drunkards or cause riots. Apart from that, two of the world's richest people were Hindus based in London. And so the British politicians noted that it was not wise to ignore the Hindus.

Devotees Become Unofficial Leaders of UK Hindus

Consequently, apart from the immediate effect of keeping the Manor open, the Manor campaign united the UK Hindus in an unprecedented manner. Previously they had never had any issue to unite around, so this campaign gave them a new identity, respectability, and voice. In many ways it also caused the devotees to become the Hindus' leaders, not only in the eyes of the Hindus themselves, but also in those of politicians, the press, and what you might call "respectable people." The Hare Kṛṣṇas were no longer just some ragtag dropouts, but the unofficial leaders of an important constituency of British citizens. And the devotees also realized: "Hey! We're mainstream! We're establishment!"

Continuing to "Play the Hindu Card"

Having won the Manor campaign, the devotees found themselves with a new, advantageous identity. The campaign had generated much favorable publicity, and the devotees were now seen as a group with much influential support and not to be pushed around. Hence, the devotees continued to represent themselves as Hindus. There were certain advantages to that, being that most people who came to them were Hindus. Non-Hindu visitors to the Manor were likely to think that they were in a Hindu temple, because at any time of the day or night at the Manor there were many Hindus present. And anyway, in the public estimation, a temple of Kṛṣṇa is a specifically Hindu place of worship.

Further Influence of Hinduism within ISKCON

Establishment of Oxford Centre for Hindu Studies

Eventually, the Oxford Centre for Hindu Studies was established by devotees. And significantly, it was called the Oxford Centre for Hindu Studies, not Vedic or Vaiṣṇava studies. I saw one video presentation wherein one young Gujarati woman from England explained how she had taken a course given by the Oxford Centre for Hindu Studies. She said something to the effect of "I'm Swaminarayan by background, and they taught me the meaning of *pūjā* and this and that."* She came in as a Swaminarayan, she took the course, and she went out as a Swaminarayan. In other words, she did not learn what Śrīla Prabhupāda taught. But she understood better about Hinduism, because she had attended the Oxford Centre for Hindu Studies.

---

* Swaminarayan – a Hindu sect. *Pūjā* – a ceremony of worship.

Motorcycle Pūjās

The world's largest Hindu population is, of course, in India. And when pious Hindus in India buy a new motorcycle (the most common form of mechanical transport, since most people still cannot afford a car), they take it to a temple to have it blessed via a motorcycle *pūjā*. Hindus in the West are more likely to have car *pūjās*, and many ISKCON temples oblige. I don't think there is anything in the *śāstras* about the *pūjā* procedures; they're probably invented by the devotees who perform them. The pious Hindus are satisfied, and they offer some *dakṣiṇā* to the officiating priest, which augments the priest's income. Of course, the priests might give the *dakṣiṇā* to the temple, although I know at least one temple where they don't. There it is considered acceptable that the temple priests get extra income to supplement their allowance.

The Hindu Card in Russia and Hungary

Recently, there were international campaigns involving ISKCON devotees in Russia and Hungary. In Tomsk, Russia, local prosecutors tried to prohibit the sale of *Bhagavad-gītā As It Is*. And in Hungary, the government more or less wanted to ban the Kṛṣṇa consciousness movement. In both cases, the devotees were able to come out successful by "playing the Hindu card" – by maintaining that we are not some weird new cult but that we represent Hinduism, which is an ancient religion and should be considered bona fide.

American Centers

In America also, our movement has become Hinduized. I believe there is an official GBC ban against it, but still, Durgā-pūjā is celebrated[1] in some ISKCON temples in America, and Indian Republic Day is celebrated with the singing of "Jai Hind," the

1 http://www.harekrsna.com/sun/news/10-11/news4014.htm (retrieved 23 Dec 2014).

Indian national anthem. And in one temple, a Māyāvādī guru lectured just days prior to his being widely discredited in the Indian press as a womanizer.

Pūjās and Kalaśas for Mundane Benefits

Several ISKCON temples in South India invite people for special *pūjās* that are purported to remove *doṣas* (malefic astrological influences). And many ISKCON temples throughout India and overseas advertise for donors to sponsor a *kalaśa* at Janmāṣṭamī and thus derive all kinds of material benefits (and some spiritual benefit also).*

Benefits of a Hinduized ISKCON

Recognition by British Politicians

In some areas of the world, our movement unabashedly identifies itself with Hinduism and accommodates some facets of Hinduism that Śrīla Prabhupāda never introduced. In other words, the movement has become Hinduized. This has certain benefits, as we saw in Russia and Hungary. Also, in the British House of Commons there is an annual Janmāṣṭamī function organized by devotees. Only a handful of MPs attend, but for devotees it is a huge step up from being penniless ex-hippies getting arrested.

And at No. 10 Downing Street, the official residence of the prime minister of the United Kingdom of Great Britain and Northern Ireland, there is an annual Diwali celebration, organized by ISKCON devotees and presented as a Hindu function.† Not everyone gets invited to No. 10. You have to be well-accepted as part of the establishment to be invited to a social event at No. 10.

* *Kalaśa* – pot, especially one containing liquids used in religious ceremonies. Janmāṣṭamī – the appearance anniversary of Lord Kṛṣṇa, celebrated as a major festival.

† Another major Hindu festival.

Last year at that function, devotees presented the prime minister with a copy of the *Rāmāyaṇa.* However, it was an edition of the *Rāmāyaṇa* that does not clearly establish Rāma as the Supreme Lord, or even that there is a Supreme Lord. It is a Hindu book written by an ISKCON devotee.

Educational Interaction

Another development in the United Kingdom is that the honorable prime minister recently declared: "We need more morality in our country, so we need religious-based schools." In response to this initiative, ISKCON devotees were asked to organize religious schools for Hindus. Devotees in Britain are now running two schools, which, as far as I understand, are similar to ISKCON schools anywhere else, with government syllabi (Darwin's theory and all), and some yoga exercises and chanting of Hare Kṛṣṇa. Some of the teachers are ISKCON devotees.

One reason that devotees were asked to start schools for Hindus is that over the past several years literally thousands of schoolchildren have visited Bhaktivedanta Manor. In today's multicultural Britain, schools try to inculcate in the children a sense of respect and tolerance for all different kinds of religions. As part of the religious course, many teachers take their children on an outing to a Hindu temple. And they mostly go to Bhaktivedanta Manor. It is by far the best "Hindu temple" in Britain. It is large and set in beautiful spacious grounds in the countryside. The resident devotees are friendly and competent guides, who tell the kids about Hinduism and bring them to see the Deities, give them *prasāda,* and get them to chant Hare Kṛṣṇa. The kids get a nice impression of devotees, and the teachers are also happy, because they and the schoolchildren are well treated and it is a good educational experience.

Thanks to the Manor devotees' interaction with Hindus and schools, as also the presence of the Oxford Centre for Hindu Studies, devotees are now consulted regarding syllabi for religious studies in secular schools in the UK. Devotees get to write or review what is written about Hinduism. Compare this situation with that of some years ago in California, when the school syllabus presented Hinduism in a very bad light – it was actually blasphemous. American Hindus protested, but they were unable to change it.

Rationalization

It could be proposed: "If we hadn't taken the Hindu lead, someone else would have. It could have been the Swaminarayans or the Vishva Hindu Parishad, but it is the devotees who are recognized as the prominent voice of Hinduism in the UK." Similarly, with car *pūjās,* etc.: "If we don't do it, Hindus will get it done at some other temple. So better they come to us."

Downside of the Hindu Card

Kṛṣṇa Consciousness Presented Differently than by Śrīla Prabhupāda

That we are identified as Hindus has its utility, but – and here comes the but – it also means that we will not say very loudly many things that Śrīla Prabhupāda said. Śrīla Prabhupāda ends that essay ["Kṛṣṇa Consciousness – Hindu Cult or Divine Culture?"] by writing:

> The Kṛṣṇa consciousness movement has nothing to do with the Hindu religion or any system of religion. No Christian gentleman will be interested in changing his faith from Christian to Hindu. Similarly, no Hindu gentleman of culture will be ready to change to the Christian faith. Such changing is for men who have no particular social status. But everyone will

> be interested in understanding the philosophy and science of God and taking it seriously. One should clearly understand that the Kṛṣṇa consciousness movement is not preaching the so-called Hindu religion. We are giving a spiritual culture that can solve all the problems of life, and therefore it is being accepted all over the world.

But devotees nowadays cannot say this very clearly. A sannyasi godbrother of mine told me that one of his disciples in the United Kingdom, who is an Indian Hindu by background, makes TV shows that present Kṛṣṇa consciousness very straightforwardly. He strongly emphasizes that Kṛṣṇa consciousness is not Hinduism, but a universal spiritual culture. These shows are well received by many Hindus and non-Hindus alike, but not (so I was told by my sannyasi godbrother) by the authorities of ISKCON in UK. Why not? Because the ISKCON UK authorities are presenting Kṛṣṇa consciousness with a distinctly different slant from Śrīla Prabhupāda's direct, clear teachings. Although there are seeming advantages to doing so, still, it cannot be denied that it is a significantly different presentation of Kṛṣṇa consciousness from that which Śrīla Prabhupāda taught. By playing the Hindu card, devotees become reticent about presenting Kṛṣṇa consciousness as the ultimate spiritual science. Although from the cultural and sociological perspective, Kṛṣṇa consciousness might be viewed as a Hindu sect, and although it might be easier to present ourselves to the public as such, that is not how Śrīla Prabhupāda instructed us to present it.

Compromise with Māyāvādīs

And along with any advantages comes the caveat of having to mix with and support nondevotee Hindus. For instance, if there is a sectarian effort to close a Māyāvādī temple, we will then be obliged to support the Māyāvādīs – whom we should be opposing as great cheaters and the greatest offenders of the Lord! As devotees become constrained from even speaking against Māyāvāda, the quintessential words *nirviśeṣa-śūnyavādi-pāścātya-deśa-tāriṇe* become a mere ritual chant, with no actual meaning in our practical lives.

See also "Hindus and Hinduization," chapter eight of *Hare Krishna Transformed,* by Professor E. Burke Rochford (2007, New York University Press), for an overview of the growing importance and influence of Indian Hindus in ISKCON's North American communities.

Suggested Further Reading

A Message to the Youth of India, by Bhakti Vikāsa Swami

Glimpses of Traditional Indian Life, by Bhakti Vikāsa Swami

Varṇāśrama-dharma, compiled by Hare Kṛṣṇa Devī Dāsī (quotes by Śrīla Prabhupāda; published by BBT; featured in Bhaktivedanta VedaBase)

Varnasrama-dharma and Srila Prabhupada
by Shyamasundara das; www.dandavats.com/?p=11750

www.16108.com/dharma/
This website by Ameyātmā Dāsa offers depth-analysis of many of the points discussed in this book.

Rethinking Varṇāśrama
www.siddhanta.com/2015/01/11/rethinking-varnasrama/
This essay by Kṛṣṇa-kīrti Dāsa discusses the connection of *varṇāśrama-dharma* with ISKCON's overall preaching mission, and how its application can solve many immediate and long-term social problems both for ISKCON and for society at large.

Light for the Dark Well: Kṛṣṇa Conscious Family Life
by Mūlaprakṛti Devī Dāsī and Viśākhā Devī Dāsī; Back to Godhead #26-4, 1992 (also in the Bhaktivedanta VedaBase)

My Brief Against Feminism (Hidden Misogyny)
by Nārada-priyā Devī Dāsī. See: www.harekrsna.com/sun/editorials/03-11/editorials7136.htm

Return of the Mothers
by Nārada-priyā Devī Dāsī. See: domesticdevotion108.blogspot.in/2011/04/return-of-mothers.html

Also: www.youtube.com/watch?v=eoeYoTd46n4
A short video with good insights into feminism.

Acknowledgements

Nitāi-Caitanya Dāsa, Arnoldas Zdanevicius, and Siddharth Chivukula all helped transcribe the recording of "The Basic Mistake of All Reformers." Vṛndāvana-candra Dāsa, Viṣṇujana Dāsa, Jambavān Dāsa, and Guru-Kṛṣṇa Dāsa all helped convert the original transcript into the present essay, "The Direction of the Kṛṣṇa Consciousness Movement."

The seminar, "Women: Masters or Mothers," was transcribed by Cakrapāṇi Dāsa, Jagaddhātrī Devī Dāsī, Mohana Dāsa and Anādi Rādhikā Devī Dāsī, Nidhi Gaurāṅgī Devī Dāsī, Nitāi Caitanya Dāsa, Rasānanda Dāsa, Śaraṇāgatā Devī Dāsī, Śyāma Padmanābha Dāsa, Sarveśvara Dāsa, Viṣṇu-citta Dāsa, and Siddharth Chivukula. For the essay by that name, Priya Govinda Dāsa provided references, and Guru-Kṛṣṇa Dāsa, Madana-mohana-mohinī Devī Dāsī, Phalinī Devī Dāsī, and Sugitā Vāṇī Devī Dāsī assisted with editing and suggestions that helped convert the original transcripts into their present form. Bāsu Ghosh Dāsa, Śyāmasundara Dāsa, and Kṛṣṇa-kīrti Dāsa also provided valuable input that meliorated the essay.

Bhakta Ram Kumar, Murāri Dāsa, Madhukaṇṭha Dāsa, Nārāyana Śrīnīvāsa Dāsa, Kiśora Dāsa and Ananta Sarovara Dāsi proofread the manuscript. Dāmodara Dāsa, Govinda Datta Dāsa, Mādhava Dāsa, and Śyāmasundara Padmanābha Dāsa helped produce accompanying DVD. Rasikaśekhara Dāsa designed the cover.

Many thanks to all of you for assisting me in this service to Śrīla Prabhupāda, his followers, and his mission.

The Author

The author was born in Britain in 1957 and joined ISKCON in London in 1975. Later that year, he was formally accepted as a disciple of His Divine Grace A. C. Bhaktivedanta Swami Prabhupāda, the founder-*ācārya* of ISKCON, and renamed Ilāpati Dāsa.

From 1977 to 1979, Ilāpati Dāsa was based in India, mostly traveling in West Bengal distributing Śrīla Prabhupāda's books. He spent the following ten years helping to pioneer ISKCON's preaching in Bangladesh, Malaysia, Myanmar, and Thailand.

In 1989 he was granted the order of *sannyāsa,* receiving the name Bhakti Vikāsa Swami, and again made his base in India. Since then he has preached Kṛṣṇa consciousness throughout the subcontinent, lecturing in English, Hindi, and Bengali. He also spends a few months each year preaching in the West. His television lectures in Hindi have reached millions worldwide.

Bhakti Vikāsa Swami writes extensively on Kṛṣṇa conscious topics. His books have been translated into over twenty languages, with nearly one and a half million in print. *Women: Masters or Mothers?* is his seventeenth book.

He is also involved in developing several *gurukulas* and also Vedic rural projects based on simple living and high thinking.

CPSIA information can be obtained at www.ICGtesting.com
Printed in the USA
BVOW06s0320080516

446748BV00016B/159/P

9 789382 109297